7/3/70 Gale Research

HOWARD PYLE

A Record of
His Illustrations and Writings

Compiled by Willard S. Morse
and Gertrude Brincklé

Wilmington, Delaware
THE WILMINGTON SOCIETY OF THE FINE ARTS

1921

Detroit: Reissued by Singing Tree Press, Book Tower, 1969

Library of Congress Catalog Card Number 68-31099

Compilers' Explanation

Periodical List

This list contains both writings and illustrations by Howard Pyle. The names of the periodicals are listed alphabetically, and the names under the periodical references are arranged chronologically. There are twenty-five periodicals in which Howard Pyle's work appeared, and which contain twenty-one hundred and eighteen illustrations reproduced from original drawings and paintings.

The following facts are given in the list:

1 Name and date of periodical, together with volume and page.
2 Title and author of article illustrated, as well as the titles of writings by Howard Pyle not illustrated.
3 Title of illustration when given.
4 Reference to books with reprint illustrations.
5 Size of illustrations, width and height, given in inches and decimals. (The outside measurements of irregularly shaped illustrations are given.)
6 Method of reproduction, shown by
      w.   meaning wood-engraving.
      p.   meaning process, half-tone, etc.
    c.p.   meaning process, colored or tinted.
      c.   meaning colored.
7 The name of the engraver, when known.
   Individual decorative initial letters are indicated as illustrations.

Book List

The list is divided into two sections: first, books containing writings by Howard Pyle, thirty-four in number, with five hundred and seventy-four illustrations from original drawings, and five hundred and fifteen reprint illustrations; second, one hundred and fifty-nine books by other authors, containing five hundred and eighty-eight illustrations from original drawings, and five hundred and thirty-four reprint illustrations.

In all cases, references are made to the first edition, except where limited editions were published, in which case references are made to them.

TITLE PAGES AND COVERS. In the wording of title pages and covers, no attempt has been made to follow the varied typography of the originals.

COLLATION. Collation, full title page and copyright data are given only of books that contain Howard Pyle's writings and books containing the first publication of his illustrations. Books containing reprints of his illustrations are given with condensed title, author and publisher.

ILLUSTRATIONS NOT PREVIOUSLY PUBLISHED. These are described by page, title of illustration, size of illustration, method of reproduction, and the name of the engraver when known.

ILLUSTRATIONS PREVIOUSLY PUBLISHED. The number only is given, with the name and date of the periodical or title of the book where they first appeared.

DECORATIVE INITIAL LETTERS. These are counted as illustrations, when they stand by themselves.

In addition to the writings and illustrations of Howard Pyle contained in periodicals and books, a description is also given of seven programmes containing twelve illustrations, seven bookplates, a print and a poster, from his original drawings.

In all, this list contains a record of thirty-three hundred and one published examples of his work as an illustrator.

To this record are added a list of his mural paintings and a list of important easel paintings never reproduced.

Sincere thanks are due to the many friends and admirers of Howard Pyle for the assistance cheerfully given us in compiling this work. It has been a pleasure to find the universal high regard in which Mr. Pyle is held by the people who knew him, or came in contact with him during his busy life. He left behind him a reputation as a man fully equal to his reputation as an artist.

WILLARD S. MORSE
GERTRUDE BRINCKLÉ

Howard Pyle

HOWARD PYLE was born in Wilmington, Delaware, on March 5th, 1853. He was the son of William Pyle and Margaret Churchman Painter.

He was educated at private schools, and studied art for three years in Philadelphia and at the Art Students' League in New York.

He married Anne Poole of Wilmington in 1881, and lived in Wilmington nearly all his life. From 1876, when his first illustration appeared in the old *Scribner's Magazine*, he contributed stories and pictures to the leading periodicals in the country. In 1894 he became director of illustration at the Drexel Institute, Philadelphia, and about the same time opened a school in Wilmington and at Chadd's Ford, Pennsylvania, where he spent his summers. He also gave weekly lectures on composition at the Art Students' League.

He was a member of the National Institute of Arts and Letters and of the National Academy.

He belonged to the Century Association in New York and the Franklin Inn Club of Philadelphia.

In 1910 he went abroad with his family and lived in Florence for one year, until his death on November 9th, 1911.

A Tribute

By HENRY MILLS ALDEN

Harper's Magazine, January, 1912

HOWARD PYLE was distinguished by marked individual peculiarities from all the other artists of his time. Indeed, for any so peculiar type of genius we must revert to William Blake. Pyle was most like Blake in this—that in the representation of life and things he caught native aspects and meanings. He had no interest in the institutional fabric of our civilization, or of any other. Of Quaker parentage and an enthusiastic disciple of Swedenborg, it was natural that he should listen to the inner voice and reject the traditions of men and the authority of the schools—also that he should seek the inward and spiritual meanings of all things. Yet, without being at all picaresque, he often chose to portray the elemental passions of our human nature.

It was not with Pyle the love of the tragedy which grows out of evil passions that prompted him. He reverted to the elements of tragedy rather than to its scheme, allured by what was native in it, haunting, and antique. Comedy has always been concerned with the contemporaneous. Pyle, in his quaint and antique humor, would have nothing of this contemporaneity, and he was quite as averse from contemporary adventure. The boldly rough aspects of our pioneer Western life did not tempt him. His saunterings were confined to the Atlantic seaboard and the West Indies, in search of old romance, of peculiar people, and of the haunts of pirates. Europe, whether in the Cromwellian era or in the remoter period of chivalry, was sufficiently disclosed to him and for his purpose in the annals of history. His imagination filled out the scene and supplied the temper and atmosphere of the story. For it was always the story he demanded, in all its spiritual meanings as interpreted in the terms of our fallible but heroically striving human nature—but yet the story in its concrete and clearly projected embodiment.

[vi]

We are glad that at the last, and after he had disclosed the possibilities of his peculiar genius, he had sixteen months of Europe, and that he had this aftermath of his life in Italy. But, for the kind of work which gave him a distinction wholly his own, he had no need of the actual European scene. It was different with Abbey, who, with a more purely esthetic sense of form and detail, felt that he must fulfil himself wholly within the precinct of art itself.

Pyle, on the other hand, was first of all and always an illustrator. Because he was transcendently that, he was something more than that, especially in his sense and handling of color and in the spirit which animated and informed his creations. He never failed to give his meaning in the picture itself, whether illustration or mural painting; but he delighted in correlating his meanings by means of the written story, which was always virile, significant, and charmingly antique and idiomatic.

His work as author and artist was, for us all, and a good part of it especially for youth, a fresh revival of the Romantic. But, though it occupied the field of wonder, it had no Rossetti-like transfiguration and exaltation, no vagueness. Without any loss of the wonder, his meanings were plain. We shall not see his like again.

Table of Contents

TABLE OF CONTENTS—*Continued*

Illustrations and Writings of

HOWARD PYLE

Published in Periodicals

THE AUTOGRAPH

I. 47 Jan.-Feb. 1912 YE PIRATE BOLD   *Howard Pyle*
    1 Ye Pirate Bold   p 6.0 x 7.5

THE BOOK BUYER

IV. 394 Dec. 1887 AMERICAN WOOD ENGRAVING OF THE
          PRESENT   *Howard Pyle*
    No illustrations by Pyle

XI. 625 Dec. 1894 HOLIDAY BOOKS FOR YOUNG PEOPLE *Howard Pyle*
    No illustrations by Pyle

XV. 442 Dec. 1897 AN OLD FRIEND WITH A NEW FACE   *Howard Pyle*
    Illustrations by Albert Herter

BOOK NEWS

XXIII. 251 Dec. 1904 FAIRY TALES   *Howard Pyle*
    No illustrations

THE CENTURY MAGAZINE

XLVI. 73 May 1893. THE CHEVALIER DE RESSEGUIER
                          Thomas Bailey Aldrich
    In the Bookseller's Shop   w 5.2 x 8.0
                               Chas. State, Sc.
XLVII. 210 Dec. 1893. A SET OF SKETCHES   *Howard Pyle*
    1 The Rivals   w 4.6 x 7.2
                           E. H. Del'Orme, Sc.
    2 The First Sketch   p 5.2 x 4.0
    3 Initial A   p 0.7 x 0.7
    4 The Second Sketch   p 5.0 x 3.0
    5 Initial A   p 0.7 x 0.7
    6 The Third Sketch [1]   p 5.0 x 5.3
    7 Initial T   p 0.7 x 0.7
    8 The Fourth Sketch   p 5.2 x 3.2
    9 Initial T   p 0.7 x 0.7
    10 The Fifth Sketch   p 4.5 x 1.2
    11 Initial A   p 0.7 x 0.7
    12 The Sixth Sketch   p 5.2 x 2.6
    13 Initial T   p 0.7 x 0.7

---

[1] Reproduced in "Modern Illustration." Joseph Pennell, Bell, London. 1895.

[1] Reproduced in "The Book of the Ocean." Ernest Ingersoll, Century Co., New York. 1898.
[2] Reproduced in "Hugh Wynne." S. Weir Mitchell, Edition of 60 copies, Century Co., New York. 1897.

LIII. 525 Feb. 1897 THE BATTLE OF COPENHAGEN   *A. T. Mahan*
1 Headpiece with title   p 5.2 x 4.5
2 Nelson sealing his letter to the Crown Prince of
   Denmark 1,2   p 8.1 x 4.9
3 Tailpiece   p 4.0 x 2.3

LIII. 741 March 1897 NELSON AT TRAFALGAR   *A. T. Mahan*
1 The Mizzen Top of the "Redoubtable"   p 3.5 x 5.4

LXIII. 41 Nov. 1901 THREE PICTURES OF DON QUIXOTE
1 Don Quixote's Encounter with the Windmill   c.p 5.0 x 7.6
          F. H. Wellington, Sc.
LXIII. 108 Nov. 1901 HOPE AND MEMORY   *Howard Pyle*
1 Headpiece with decorated border   c.p 5.2 x 8.2
2 Full page illustration—no title   c.p 5.2 x 7.9
3 Headpiece   c.p 5.1 x 1.4
4 Tailpiece   c.p 5.1 x 1.4
5 Marginal decoration   c.p 0.3 x 5.2
6 Marginal decoration   c.p 0.3 x 5.2

LXV. 167 Dec. 1902 THE TRAVELS OF THE SOUL   *Howard Pyle*

Color plates:
1 The Wicket of Paradise   c 4.7 x 8.3
       H. Davidson, Sc.
2 In the Meadows of Youth   c 4.7 x 8.3
       H. Davidson, Sc.
3 In the Valley of the Shadows   c 4.7 x 8.3
       H. Davidson, Sc.
4 At the Gates of Life   c 4.7 x 8.3
       H. Davidson, Sc.

In black and white:
5 Title page with decorations   p 3.5 x 3.7
6 First page text with headpiece   p 4.4 x 1.3
7 Initial T   p 0.6 x 0.6
8 Second page text with headpiece   p 4.6 x 2.1
9 Initial O   p 0.6 x 0.6
10 Tailpiece   p 2.1 x 2.1
11 Third page text with headpiece   p 4.7 x 2.1
12 Initial N   p 0.6 x 0.6

[1] Reproduced in "Catalogue of Drawings," etc., by Howard Pyle, Philadelphia. 1897.
[2] Reproduced in "Catalogue of Drawings," etc., by Howard Pyle, Boston. 1897.

[1] Reproduced in "The Price of Blood." Howard Pyle, Richard G. Badger & Co., Boston. 1899.

THE COSMOPOLITAN

[1] Reproduced in "American Art by American Artists." Collier, New York. 1915.

2 "The young fellow lounged in a rattan chair"   p 2.7 x 3.2
3 "Their first meeting happened at the club"   p 2.2 x 3.5
4 "DuMoreau was leaning part way across the table" p 2.7 x 2.9
5 "He glared at the girl in the dim light"   p 2.4 x 4.1
6 "Then there was the crash and clatter of an
    overturned chair"   p 2.7 x 3.4

EVERYBODY'S MAGAZINE

VI. 585 June 1902 THE FIRST SELF-MADE AMERICAN
                                        Adele Marie Shaw
    1 "His Majesty would furnish no more money for
        treasure hunting"   p 5.2 x 3.5
    2 The settler   p 2.0 x 4.0
    3 "He fell in love"   p 1.8 x 2.0
    4 "A fair brick house in the Green Lane of North
        Boston"   p 3.0 x 1.2
    5 "Stand off, ye wretches"   p 3.0 x 3.2
    6 "He had seen great guns in the bottom of the sea" p 2.9 x 2.2
    7 "Soberly joined himself to the North Church"   p 2.5 x 3.5
    8 "The ships rolled and wallowed in the river"   p 3.0 x 1.4
    9 "Why, what is this? whence came this?"   p 5.2 x 8.0
   10 "An 'Eminent Person from Whitehall' visited
        him in his chambers"   p 3.0 x 4.0
   11 "The victims of the witchcraft delusion"   p 2.5 x 3.5
   12 "The Queen granted him an audience"   p 5.0 x 2.9

XXVIII. 3 Jan. 1913 THE MADONNA OF THE BLACKBIRD *Arthur Train*
    1 He had lost the soul of M. Fournier   c 5.0 x 7.7
    2 Over her gleaming shoulder her chalky face
        lowered at him, with a look of sullen hatred   c 5.2 x 7.7

FRANK LESLIE'S POPULAR MONTHLY

LVI. 402 Aug. 1903 THE ROMANCE—A Picture   *Howard Pyle*
        Illustration by Henry J. Peck

[1] Reproduced in "A Modern Aladdin." Howard Pyle, Harper, New York. 1892.

3 "Such was the workshop in which the two labored
  together"[1]   p 3.2 x 3.8
4 "She held the book to the flames whilest talking,
  her eyes fixed intently upon it"[1]   p 2.7 x 4.8

xxiv. 459 June 13, 1891
  1 "He leaned over and looked into her face"[1]   p 3.2 x 4.3
  2 "He saw within an oval mirror, set in a heavy
    frame of copper"[1]   p 2.5 x 4.4
  3 "And stripped the false body off of him as you
    would strip off a man's coat"[1]   p 2.0 x 5.4
  4 "The innkeeper served him in person"[1]   p 3.2 x 3.8

xxiv. 483 June 20, 1891
  1 " 'Mad!' said Oliver, 'why am I mad?' "[1]   p 2.6 x 4.0
  2 "Oliver spread out the gems upon the table with
    his hand"[1]   p 3.3 x 3.5
  3 "He is clad in a loose dressing-robe of figured
    cloth and lies in bed reading his book"[1]   p 3.3 x 4.3

xxiv. 499 June 27, 1891
  1 " 'Do you know,' said the Marquis, 'what a thing
    it is that you ask?' "[1]   p 3.4 x 3.6
  2 "He sank upon his knees beside her"[1]   p 2.7 x 5.5
  3 "She drew her down until the girl kneeled upon
    the floor beside the sofa"[1]   p 3.0 x 3.8
  4 "Monsieur the Count de St. Germaine"[1]   p 1.8 x 5.2

xxiv. 522 July 4, 1891
  1 "The Count de St. Germaine, without removing
    his eyes from his victim, took another deep,
    luxurious pinch of snuff"[1]   p 3.2 x 4.4
  2 "Oliver fixed his gaze upon the smooth brilliant
    surface of the glass"[1]   p 2.8 x 4.8
  3 "He saw a dull heavy yellow smoke arise to the
    ceiling"[1]   p 3.4 x 5.6
  4 "They beheld their master lying upon his face
    under the table"[1]   p 3.2 x 4.0

---

[1] Reproduced in "A Modern Aladdin." Howard Pyle, Harper, New York. 1892.

XXIV. 542 July 11, 1891
1 "Suddenly someone touched Oliver lightly upon
the shoulder"[1]   p 3.1 x 4.9
2 "He found in his clinched hand a lace cravat"[1]   p 2.9 x 4.3
3 "'Celeste!' breathed Oliver through the crack in the
door"[1]   p 2.3 x 5.2
4 "Over his shoulder he carried something limp,
like an empty skin, or a bundle of clothes
tied together"[1]   p 2.3 x 4.3

XXIV. 930 Dec. 5, 1891 THE FIRST THANKSGIVING   *Theron Brown*
1 Headpiece   p 9.0 x 10.0
2 Initial O   p 0.9 x 0.9

HARPER'S NEW MONTHLY MAGAZINE

LVII. 29 June 1878 THE BATTLE OF MONMOUTH COURT-HOUSE
                                            Benson J. Lossing
1 Carnival, Philadelphia, 1778   w 6.5 x 4.4
                                                      R. A. Muller, Sc.
LVII. 38 July 1878 DADDY WILL   *Charles D. Deshler*
1 "The little pink finger and the huge black index
came to a full stop under this commandment" w 4.4 x 4.4
                                                      F. Juengling, Sc.
LVII. 199 July 1878 OWLET   *John Esten Cooke*
1 At Daddy Bayne's   w 4.5 x 3.4
2 "She walked on after saying this, musing"   w 4.0 x 5.4

LVII. 337 Aug. 1878 MANUEL MENENDEZ   *Charles Carroll*
1 "She went by without looking at him"   w 4.0 x 5.4
2 Fermina opens the casket   w 4.0 x 5.8

LVII. 489 Sept. 1878 AB'M: A GLIMPSE OF MODERN DIXIE
                                            Charles D. Deshler
1 "Well, dat nigger cheat de burer—he s-t-o-l-e,
Massa!"   w 3.8 x 3.5
2 "Then came the tug of war"   w 4.5 x 4.3
                                                      R. A. Muller, Sc.

[1] Reproduced in "A Modern Aladdin." Howard Pyle, Harper, New York. 1892.

[1] Reproduced in "Art in America." S. G. W. Benjamin, Harper, New York. 1880.

[2] Reproduced with title "Address to Old Hickory" in "Building the Nation." Charles Carleton Coffin, Harper, New York. 1882.

[3] Reproduced with title "Government Toll Gate on Cumberland Road" in "Harper's Ency. U. S. History," Vol. V. Harper, New York. 1902.

[4] Reproduced with title "Travelling by Stage Coach" in "Harper's Ency. U. S. History," Vol. VIII. Harper, New York. 1902.

[5] Reproduced with title "The Toll Gate" in "Building the Nation." Charles Carleton Coffin, Harper, New York. 1882.

[6] Reproduced with title "The Stage" in "Building the Nation." Charles Carleton Coffin, Harper, New York. 1882.

[7] Reproduced with title "Government Toll Gate on the Cumberland" in "Harper's Popular Cyclopædia of U. S. History." B. J. Lossing, Harper, New York. 1881.

---

[1] Reproduced in "Building the Nation." Charles Carleton Coffin, Harper, New York. 1882.

[2] Reproduced with title "A Witch" in "Harper's Ency. U. S. History," Vol. X. Harper, New York. 1902.

[3] Reproduced with title "The idea was abroad that she had a malignant touch" in "Old Times in the Colonies." Charles Carleton Coffin, Harper, New York. 1880.

[4] Reproduced in "Building the Nation." Charles Carleton Coffin, Harper, New York. 1882.

[5] Reproduced in "Old Times in the Colonies." Charles Carleton Coffin, Harper, New York. 1880.

[6] Reproduced with title "Quakers doing their duty" in "Old Times in the Colonies." Charles Carleton Coffin, Harper, New York. 1880.

---

[1] Reproduced in "Harper's Ency. U. S. History," Vol. X. Harper, New York. 1902.

[2] Reproduced in "Building the Nation." Charles Carleton Coffin, Harper, New York. 1882.

[3] Reproduced with title "Dutch Courting" and

[4] Reproduced with title "After Dinner" in "Building the Nation." Charles Carleton Coffin, Harper, New York. 1882.

2 "I only regret that I have but one life to lose for
my country" [1]   w 4.7 x 3.5

LXI. 888 Nov. 1880 THE DRIFTWOOD FIRE   *Harriet Prescott Spofford*
1 "I saw her face white even in all that immense
ruddy glare"   w 4.8 x 4.4
                                                   J. P. Davis, Sc.

LXII. 178 Jan. 1881 OLD-TIME LIFE IN A QUAKER TOWN *Howard Pyle*
1 Old Swedes' Church, Wilmington [7] [3] [2]   w 3.7 x 4.8
2 Going to Church [4]   w 4.7 x 4.6
                                                   J. P. Davis, Sc.
3 At Evening [5]   w 4.7 x 2.6
4 The Umbrella—A Curious Present   w 4.7 x 4.7
5 William Cobbett's School [6]   w 4.7 x 4.0
                                                   H. Wolf, Sc.
6 The Destruction of the Sign   w 4.6 x 5.9
                                                   H. Wolf, Sc.
7 The British in Wilmington   w 4.7 x 2.5

LXII. 248 Jan. 1881 PATIENT MERCY JONES   *James T. Fields*
1 "I never had wood that I liked half so well—do
see who has nice crooked fuel to sell"   w 4.7 x 4.1

LXII. 524 March 1881 A GLIMPSE OF AN OLD DUTCH TOWN
1 New Year's Hymn to St. Nicholas [8]   w 4.7 x 3.5
                                                   C. Mayer, Sc.
2 Mynheer's morning horn [8]   w 3.4 x 5.6

LXIII. 836 Nov. 1881 TILGHMAN'S RIDE FROM YORKTOWN
        TO PHILADELPHIA*   *Howard Pyle*
1 "He stops at the Sign of the Weathervane"   w 4.6 x 5.8
                                                   A. Hayman, Sc.
2 "Then he tells his news, in the ruddy glow"   w 4.0 x 3.7

[1] Reproduced with title "Hale's Execution" in "Harper's Ency. U. S. History," Vol. IV. Harper, New York. 1902.
[2] Reproduced in "Harper's Ency. U. S. History," Vol. III. Harper, New York. 1902.
[3] Reproduced in "A History of the American People," Vol. II. Woodrow Wilson, Harper, New York. 1902.
[4] Reproduced with title "Quakers on Their Way to Church," etc., in "Harper's Ency. U.S. History," Vol. I. Harper, New York. 1902.
[5] Reproduced with title "Scene in an Old Quaker Town" in "Harper's Ency. U. S. History," Vol. VII. Harper, New York. 1902.
[6] Reproduced with title "Old Time School in Pennsylvania" in "Building the Nation." Charles Carleton Coffin, Harper, New York. 1882.
[7] Reproduced in "Documentary Edition," Vol. III, "A History of the American People." Woodrow Wilson, Harper, New York. 1918.
[8] Reproduced in "Building the Nation." Charles Carleton Coffin, Harper, New York. 1882.
* Verses republished without illustrations in "Elocutionist's Annual No. 10." Philadelphia. 1882.

LXIV. 88 Dec. 1881 AUTUMN SKETCHES IN THE PENNSYLVANIA
        HIGHLANDS   *Howard Pyle*

1 A Mountain Farm-house   w 4.7 x 6.4
2 The Lowland Brook   w 3.7 x 5.2
3 An Autumn Evening   w 4.6 x 6.7
4 The Mountain Orchard   w 4.7 x 4.3
5 The Corn Fields on the Hillside   w 4.7 x 4.6
                                    G. P. Williams, Sc.

LXIV. 481 March 1882 OLD NEW YORK COFFEE-HOUSES
                          John Austin Stevens

1 Isaac Sears Addressing the Mob   w 4.3 x 6.3
2 The Press-Gang in New York   w 4.8 x 3.5
                       Smithwick & French, Sc.
3 Theophylact Bache saving Graydon from the Mob
   in 1776   w 4.8 x 3.4
                            J. P. Davis, Sc.

LXV. 811 Nov. 1882 THE EARLY QUAKERS IN ENGLAND
        AND PENNSYLVANIA   *Howard Pyle*

1 The Tile House, New Castle, Delaware [1] w 3.5 x 4.0
2 "I often took my Bible and sat in hollow trees" w 4.2 x 3.1
                             Sharp, Sc.
3 "The Word of the Lord came to me, saying 'Cry,
   Woe to the bloody City of Litchfield!' " [2] w 4.7 x 3.3
4 "I sat in a hay-stack and said nothing for some
   hours"   w 2.4 x 6.1
5 "They led me, taking hold of my collar and by
   my arms" [3]   w 4.8 x 3.3
                             G. Kruell, Sc.
6 "The Admiral lost all control of himself, and in a
   rage ordered his son to quit the house" w 4.8 x 3.4
                             J. P. Davis, Sc.
7 Quaker and King at Whitehall 1681 [4] w 4.8 x 6.7
                           Frank French, Sc.

---

[1] Reproduced with title "Old Quaker House, New Castle, Delaware."
[2] Reproduced with title "A Quaker in Litchfield, England."
[3] Reproduced with title "Persecuting a Quaker."
[4] Reproduced with title "A Quaker at the Court of Charles II" in "Harper's Ency. U. S. History," Vol. VII. Harper, New York. 1902.

8 The Departure of the "Welcome" [1]   w 3.5 x 5.9
F. S. King, Sc.

9 A burial at sea on board the "Welcome"   w 4.8 x 3.2

10 William Penn and his Commissioners in the cabin
of the "Welcome"   w 4.9 x 4.0

LXVI. 217 Jan. 1883 THE OLD ENGLISH SEAMEN
Thomas Wentworth Higginson

1 "Thomas Moon began to lay about him with his
sword" [3] [2]   w 4.8 x 4.3
H. Wolf, Sc.

2 Drake's attack upon San Domingo [3] [2]   w 4.3 x 5.6
A. Hayman, Sc.

LXVI. 505 March 1883 THE FRENCH VOYAGEURS
Thomas Wentworth Higginson

1 "Jacques Cartier setting up a cross at Gaspé" [7] [4] [2] w 4.8 x 7.1

2 Dominique de Gourgues avenging the murder of the
Huguenot colony [5] [2]   w 4.6 x 2.4
F. H. Wellington, Sc.

3 "He brought both Catholic priests and Huguenot
ministers, who disputed heartily on the way" [6] [2] w 4.8 x 2.9

4 "He rested his musket" [2]   w 4.8 x 3.5

LXVI. 706 April 1883 AN ENGLISH NATION
Thomas Wentworth Higginson

1 The Landing of the Pilgrims [8] [4] [2]   w 6.9 x 4.7
Hoskin, Sc.

---

[1] Reproduced with title "The Departure of the 'Welcome'" in "Harper's Ency. U. S. History," Vol. VII. Harper, New York. 1902.

[2] Reproduced in "A Larger History of the United States." Thomas Wentworth Higginson, Harper, New York. 1886.

[3] Reproduced in "Adventures of Pirates and Sea Rovers." Howard Pyle, Harper, New York. 1908.

[4] Reproduced in "Harper's Ency. U. S. History," Vol. II. Harper, New York. 1902.

[5] Reproduced with title "DeGourgues Avenging the Massacre of the Huguenots," etc., in "Harper's Ency. U. S. History," Vol. VI. Harper, New York. 1902.

[6] Reproduced with title "Mendindez's Expedition on the Way to the New World" in "Harper's Ency. U. S. History," Vol. VI. Harper, New York. 1902.

[7] Reproduced in "Indian History for Young Folks." Francis S. Drake, Harper, New York. 1885.

[8] Reproduced in "Documentary Edition," Vol. I, "A History of the American People." Woodrow Wilson, Harper, New York. 1918.

2 Arrival of the Young Women at Jamestown [2] [1]   w 4.9 x 3.7

3 Endicott cutting the cross out of the English flag [3] w 4.7 x 5.5

LXVII. 20 June 1883 THE HUNDRED YEARS' WAR

Thomas Wentworth Higginson

1 Death of King Philip [5] [4] [1]   w 4.5 x 5.6
A. Hayman, Sc.

2 Governor Andros and the Boston People [3] [1]   w 4.5 x 5.3
A. Whitney, Sc.

LXVII. 213 July 1883 THE SECOND GENERATION OF ENGLISHMEN IN

AMERICA   *Thomas Wentworth Higginson*

1 A Quaker Exhorter in New England [6] [1]   w 4.7 x 6.1
F. H. Wellington, Sc.

2 Arresting a Witch [6] [1]   w 4.7 x 5.8
F. Bernstrom, Sc.

3 Peter Stuyvesant tearing the letter demanding the
surrender of New York [6] [1]   w 4.7 x 5.1

LXVII. 428 Aug. 1883 THE BRITISH YOKE

Thomas Wentworth Higginson

1 The "Boston Massacre" [7] [1]   w 4.8 x 5.3
F. Bernstrom, Sc.

2 An Out-of-door Tea Party in Colonial New
England [1]   w 4.9 x 4.7

LXVII. 651 Oct. 1883 LAST DAYS OF WASHINGTON'S ARMY

AT NEWBURGH   *J. T. Headley*

1 Washington refusing a dictatorship [9] [8] [6]   w 4.8 x 6.5
H. Wolf, Sc.

---

[1] Reproduced in "A Larger History of the United States." Thomas Wentworth Higginson, Harper, New York. 1886.

[2] Reproduced in "Harper's Ency. U. S. History," Vol. V. Harper, New York. 1902.

[3] Reproduced in "Harper's Ency. U. S. History," Vol. VI. Harper, New York. 1902.

[4] Reproduced in "Harper's Ency. U. S. History," Vol. VII. Harper, New York. 1902.

[5] Reproduced in "Indian History for Young Folks." Francis S. Drake, Harper, New York. 1885.

[6] Reproduced in "Harper's Ency. U. S. History," Vol. X. Harper, New York. 1902.

[7] Reproduced in "Harper's Ency. U. S. History," Vol. I. Harper, New York. 1902.

[8] Reproduced with title "The Man is Grander than the King" in "Old Homestead Poems." Wallace Bruce, Harper, New York. 1888.

[9] Reproduced in "Documentary Edition," Vol. V in "A History of the American People." Woodrow Wilson, Harper, New York. 1918.

2 Washington and his generals in consultation
March 15, 1783 [1] [2]
                                          w 4.7 x 3.5
                                          S. G. Putnam, Sc.

LXVII. 731 Oct. 1883 THE DAWNING OF INDEPENDENCE
                                          Thomas Wentworth Higginson

1 Lexington Green—"If they want a War, let it begin
here" [3] [4]
                                          w 4.6 x 5.5
                                          F. H. Wellington, Sc.

2 Sergeant Jasper at the Battle of Fort Moultrie [3] [5] w 4.8 x 6.0
                                          Hoskin, Sc.

LXVII. 909 Nov. 1883 EVACUATION OF NEW YORK BY THE
BRITISH, 1783   *Henry P. Johnson*

1 The last boatload of the British leaving New York [5] w 4.7 x 5.2
2 The civil procession, headed by General Washington
and Governor Clinton [5]
                                          w 4.8 x 6.4
                                          H. Wolf, Sc.

LXVIII. 3 Dec. 1883 CHRISTMAS   *George William Curtis*

1 "The Master caused us to have some Beere"   w 4.7 x 5.4
2 The Puritan Governor interrupting the Christmas
sports
                                          w 7.1 x 4.6
                                          J. Bernstrom, Sc.

LXVIII. 238 Jan. 1884 THE BIRTH OF A NATION
                                          Thomas Wentworth Higginson

1 The French Officers at Newport [4]   w 4.7 x 5.1
2 Shay's Mob in possession of a Court House [4] [6] [7] [2] w 4.8 x 6.4
                                          A. Hayman, Sc.

---

[1] Reproduced in "Harper's Ency. U. S. History," Vol. X. Harper, New York. 1902.

[2] Reproduced in "Documentary Edition," Vol. V, "A History of the American People." Woodrow Wilson, Harper, New York. 1918.

[3] Reproduced in "History of the United States." Thomas Wentworth Higginson, Harper, New York. 1905.

[4] Reproduced in "A Larger History of the United States." Thomas Wentworth Higginson, Harper, New York. 1886.

[5] Reproduced in "Harper's Ency. U. S. History," Vol. VI. Harper, New York. 1902.

[6] Reproduced in "Harper's Ency. U. S. History," Vol. VIII. Harper, New York. 1902.

[7] Reproduced in "A History of the American People," Vol. III. Woodrow Wilson, Harper, New York. 1902.

[1] Reproduced in "A Larger History of the United States." Thomas Wentworth Higginson, Harper, New York. 1886.
[2] Reproduced in "Harper's Ency. U. S. History," Vol. V. Harper, New York. 1902.
[3] Reproduced in "A History of the American People," Vol. III. Woodrow Wilson, Harper, New York. 1902.
[4] Reproduced in "Documentary Edition," Vol. VI, "A History of the American People." Woodrow Wilson, Harper, New York. 1918.
[5] Reproduced in "Harper's Ency. U. S. History," Vol. IX. Harper, New York. 1902.

LXXI. 813 Nov. 1885 AN INDIAN JOURNEY   *Lucy C. Lillie*
  1 Death of the Indian Chief Alexander   w 7.3 x 4.8
                                      F. H. Wellington, Sc.

LXXII. 53 Dec. 1885 ESTHER FEVEREL   *Brander Mathews*
  1 "Roger Feverel had kindled it for the first time"   w 4.9 x 6.2
                        French, Sc.
  2 "Her glance fell, under his steady gaze"   w 4.9 x 6.2
                        J. Tinkey, Sc.

LXXII. 561 March 1886 THE CITY OF CLEVELAND   *Edmund Kirke*
  1 Travelling in the Olden Time   w 4.8 x 6.8
                        Hoskin, Sc.
  2 Governor Huntington attacked by Wolves   w 4.8 x 6.5
                      F. H. Wellington, Sc.

LXXIII. 236 July 1886 THE GUNPOWDER FOR BUNKER
        HILL   *Ballard Smith*
  1 Paul Revere bringing news to Sullivan [1]   w 4.7 x 7.2
                      F. H. Wellington, Sc.
  2 Surrender of Fort William and Mary [1]   w 4.8 x 5.5
  3 Transporting Powder from the Fort [1]   w 4.8 x 3.3
                      W. R. B., Sc.
  4 Bringing the Powder to Bunker Hill [1]   w 4.7 x 3.3
                      J. Tinkey, Sc.

LXXIII. 327 Aug. 1886 THE CITY OF THE STRAIT   *Edmund Kirke*
  1 The Landing of Cadillac [2]   w 7.7 x 4.8
                      A. Lindsay, Sc.
  2 The Ojibway Maiden disclosing Pontiac's Plot   w 7.3 x 4.9
                      J. Tinkey, Sc.

LXXIV. 659 April 1887 THE SOUTHERN GATEWAY TO THE
        ALLEGHANIES   *Edmund Kirke*
  1 "The woman turned fiercely upon the Chieftain"   w 4.8 x 7.0
                      F. S. King, Sc.
  2 Joseph Brown leading his company to Nicojack   w 4.7 x 6.3
                      Hoskin, Sc.

LXXV. 29 June 1887 STEPHEN WYCHERLIE   *Howard Pyle*
  1 "I sat gazing upon her as she leaned forward"   w 4.8 x 7.3
                      F. S. King, Sc.
  2 "Thereupon, lifting up his eyes again, he began
     once more wrestling with the spirit in prayer"   w 4.8 x 6.4
                      R. A. Muller, Sc.

[1] Reproduced in "Harper's Ency. U. S. History," Vol. X. Harper, New York. 1902.
[2] Reproduced in "Harper's Ency. U. S. History," Vol. III. Harper, New York. 1902.

3 "Still she looked upon me, though silently and
    pale as death"   w 4.8 x 3.2
4 "Then came Mistress Margaret unto me and put
    a letter into my hand"   w 4.7 x 3.6
                                                        Hoskin, Sc.

LXXV. 48 June 1887 THE KENTUCKY PIONEERS   *John Mason Brown*
  1 The Capture of Elizabeth and Frances Callaway
    and Jemima Boone [1]   w 4.7 x 5.8
                                                    F. H. Wellington, Sc.
  2 Defense of the Station   w 4.8 x 7.3

LXXV. 357 Aug. 1887 BUCCANEERS AND MAROONERS OF
          THE SPANISH MAIN   *Howard Pyle*
  1 On the Tortugas   w 7.6 x 4.8
                                                        H. Wolf, Sc.
  2 Capture of the Galleon   w 7.6 x 4.9
                                                      S. G. Putnam, Sc.
  3 Henry Morgan Recruiting for the Attack [2]   w 7.2 x 4.8
                                                        King, Sc.
  4 The Sacking of Panama   w 7.4 x 4.8
                                                     F. Bernstrom, Sc.

LXXV. 502 Sept. 1887 BUCCANEERS AND MAROONERS OF THE
            SPANISH MAIN   *Howard Pyle*
  1 Avary sells his jewels   w 4.8 x 3.7
                                                        Aikman, Sc.
  2 Marooned   w 7.5 x 4.8
                                                        H. Wolf, Sc.
  3 Blackbeard buries his treasure   w 7.8 x 4.8
                                                        G. Kruell, Sc.
  4 Walking the plank   w 4.8 x 7.4
                                                      H. F. Anderson, Sc.

LXXV. 666 Oct. 1887 AARON BURR'S WOOING   *Edmund C. Stedman*
  1 Aaron Burr's Wooing   w 4.8 x 6.3
                                                        J. Tinkey, Sc.

LXXVI. 420 Feb. 1888 ON THE OUTPOSTS—1780   *Howard Pyle*
  1 "They ploughed their fields with an armed sentry
    beside them" [3]   w 4.7 x 4.3
  2 Finding the body of Joseph Hay in the Trail   w 4.8 x 6.9
                                                    F. H. Wellington, Sc.

---

[1] Reproduced in "Abraham Lincoln." Charles C. Coffin, Harper & Brothers, New York. 1893.
[2] Reproduced as frontispiece in "The Buccaneers and Marooners of America." Edited by Howard Pyle, MacMillan, New York. 1891.
[3] Reproduced with title "Pioneers Farming" in "Harper's Ency. U. S. History," Vol. IV. Harper, New York. 1902.

LXXVI. 536 March 1888 CANADIAN VOYAGEURS ON THE
SAGUENAY   *C. H. Farnham*
   1 Coureurs de Bois   w 4.8 x 7.2
                                       Johnson, Sc.

LXXVII. 12 Dec. 1888 MORGAN   *Edmund C. Stedman*
   1 Morgan at Porto Bello   w 7.8 x 4.9

LXXVIII. 671 April 1889 WASHINGTON'S INAUGURATION
                                John Bach McMaster
   1 Washington met by his Neighbors on his way to
     the Inauguration   w 7.6 x 4.7
                              F. H. Wellington, Sc.
   2 The Inauguration [1] [4]   w 4.8 x 7.1
                              F. S. King, Sc.
   3 Celebration on the Night of the Inauguration [5] [4] [3] [2] w 4.8 x 7.6
                              H. W. Peckwell, Sc.

LXXIX. 776 Oct. 1889 A PECULIAR PEOPLE   *Howard Pyle*
   1 An Old Lancaster House   w 4.6 x 3.4
   2 A Dormitory in the Sisters' House, Ephrata   w 3.1 x 4.3
   3 The Kloster   w 4.7 x 3.3
   4 Going to Meeting   w 3.7 x 5.7
   5 The Kiss of Peace   w 3.2 x 4.3
   6 My Cicerone   w 2.2 x 4.4
                          Smithfield & French, Sc.
   7 "It was to represent the Narrow Way"   w 3.3 x 4.7
                        Smithfield & French, Sc.
   8 "It was along this wall that the wounded soldiers
     sat"   w 4.6 x 3.4
   9 Interior of Chapel   w 3.8 x 5.1
                          J. P. Davis, Sc.

LXXX. 218 Jan. 1890 YOUMA   *Lafcadio Hearn*
   1 "She stood like a bronze. Gabriel was beside her,
     his naked cutlass in his hand" [6]   w 4.8 x 6.9

---

[1] Reproduced in color in "Harper's Ency. U. S. History," Vol. IV. Harper, New York. 1902.

[2] Reproduced in "Harper's Ency. U. S. History," Vol. X. Harper, New York. 1902.

[3] Reproduced in "A History of the American People," Vol. III. Woodrow Wilson, Harper, New York. 1902.

[4] Reproduced in "A Tour Around New York." John Flavel Mines, Harper, New York. 1893.

[5] Reproduced in "Documentary Edition," Vol. V, "A History of the American People." Woodrow Wilson, Harper, New York. 1918.

[6] Reproduced in "Youma." Lafcadio Hearn, Harper, New York. 1890.

LXXX. 408 Feb. 1890 YOUMA   *Lafcadio Hearn*
1 " 'And you would not give me a chance to tell you,'
    she repeated, pleadingly, touching his arm"   w 7.2 x 4.8
                                                    L. Faber, Sc.

LXXX. 169 Jan. 1890 JAMAICA, NEW AND OLD. I.   *Howard Pyle*
1 Illustrated initial I   w 1.5 x 4.4
2 "Popping ineffectual round-shot after her"   w 3.1 x 3.0
                                                  A. E. Wood, Sc.
3 "The dim, shadowy forms of vessels riding at
    anchor in the night"   w 3.6 x 1.5
4 "A hot, broad, all-pervading glare of sunlight" w 4.8 x 5.8
5 "A lodging-house very well known to all Jamaica
    travellers"   w 4.8 x 5.7
                                                  A. Lindsay, Sc.
6 Spanish Galleon   w 4.8 x 2.1
7 "That prince or potentate of the old sugar king
    period"   w 1.7 x 3.3
8 "A turbaned coolie and his wife"   w 1.8 x 3.3
9 "Where they sit in long rows with baskets of
    oranges"   w 4.7 x 1.5
10 "Sitting with piles of great pots and bowls and
    queer jars of red earthenware"   w 4.7 x 2.9
                                                  Witte, Sc.
11 "A curious group travelling along a hot dusty
    road"   w 3.0 x 2.1
12 In the market place   w 3.1 x 5.7
                                                  T. H. Heard, Sc.
13 "In mid-harbor the tainted crafts were burned in
    sight of all"   w 3.3 x 5.2
                                                  J. Tinkey, Sc.
14 Gallows Point   w 1.2 x 3.2
                                                  F. S. King, Sc.
15 "The beautiful sweeping curve of harbor"   w 3.7 x 2.9
16 "Squatted on a log, and talked in a sad, melancholy
    manner"   w 4.2 x 5.1
17 "The abbot and the town major personating con-
    quered Spain"   w 4.5 x 3.6
18 The Mangrove   w 2.9 x 4.9
                                                  J. Tinkey, Sc.
19 "One time it was alive with the great lumbering
    coaches"   w 4.8 x 2.2

20 "Around the archways and the square stone pillars,
buzzing like angry hornets"   w 4.7 x 4.5
21 "It is the Cathedral of St. Katherine"   w 2.9 x 3.2
22 "Sic transit gloria mundi"   w 3.7 x 3.4

LXXX. 378 Feb. 1890 JAMAICA, NEW AND OLD. II.   *Howard Pyle*
1 Headpiece   w 4.7 x 1.8
2 Illustrated initial P   w 1.2 x 2.6
3 "The Governor was among the very first to set
foot upon the deck"   w 4.6 x 7.8
4 "The embrasures are blind and empty"   w 3.1 x 6.4
                                                 F. Levin, Sc.
5 "Here and there one comes upon an old house"   w 4.8 x 3.1
6 "They were dressed in loose sackcloth shirt and
drawers"   w 4.8 x 6.0
                                                 Witte, Sc.
7 "A store stood with open front toward the road" w 4.8 x 3.8
8 "An old man, lean and naked"   w 2.2 x 3.2
9 "An ancient sibyl-like figure"   w 2.3 x 3.7
10 "A crowd gathered around"   w 4.8 x 4.5
11 "Plantation houses standing back from the road-
side"   w 4.8 x 4.3
                                                 A. Lindsay, Sc.
12 "It is the leader, and all the others follow it" w 4.8 x 4.2
13 "The long straggling aqueduct"   w 4.8 x 1.6
14 "A turbaned negro woman sat with her knitting" w 3.0 x 4.3
                                                 Witte, Sc.
15 "The crooked winding road that leads into the
village"   w 4.8 x 2.7
16 "He sat down by the garden gate"   w 2.3 x 3.4
                                                 Witte, Sc.
17 "And thither children brought donkeys every
morning"   w 2.3 x 3.0
                                                 Grimley, Sc.
18 "In all houses one finds the filter and the water
jar"   w 2.3 x 3.8
19 "Coffee mill, surrounded by flat stone terraces" w 3.0 x 5.2
20 "A great section of bamboo trunk balanced upon
her head"   w 1.7 x 3.4
21 "Two negro women stood gossiping and cooling
their feet"   w 2.4 x 3.4

22 "The only picturesque object in the whole horrid
  expanse"   w.-3.7 x 3.8
23 The bugle call   w 1.6 x 3.4

LXXX. 842 May 1890 OLD NEW YORK TAVERNS *John Austin Stevens*
 1 Initial A   w 1.2 x 2.0
 2 The Old-time Landlord   w 2.3 x 3.4
 3 "The King's Head, kept by one Roger Baker"   w 2.4 x 4.7
 4 "Elizabeth Jourdain, who lodged Her Majesty's
  soldiers"   w 4.5 x 3.4
 5 Game of Bowls   w 7.0 x 4.8
                  A. Lindsay, Sc.
 6 " 'The Dog's Head in the Pot' (of great
  antiquity)"   w 1.8 x 3.1
 7 "It crossed the river to the Long Island side of the
  Brooklyn Ferry"   w 3.7 x 2.5
 8 Brownejohn's Wharf   w 4.8 x 6.9
                H. W. Peckwell, Sc.
 9 "Each to be honored with bumpers innumerable
  of rich wine and punch"   w 4.7 x 4.0
10 In the reading-room   w 7.0 x 4.7
                A. Anderson, Sc.
11 "The rival editors"   w 2.4 x 2.6
12 "John Still, 'an honest barber and peruke-maker
  from London' "   w 2.4 x 3.1
13 "The ball began with French dances"   w 3.6 x 3.0
14 "The chair was carried by hand and the harness
  was worn by the bearers"   w 3.7 x 2.8
15 "Cards and gaming were features"   w 3.0 x 3.0
16 The ferry   w 2.7 x 4.2
17 "Cargoes of favorite vintages"   w 2.3 x 2.9
18 "The drum beat in the streets of the city"   w 2.9 x 4.4
19 "The first violin would be played by a 'gentleman
  lately arrived' "   w 2.0 x 3.5
20 At the Vauxhall   w 3.0 x 5.1
21 "Exchanged thrusts with the merciless Junius"   w 3.0 x 2.8
22 "The variety and fatigues of his business"   w 3.5 x 2.6
23 Meeting of Captain Tollemache and Captain
  Pennington at the New York Arms   w 6.9 x 4.8

24 "John Cape takes down the quaint old sign" w 1.8 x 2.8
25 "The men who met at Hampden Hall" w 3.8 x 1.6
26 Tailpiece w 2.5 x 1.7

LXXXI. 123 June 1890 CHAPBOOK HEROES *Howard Pyle*
  1 The Chapman w 4.7 x 7.2
    F. Bernstrom, Sc.
  2 Claude DuVal proposes a Dance on the Heath w 7.4 x 4.7
    F. H. Wellington, Sc.
  3 Sir James Thornhill painting Jack Sheppard's
    Portrait w 4.8 x 6.2
  4 Turpin and King w 4.8 x 7.2
    A. E. Anderson, Sc.

LXXXI. 186 July 1890 A FAMOUS CHAPBOOK VILLAIN *Howard Pyle*
  1 Jonathan in the Wood Street Compter Prison w 4.8 x 7.2
    J. Tinkey, Sc.
  2 Jonathan as an Enemy arresting a Thief w 4.8 x 6.8
    R. A. Muller, Sc.
  3 Jonathan and a Client—The Lady with the Green
    Pocket-book w 4.8 x 6.3
    H. Wolf, Sc.
  4 On the Way to Tyburn w 7.6 x 4.7

LXXXI. 933 Nov. 1890 THE QUAKER LADY *S. Weir Mitchell*
  1 Headpiece with title p 2.0 x 1.5
  2 First page—Vignette p 1.4 x 3.3
  3 First page—Vignette p 2.3 x 3.2
  4 First page—Vignette p 1.5 x 2.3
  5 First page—Vignette p 1.4 x 1.3
  6 First page—Vignette p 0.8 x 1.9
  7 Second page—Vignette p 2.5 x 1.5
  8 Second page—Vignette p 1.3 x 3.4
  9 Second page—Vignette p 1.0 x 2.2
10 Second page—Vignette p 2.5 x 1.0
11 Second page—Vignette p 2.8 x 3.3
12 Third page—Vignette p 1.1 x 1.1
13 Third page—Vignette p 1.6 x 3.7
14 Third page—Vignette p 2.4 x 3.4
15 Third page—Vignette p 2.5 x 2.0
16 Third page—Vignette p 1.9 x 2.1
17 Third page—Vignette p 2.3 x 0.9

LXXXII. 38 Dec. 1890 FLUTE AND VIOLIN   *James Lane Allen*

1	The Magic Flute [1]	w 4.8 x 7.1
2	"He had beautiful manners" [1]	p 4.2 x 3.1
3	"His long nightly labors" [1]	p 3.0 x 2.7
4	The Widow Spurlock [1]	p 1.2 x 1.6
5	Old Arsena	p 1.6 x 2.3
6	"With their heads close together" [1]	p 1.8 x 2.6
7	"He began to play" [1]	p 3.1 x 3.5
8	Hanging the violin [1]	p 2.0 x 3.9
9	David [1]	p 1.7 x 2.0
10	"He played with unusual fervor" [1]	p 2.9 x 3.4
11	Mr. Leuba	p 1.8 x 1.9
12	"Executing an intricate passage" [1]	p 3.4 x 3.1
13	"A small crowd had collected around the entrance to the Museum"	p 4.3 x 3.0
14	"The widow dropped her eyes" [1]	p 2.4 x 4.1
15	"It was a very gay dinner" [1]	p 4.3 x 2.5
16	The parson came down the street driving his flock of boys [1]	p 4.2 x 3.9
17	Before the picture [1]	p 3.1 x 3.7
18	"Toiled homeward with his treasure"	p 2.4 x 4.7
19	"Buried his head on her bosom" [1]	p 2.4 x 3.4
20	At David's bedside [1]	p 3.0 x 2.7
21	"His head bowed on his folded arms" [1]	p 2.3 x 2.6

LXXXIV. 16 Dec. 1891 A MAID'S CHOICE   *W. W. Gilchrist*

Eleven pages illustrated and decorated—Music with words
Five pages, each with elliptical illustrations surrounded
    by decorations and music below, as follows:

1	Headpiece with title	p 5.0 x 7.8 Aikman, Sc.
2	Headpiece Verse 1—Ye Jovial Huntsman	p 5.0 x 7.8 Kilifair, Sc.
3	Headpiece Verse 2—Ye Fat, Rich Man	p 5.0 x 7.8 Anderson, Sc.
4	Headpiece Verse 3—Ye Gallant Soldier	p 5.0 x 7.8 J. Bernstrom, Sc.
5	Headpiece Verse 4—Ye Jolly Country Boy	p 5.0 x 7.8 F. French, Sc.

Six pages music and words, and interspersed with
    36 small illustrations about 1.5 x 1.5. Total 41 illustrations.

---

[1] Reproduced in "Flute and Violin." James Lane Allen, Harper, New York. 1891.

LXXXIV. 349 Feb. 1892 THE LITTLE MAID AT THE DOOR

Mary E. Wilkins

  1 Headpiece above title   p 4.3 x 4.0
  2 Initial J   p 0.8 x 0.8
  3 "I see naught but a little maid at the door"[1]   w 4.8 x 7.1
       A. Lindsay, Sc.

LXXXV. 165 July 1892 HOW THE DECLARATION WAS RECEIVED
       IN THE OLD THIRTEEN   *Chas. D. Deshler*

  1 Reading the Declaration before Washington's Army,
       New York, July 9, 1776[2]   w 4.8 x 6.5
       A. Lindsay, Sc.
  2 Headpiece with title   p 4.4 x 3.0
  3 At Philadelphia, Pennsylvania   p 4.8 x 2.0
  4 At Princeton, New Jersey   p 3.5 x 1.8
  5 At Dover, Delaware   p 4.7 x 1.7
  6 In New York. (At Headquarters)   p 4.8 x 3.0
  7 At Boston, Massachusetts   p 4.8 x 2.9
  8 At Portsmouth, New Hampshire   p 3.3 x 1.8
  9 At Newport, Rhode Island   p 4.8 x 2.8
 10 In Connecticut   p 2.3 x 2.1
 11 At Williamsburg, Virginia   p 4.8 x 2.0
 12 At Halifax, North Carolina   p 2.3 x 3.4
 13 At Baltimore, Maryland   p 3.3 x 2.5
 14 At Charleston, South Carolina   p 4.8 x 1.8
 15 At Savannah, Georgia   p 2.4 x 2.5

LXXXV. 278 July 1892 TWO MOODS   *Thomas B. Aldrich*
Full page. Border with illustrations above and poem
       inserted   p 4.8 x 7.4

LXXXV. 586 Sept. 1892 AMONG THE SAND HILLS   *Howard Pyle*
  1 Headpiece   p 4.8 x 3.0
  2 Initial T   p 0.3 x 0.3
  3 No title   p 2.3 x 0.6
  4 Initial S   p 0.3 x 0.3

---

[1] Reproduced in "Silence and Other Stories." Mary E. Wilkins, Harper & Brothers, New York. 1898.

[2] Reproduced in "Documentary Edition," Vol. IV, "A History of the American People." Woodrow Wilson, Harper, New York. 1918.

5 No title	p 4.8 x 0.6	
6 Initial T	p 0.3 x 0.3	
7 The Sand Hills	p 4.8 x 7.2	
8 No title	p 2.3 x 1.0	
9 Initial F	p 0.3 x 0.3	
10 No title	p 2.3 x 0.3	
11 Initial B	p 0.3 x 0.3	
12 No title	p 4.8 x 2.0	
13 No title	p 2.3 x 1.3	
14 Initial S	p 0.3 x 0.3	
15 No title	p 2.3 x 0.3	
16 The Wreck	p 4.8 x 3.3 Anderson, Sc.	
17 Initial C	p 0.3 x 0.3	
18 No title	p 2.3 x 0.5	
19 Initial B	p 0.3 x 0.3	
20 No title	p 1.2 x 0.9	
21 No title	p 2.3 x 0.5	
22 No title	p 4.8 x 1.5	
23 Initial T	p 0.3 x 0.3	
24 No title	p 0.8 x 1.1	
25 No title	p 2.3 x 0.4	
26 Initial N	p 0.3 x 0.3	
27 No title	p 2.3 x 1.0	
28 The Lily Lake	p 4.7 x 5.4	

LXXXVI. 20 Dec. 1892 GILES COREY, YEOMAN — *Mary E. Wilkins*

1 "This is no courting night" [1] — w 4.8 x 3.5

2 "Hey, black cat! hey, my pretty black cat" [1] — w 4.8 x 7.2 Anderson, Sc.

3 "There is a flock of yellow birds around her head" [1] — w 4.8 x 7.3

4 "Father, Father!" [1] — w 4.8 x 7.5 F. French, Sc.

LXXXVI. 547 March 1893 MONOCHROMES — *W. D. Howells*

1 Frontispiece. Question [2] — w 4.8 x 7.6 F. French, Sc.

2 Headpiece with title [2] — p 4.8 x 2.6

---

[1] Reproduced in "Giles Corey, Yeoman." Mary E. Wilkins, Harper, New York. 1893.
[2] Reproduced in "Stops of Various Quills." W. D. Howells, Harper, New York. 1895.

3	Question. Initial S [1]	p 0.6 x 0.6
4	Tailpiece [1]	p 2.4 x 0.9
5	Living. Headpiece [1]	p 4.9 x 0.9
6	Initial H [1]	p 0.6 x 0.6
7	Tomorrow. Headpiece [1]	p 3.7 x 0.9
8	Initial O [1]	p 0.6 x 0.6
9	Tailpiece [1]	p 1.6 x 0.9
10	From Generation to Generation. Headpiece [1]	p 4.9 x 1.4
11	Initial I [1]	p 0.6 x 0.6
12	Tailpiece [1]	p 1.3 x 1.2
13	The Bewildered Guest. Headpiece [1]	p 2.8 x 1.0
14	Initial I [1]	p 0.6 x 0.6
15	Hope. Headpiece [1]	p 4.9 x 1.7
16	Initial Y [1]	p 0.6 x 0.6
17	Tailpiece [1]	p 1.3 x 0.5
18	Respite. Initial D	p 0.6 x 0.6
19	Tailpiece [1]	p 2.3 x 1.2

LXXXVI. 683 April 1893 RETRIBUTION   *Howard Pyle*

1 "He sat down beside her on the bench"   w 4.7 x 6.9
J. Bernstrom, Sc.

2 "Thereupon the poor woman screamed aloud, and cried out that he was a Murderer"   w 6.8 x 4.8
F. H. Wellington, Sc.

LXXXVI. 813 May 1893 THE EVOLUTION OF NEW YORK. I.

Thomas A. Janvier

1 Along the Canal in Old Manhattan [2]   w 4.7 x 7.4
F. S. King, Sc.

2 Headpiece with title and initial [3]   p 4.8 x 3.8

3 On the River Front [6] [5] [4] [2]   w 4.7 x 7.3
J. Tinkey, Sc.

4 Tailpiece [3] [2]   p 4.4 x 4.5

[1] Reproduced in "Stops of Various Quills." W. D. Howells, Harper, New York. 1895.

[2] Reproduced in "In Old New York." Thomas A. Janvier, Harper, New York. 1894.

[3] Reproduced in "Harper's Ency. U. S. History," Vol. VI. Harper, New York. 1902.

[4] Reproduced with title "Along the Water Front in Old New York" in "Harper's Ency. U. S. History," Vol. VI. Harper, New York. 1902.

[5] Reproduced in "A History of the American People," Vol. III. Woodrow Wilson, Harper, New York. 1902.

[6] Reproduced in "Documentary Edition," Vol. V, "A History of the American People." Woodrow Wilson, Harper, New York. 1918.

LXXXVII. 15 June 1893 THE EVOLUTION OF NEW YORK. II.

Thomas A. Janvier

1 Headpiece—In 1776—The Conflagration [2] [1]   p 4.4 x 4.1
2 A Privateersman Ashore [1]   w 4.7 x 7.4
A. Lindsay, Sc.
3 Opening of the Erie Canal [1]   w 4.7 x 7.4
Anderson, Sc.
4 Tailpiece   p 4.4 x 3.0

LXXXVII. 327 Aug. 1893 THE COCKLANE GHOST   *Howard Pyle*
1 Headpiece with title and initial   p 4.8 x 3.7
2 Vignette   p 4.4 x 3.1
3 Vignette   p 3.1 x 4.0
4 Vignette   p 4.8 x 2.4
5 Vignette   p 4.8 x 3.2
6 Vignette   p 2.3 x 2.2
7 Vignette   p 2.3 x 3.4
8 Vignette   p 4.8 x 2.5
9 Vignette   p 2.4 x 3.5
10 Vignette   p 3.2 x 3.3
11 Vignette   p 4.8 x 2.5
12 Vignette   p 4.8 x 2.4
13 Tailpiece   p 1.6 x 1.7

LXXXVIII. 103 Dec. 1893 A SOLDIER OF FORTUNE   *Howard Pyle*
1 Headpiece with initial O   p 1.0 x 1.5
2 Vignette   p 2.6 x 1.9
3 Vignette   p 1.5 x 2.2
4 A Night in the Village Street   w 4.8 x 6.4
Peckwell, Sc.
5 Vignette   p 2.3 x 1.5
6 Vignette   p 1.9 x 3.3
7 Dragging the Duke out of the Coach   w 4.8 x 7.0
A. Lindsay, Sc.
8 Vignette   p 1.5 x 1.9
9 Vignette   p 3.2 x 1.4
10 Vignette   p 2.2 x 1.8
11 Vignette   p 0.8 x 1.7

[1] Reproduced in "In Old New York." Thomas A. Janvier, Harper, New York. 1894.
[2] Reproduced in "Harper's Ency. U. S. History," Vol. VI. Harper, New York. 1902.

12 The Fight for the Crown   w 4.8 x 7.2
    F. French, Sc.

13 Vignette   p 2.0 x 2.0

14 Vignette   p 1.7 x 2.1

15 Vignette   p 2.3 x 0.8

16 Vignette   p 2.7 x 2.5

LXXXVIII. 392 Feb. 1894 IN TENEBRAS [1]   *Howard Pyle*
No illustrations

LXXXIX. 813 Nov. 1894 THE SEA ROBBERS OF NEW YORK
    Thomas A. Janvier

1 "He had found the Captain agreeable and companionable"   w 4.8 x 7.2
    Aikman, Sc.

2 Headpiece—New York as it appeared about 1690 (with initial T)   p 4.8 x 4.5

3 "Pirates used to do that to their Captains now and then"   p 7.7 x 4.1

4 Kidd at Gardiner's Island   p 4.7 x 7.2

5 Tailpiece   p 4.5 x 2.4

XC. 34 Dec. 1894 STOPS OF VARIOUS QUILLS   *Wm. D. Howells*

1 Frontispiece. No title [2]   p 3.7 x 7.6
    Kurtz, Sc.

2 Headpiece with title [2]   p 4.8 x 3.2

3 Sphinx. Initial W [2]   p 0.6 x 0.6

4 Tailpiece [2]   p 1.2 x 1.0

5 Headpiece [2]   p 3.6 x 1.8

6 Time. Initial D [2]   p 0.6 x 0.6

7 Headpiece [2]   p 3.0 x 0.8

8 Society. Initial Y   p 0.6 x 0.6

9 Tailpiece [2]   p 1.3 x 0.4

10 Headpiece [2]   p 4.6 x 1.1

11 Heredity. Initial T [2]   p 0.6 x 0.6

12 Tailpiece [2]   p 2.0 x 0.6

13 Headpiece [2]   p 4.7 x 2.3

14 Solitude. Initial A [2]   p 0.6 x 0.6

---

[1] Republished in "Shapes that Haunt the Dusk." Harper, New York. 1907.
[2] Reproduced in "Stops of Various Quills." W. D. Howells, Harper, New York. 1895.

15	Headpiece [1]	p 3.6 x 1.0
16	Change. Initial S [1]	p 0.6 x 0.6
17	Tailpiece [1]	p 3.9 x 0.8
18	Headpiece [1]	p 3.6 x 1.6
19	Midway. Initial S [1]	p 0.6 x 0.6
20	Headpiece [1]	p 2.3 x 1.3
21	Calvary. Initial I [1]	p 0.6 x 0.6

xc. 293 Jan. 1895 NEW YORK SLAVE TRADERS *Thomas A. Janvier*

1 "Some of the by-standers said 'She is drunk, it will soon pass away' " w 4.8 x 7.4
King, Sc.

2 "The choicest pieces of her cargo were sold at auction" w 4.8 x 7.4
A. Lindsay, Sc.

3 "We escaped in the boat" p 4.8 x 7.4
Kurtz, Sc.

xc. 333 Feb. 1895 NEW YORK COLONIAL PRIVATEERS
Thomas A. Janvier

1 "Again my Captain took the biggest" w 4.8 x 7.4
Kurtz, Sc.

2 Headpiece with title and initial O p 4.7 x 5.2

3 "Barbarously murdered the first, and grievously wounded the latter." p 4.8 x 7.3
A. Lindsay, Sc.

4 Tailpiece p 1.7 x 1.9

xc. 630 March 1895 SOCIETY *W. D. Howells*

1 Headpiece [1] p 4.8 x 1.9
2 Marginal decoration p 1.2 x 5.5
3 Tailpiece [1] p 4.3 x 1.2

xci. 517 Sept. 1895 PEBBLES *W. D. Howells*

1 Frontispiece—No title [1] p 4.8 x 7.2
Kurtz, Sc.

2 Headpiece with title [1] p 4.7 x 6.2
3 The Burden. Initial I [1] p 0.4 x 0.4
4 Tailpiece [1] p 3.3 x 1.0
5 Headpiece [1] p 4.4 x 3.3
6 Sympathy. Initial F [1] p 0.4 x 0.4

[1] Reproduced in "Stops of Various Quills." W. D. Howells, Harper, New York. 1895.

[1] Reproduced in "Stops of Various Quills." W. D. Howells, Harper, New York. 1895.
[2] Reproduced in The Wilmington Society of the Fine Arts Catalogue, Wilmington. 1912.
[3] Reproduced in "George Washington." Woodrow Wilson, Harper, New York. 1897.
[4] Reproduced with title "Scene on a Colonial Plantation" in "Harper's Ency. U. S. History," Vol. IX. Harper, New York. 1902.

XCII. 549 March 1896 COLONEL WASHINGTON *Woodrow Wilson*
1 Washington's Retreat from Great Meadows [1] p 4.8 x 7.2
2 Headpiece with title [1] p 4.8 x 3.7
3 The Burial of Braddock [3] [2] [1] p 4.8 x 7.4
4 Washington and Mary Philipse [1] p 4.8 x 7.6
5 Tailpiece [1] p 2.0 x 0.8

XCII. 931 May 1896 AT HOME IN VIRGINIA *Woodrow Wilson*
1 Leaving Mount Vernon for the Congress of the
　Colonies [5] [1] p 4.8 x 7.2
2 The Old Capital at Williamsburg [6] [4] [1] p 4.8 x 3.7
3 In the Old Raleigh Tavern [1] p 4.8 x 7.4

XCII. 828 May 1896 THROUGH INLAND WATERS. I. *Howard Pyle*
1 Head and sidepiece (with initial T) p 4.7 x 7.5
2 Vignette p 2.4 x 3.0
3 Vignette p 4.0 x 0.9
4 Full page. No title p 6.7 x 4.8
5 Headpiece with sub-title p 4.7 x 2.8
6 Vignette p 4.7 x 3.6
7 Vignette p 1.0 x 1.0
8 Vignette p 2.5 x 3.5
9 Vignette p 3.3 x 1.5
10 Vignette p 1.7 x 2.0
11 Vignette p 1.5 x 2.0
12 Vignette p 3.5 x 2.8
13 Vignette p 1.8 x 2.7
14 Vignette p 1.7 x 2.2
15 Vignette p 1.3 x 2.7
16 Tailpiece p 1.0 x 1.3

---

[1] Reproduced in "George Washington." Woodrow Wilson, Harper, New York. 1897.
[2] Reproduced in "A History of the American People," Vol. III. Woodrow Wilson, Harper, New York. 1902.
[3] Reproduced in "Documentary Edition," Vol. V, "A History of the American People." Woodrow Wilson, Harper, New York. 1918.
[4] Reproduced in "A History of the American People," Vol. II. Woodrow Wilson, Harper, New York. 1902.
[5] Reproduced in "Documentary Edition," Vol. VI, "A History of the American People." Woodrow Wilson, Harper, New York. 1918.
[6] Reproduced in "Documentary Edition," Vol. III, "A History of the American People." Woodrow Wilson, Harper, New York. 1918.

XCIII. 63 June 1896 THROUGH INLAND WATERS. II.   *Howard Pyle*

 1 Headpiece with title (and initial T)   p 4.8 x 6.2
 2 Vignette   p 4.8 x 4.0
 3 Vignette   p 3.1 x 1.0
 4 Vignette   p 4.3 x 2.3
 5 Vignette   p 2.5 x 2.5
 6 Vignette   p 4.5 x 5.3
 7 Full page. No title   p 6.8 x 4.9
 8 Vignette   p 1.9 x 1.6
 9 Vignette   p 1.8 x 3.1
 10 Vignette   p 4.5 x 2.0
 11 Vignette   p 1.8 x 1.8
 12 Vignette   p 4.8 x 4.2
 13 Illustration. No title   p 4.8 x 3.4
 14 Vignette   p 4.8 x 4.2
 15 Vignette   p 2.2 x 1.7
 16 Tailpiece   p 4.8 x 3.5

XCIII. 165 July 1896 GENERAL WASHINGTON   *Woodrow Wilson*

 1 Headpiece with title [3][2][1]   p 4.7 x 3.0
 2 Washington and Steuben at Valley Forge [3][2][1]   p 4.8 x 7.4
 3 Lady Washington's Arrival at Headquarters, Cambridge [1]   p 7.4 x 4.8
 4 The Escape of Arnold [1]   p 4.9 x 7.4
 5 Carpenters' Hall, Philadelphia [4][1]   p 4.5 x 3.8

XCIII. 489 Sept. 1896 FIRST IN PEACE   *Woodrow Wilson*

 1 Washington in the Garden at Mount Vernon [3][2][1] p 4.8 x 6.7
 2 Headpiece with title [1]   p 4.8 x 3.0
 3 Washington bringing his Mother into the Ballroom.
   Fredericksburg [1]   p 4.8 x 7.3
 4 Mustered out—A rest on the way home [1]   p 7.3 x 4.8
 5 Tailpiece [1]   p 2.0 x 0.9

---

[1] Reproduced in "George Washington." Woodrow Wilson, Harper, New York. 1897.
[2] Reproduced in "Catalogue of Drawings," etc. Howard Pyle, Philadelphia. 1897.
[3] Reproduced in "Catalogue of Drawings," etc. Howard Pyle, Boston. 1897.
[4] Reproduced in "Harper's Ency. U. S. History," Vol. VII. Harper, New York. 1902.

XCIII. 843 Nov. 1896 THE FIRST PRESIDENT OF THE
        UNITED STATES   *Woodrow Wilson*
  1 Washington and Nellie Custis [1]   p 4.8 x 7.3
  2 Headpiece with title [1]   p 4.8 x 3.1
  3 Thompson, the Clerk of Congress, announcing to
      Washington, at Mount Vernon, his election to
      the Presidency [4] [3] [2] [1]   p 4.9 x 7.3
  4 The Death of Washington [1]   p 4.8 x 7.0
  5 Tailpiece   p 2.6 x 1.2

XCIV. Dec. 1896 COVER DESIGN   c 6.0 x 8.0

XCIV. 11 Dec. 1896 THE ROMANCE OF AN AMBROTYPE   *Howard Pyle*
  1 Headpiece with title   p 4.8 x 3.4
  2 Initial T   p 0.6 x 0.6
  3 Vignette   p 2.7 x 4.1
  4 Vignette   p 4.8 x 3.4
  5 Vignette   p 4.8 x 2.7
  6 Vignette   p 1.9 x 2.8
  7 Vignette   p 4.6 x 2.3
  8 Vignette   p 2.2 x 3.2
  9 Vignette   p 4.8 x 1.2
 10 Vignette   p 3.6 x 2.1
 11 Vignette   p 2.3 x 2.0
 12 Vignette   p 4.8 x 2.8
 13 Vignette   p 2.0 x 2.1
 14 Tailpiece   p 2.5 x 1.5

XCIV. 443 Feb. 1897 THE ASSEMBLY BALL *Sarah Beaumont Kennedy*
  1 The Assembly Ball   p 4.9 x 7.3
  2 Headpiece with title   p 4.8 x 3.2
  3 Initial I   p 0.5 x 0.5
  4 Tailpiece   p 4.2 x 2.0

---

[1] Reproduced in "George Washington." Woodrow Wilson, Harper, New York. 1897.

[2] Reproduced with title "Washington Receiving the Announcement" in "Harper's Ency. U. S. History," Vol. IX. Harper, New York. 1902.

[3] Reproduced in "A History of the American People," Vol. III. Woodrow Wilson, Harper, New York. 1902.

[4] Reproduced in "Documentary Edition," Vol. V, "A History of the American People." Woodrow Wilson, Harper, New York. 1918.

XCIV. 497 March 1897 LOVE AND DEATH   *Howard Pyle*
    1 Love and Death   p 4.8 x 7.8
    2 Headpiece   p 4.7 x 1.7
    3 Tailpiece   p 4.7 x 1.3

XCIV. 659 April 1897 WASHINGTON AND THE FRENCH
         CRAZE OF '93   *John Bach McMaster*
    1 A Banquet to Genet [3] [1]   c 4.9 x 7.4
    2 Headpiece. Arrival of Genet at Gray's Ferry   p 4.8 x 3.0
    3 The News of the Execution of Louis XVI   p 4.8 x 7.3
    4 Citizen Genet formally presented to Washington [3] [2]   p 4.8 x 7.3
    5 Tailpiece   p 2.6 x 3.0

OLD CHESTER TALES   *Margaret Deland*
XCVI. 644 April 1898
    1 Decoration with title   p 4.8 x 0.7
    2 Headpiece [4]   p 4.8 x 4.1
    3 "She seemed 'a tall white lily,' he said" [4]   p 4.8 x 7.3

XCVI. 880 May 1898
    4 " 'Change it? My name?' she said" [6] [4]   p 4.8 x 7.7
    5 Headpiece [6] [5] [4]   p 4.8 x 3.7

XCVII. 25 June 1898
    6 Headpiece [4]   p 4.8 x 3.5
    7 " 'And who's going to support 'em?' demanded
      Mrs. Barkley" [4]   p 4.8 x 7.2

XCVII. 260 July 1898
    8 "Judge Morrison read these harmless jingles,
      chuckling and sneering" [5]   p 4.8 x 7.3
    9 Headpiece   p 4.8 x 4.0

[1] Reproduced in "A History of the American People," Vol. III. Woodrow Wilson, Harper, New York. 1902.

[2] Reproduced with title "Interview between Washington," etc., in "A History of the American People," Vol. III. Woodrow Wilson, Harper, New York. 1902.

[3] Reproduced in "Documentary Edition," Vol. VI, "A History of the American People." Woodrow Wilson, Harper, New York. 1918.

[4] Reproduced in "Old Chester Tales." Margaret Deland, Harper, New York. 1899.

[5] Reproduced in "Around Old Chester." Margaret Deland, Harper, New York. 1915.

[6] Reproduced in "Good for the Soul." Margaret Deland, Harper, New York. 1899.

xcvii. 406 Aug. 1898
  10 Headpiece [1]   p 4.8 x 4.4
  11 "Mary turned white; then she dropped down at
       his feet" [1]   p 4.8 x 7.3

xcvii. 522 Sept. 1898
  12 Headpiece [1]   p 4.8 x 4.4
  13 " 'So you're hanging the locusts?' inquired the
       Judge, contemptuously" [1]   p 4.8 x 7.3

xcvii. 780 Oct. 1898
  14 Headpiece [1]   p 4.8 x 4.0
  15 "I had enemies in my line" [1]   p 4.8 x 7.1

xcvii. 863 Nov. 1898
  16 Headpiece [1]   p 4.8 x 4.0
  17 "They told each other about it" [1]   p 4.8 x 7.1

xcviii. 142 Dec. 1898
  18 Headpiece [1]   p 4.8 x 3.1
  19 "Mr. Horace looked at her with instant
       sympathy" [1]   p 4.8 x 7.2

xcviii. 3 Dec. 1898 OLD CAPTAIN   *Myles Hemenway*
  1 "And you shall not hinder me"   c 5.0 x 7.3
  2 Headpiece   p 4.7 x 2.8
  3 Illustration. No title   p 4.8 x 3.0
  4 Illustration. No title   p 4.7 x 1.6
  5 Illustration. No title   p 4.5 x 3.3
  6 Illustration. No title   p 4.8 x 1.2
  7 Illustration. No title   p 4.8 x 3.2
  8 Illustration. No title   p 4.8 x 1.5
  9 Illustration. No title   p 4.8 x 2.2
  10 Illustration. No title   p 4.8 x 2.3
  11 Tailpiece   p 4.7 x 2.1

xcix. 399 Aug. 1899 THE BODY TO THE SOUL   *Ellen M. Gates*
  1 Frontispiece   p 3.5 x 7.7
  2 Headband with title   p 4.9 x 3.3

[1] Reproduced in "Old Chester Tales." Margaret Deland, Harper, New York. 1899.

3	Side decoration	p 1.1 x 5.7
4	Decoration	p 1.2 x 1.3
5	Side decoration	p 1.1 x 7.7
6	Side decoration	p 1.1 x 7.7
7	Tailpiece	p 2.5 x 2.5

c. 69 Dec. 1899 A PUPPET OF FATE — *Howard Pyle*

1	Headpiece with title with initial T	c 4.9 x 5.0
2	Vignette	c 1.0 x 8.0
3	Chapter heading with initial N	c 0.7 x 2.7
4	Vignette	c 2.3 x 5.5
5	Vignette	c 1.5 x 2.1
6	Vignette	c 2.0 x 7.7
7	Vignette	c 2.4 x 8.0
8	Chapter heading with initial F	c 1.0 x 2.8
9	Vignette	c 2.0 x 7.8
10	Full page	c 4.8 x 7.2
11	Chapter heading with initial A	c 0.8 x 2.8
12	Vignette	c 1.6 x 4.1

c. 667 April 1900 A PRELUDE — *Bliss Carmen*

1	Headpiece with title	p 4.3 x 3.9
2	Initial T	p 0.5 x 0.5
3	In Springtime	p 4.8 x 7.5
4	Tailpiece	p 4.3 x 2.9

c. 930 May 1900 THE ANGEL AND THE CHILD — *Howard Pyle*
Illustrations by Sarah S. Stilwell

CI. 892 Nov. 1900 THE YELLOW OF THE LEAF — *Bliss Carmen*

1	Headpiece	p 4.8 x 2.3
2	Title with decorations	p 4.8 x 0.3
3	Initial T	p 0.6 x 0.6
4	"The falling leaf is at the door"	p 3.2 x 8.0
5	Tailpiece	p 1.1 x 4.8

CII. 3 Dec. 1900 THE PILGRIMAGE OF TRUTH — *Erik Bogh*

1	Truth Leaves the Fairies' Wonderland	c 4.8 x 7.3
2	Truth before the King	c 4.8 x 7.1
3	Truth in the Temple	c 4.8 x 7.0

4	Truth before the Seer	c 4.8 x 7.2
5	Truth Went on Her Way Alone	c 4.8 x 7.2
6	Truth in the Fool's Lodge	c 4.8 x 7.1
	In black—initials in red:	
1	Headpiece with title	p 4.8 x 4.7
2	Initial F	p 1.2 x 1.2
3	Tailpiece	p 1.2 x 4.9
4	Initial T	p 1.2 x 1.2
5	Tailpiece	p 2.0 x 4.9
6	Initial T	p 1.2 x 1.2
7	Headband	p 1.4 x 4.9
8	Headband	p 1.4 x 4.9
9	Initial B	p 1.2 x 1.2
10	Initial O	p 1.2 x 1.2
11	Initial H	p 1.2 x 1.2

HARPER'S MONTHLY MAGAZINE

COLONIES AND NATION   *Woodrow Wilson*

CII. 143 Jan. 1901
1 Headpiece with decoration and title [1]   p 4.9 x 4.5
2 Landing negroes at Jamestown from Dutch man-
   of-war, 1619 [8] [4] [2]   p 4.8 x 7.3

CII. 335 Feb. 1901
3 Anne Hutchinson preaching in her house in
   Boston [8] [2]   p 4.7 x 7.0
4 Arrival of Stuyvesant in New Amsterdam [9] [2]   p 4.7 x 7.2

CII. 531 March 1901
5 The Burning of Jamestown [9] [5] [2]   p 4.7 x 7.0
6 Ships loading in Albemarle Sound [9] [2]   p 4.8 x 7.1
7 On the War Path [9] [6] [2]   p 4.7 x 7.1

CII. 709 April 1901
8 A Pennsylvania Cave-Dwelling XVIIth Century [9][2] p 7.2 x 4.7
9 An interview between Sir Edmund Andros and
   James Blair [9] [2]   p 4.7 x 7.1
10 Phips recovering the sunken treasure [9] [2]   p 4.6 x 7.1
11 Slaughter signing the death warrant of Leisler [9] [2] p 4.7 x 7.1

For footnotes see end of series on pages following.

[1] Picture only reproduced with title "Ships Were Rare" in "History of the American People," Vol. I. Woodrow Wilson, Harper, New York. 1902.

[2] Reproduced in "History of the American People," Vol. I. Woodrow Wilson, Harper, New York. 1902.

[3] Reproduced in "History of the American People," Vol. II. Woodrow Wilson, Harper, New York. 1902.

[4] Reproduced with title "Landing Slaves from a Dutch," etc., in "Harper's Ency. U. S. History," Vol. VIII. Harper, New York. 1902.

[5] Reproduced in "Harper's Ency. U. S. History," Vol. V. Harper, New York. 1902.

[6] Reproduced with title "Indians Ambuscading a Puritan Farmer" in "Harper's Ency. U. S. History," Vol. VII. Harper, New York. 1902.

[7] Reproduced in "Harper's Ency. U. S. History," Vol. I. Harper, New York. 1902.

[8] Reproduced in "Documentary Edition," Vol. I, "A History of the American People." Woodrow Wilson, Harper, New York. 1918.

[9] Reproduced in "Documentary Edition," Vol. II, "A History of the American People." Woodrow Wilson, Harper, New York. 1918.

[10] Reproduced in "Documentary Edition," Vol. III, "A History of the American People." Woodrow Wilson, Harper, New York. 1918.

[11] Reproduced in "Documentary Edition," Vol. IV, "A History of the American People." Woodrow Wilson, Harper, New York. 1918.

For other references to above see foot following page.

CIII. 2 June 1901 A DREAM OF YOUNG SUMMER   *Edith M. Thomas*
    1 A Dream of Young Summer   · c 4.2 x 7.7

CIII. 718 Oct. 1901 KING CUSTOM   *Maud S. Rawson*
    1 Headpiece   p 3.3 x 1.8
    2 Initial M   p 0.6 x 0.6
    3 Marginal decoration   p 4.3 x 7.4
    4 Vignette   p 4.7 x 4.8
    5 My Lady of Brede   c 4.5 x 7.3

CIII. 884 Nov. 1901 MARGARET OF CORTONA   *Edith Wharton*
    1 Headpiece   p 4.7 x 4.4

CIV. 27 Dec. 1901 THE SEA MAN   *Josephine D. Daskam*
    1 Headpiece with title   p 3.4 x 2.5
    2 Full page   p 3.7 x 7.2

CIV. 180 Jan. 1902 NORTH FOLK LEGENDS OF THE SEA   *Howard Pyle*
    1 Frontispiece   c 4.4 x 7.3
    2 Decoration   c 4.8 x 5.7
    3 Initial T   c 0.6 x 0.6
    4 Marginal decoration with title   c 4.8 x 7.9
    5 The Fishing of Thor and Hymir   c 4.1 x 7.8
    6 Headpiece   c 4.9 x 2.3
    7 Decorative title   c 4.9 x 0.5
    8 The Fairy Morgana   c 3.9 x 7.7
    9 Headpiece   c 4.9 x 1.5
    10 Decorative title   c 4.8 x 0.6
    11 Saint Brendan's Island   c 3.7 x 7.3
    12 Headpiece   c 4.9 x 2.6
    13 Decorative title   c 4.9 x 1.1
    14 Mother Carey's Chickens   c 4.0 x 7.6
    15 Headpiece, The Flying Dutchman   c 4.9 x 3.7

Following footnotes refer to two preceding pages:
[12] Reproduced in "History of the American People," Vol. III. Woodrow Wilson, Harper, New York. 1902.
[13] Reproduced with title "Tory Refugees" in "Harper's Ency. U. S. History," Vol. IX. Harper, New York. 1902.
[14] Reproduced in "Documentary Edition," Vol. V, "A History of the American People." Woodrow Wilson, Harper, New York. 1918.

cv. 282 July 1902 Cap'n Goldsack   *William Sharp*
1 Cap'n Goldsack   c.p 3.8 x 7.1

cv. 592 Sept. 1902 The Voice   *Margaret Deland*
1 Headpiece   p 4.7 x 3.2
2 An autumn field of which she had dreamed   p 4.0 x 7.0
3 She cried out   p 4.6 x 6.9
4 She felt her blood tingling in every vein   p 4.7 x 3.2

cvi. 27 Dec. 1902 The True Captain Kidd   *John D. Champlin, Jr.*
1 Headpiece   c 4.8 x 3.7
2 Decorative title   c 4.3 x 1.8
3 Initial W   c 0.8 x 0.8
4 Kidd on the Deck of the "Adventure Galley"[2]   c 4.6 x 7.1
5 Burning the Ship   c 4.6 x 7.4
6 Buried Treasure [1]   c 4.7 x 7.2

cvi. 319 Jan. 1903 The Chanty Man   *E. Phelps Whitmarsh*
1 The Chanty Man   c 4.2 x 7.1

cvii. 327 Aug. 1903 The Castle of Content   *James Branch Cabell*
1 "Small heed had we of the fleet, sweet hours" [3]   c 3.7 x 7.3
2 "'Twas a strange tale she had ended" [3]   c 4.8 x 7.2
3 Lady Adeliza came wondering to the balcony [3]   c 4.8 x 7.1
4 He thought of his love   c 4.5 x 2.6
5 In the night [3]   c 4.7 x 3.3

cviii. 3 Dec. 1903 Peire Vidal, Troubadour   *Olivia H. Dunbar*
1 "Nothing harms me all the day"   c 4.0 x 7.5
2 At the gate of the Castle   c 4.0 x 7.5
3 Vidal—Poet and Satirist   c 4.0 x 7.6
4 In the train of King Alfonzo [4]   c 4.0 x 7.5

---

[1] Reproduced in part on cover of "The Buccaneers." Don C. Seitz, Harper, New York. 1912.
[1] Reproduced in part on cover of "Stolen Treasures." Howard Pyle, Harper, New York. 1907.
[2] Reproduced in The Wilmington Society of the Fine Arts Catalogue, Wilmington. 1912.
[3] Reproduced in "The Line of Love." James Branch Cabell, Harper, New York. 1905.
[4] Reproduced with title "The Bishop of Montors Has Returned" in "The Soul of Melicent." James Branch Cabell, Stokes, New York. 1913. Also on cover of book.

CVIII. 199 Jan. 1904 THE STAIRWAY OF HONOR *Maud Stepney Rawson*
  1 Her whisper was so soft he only guessed the words c 4.9 x 7.3
  2 This last picture   c 4.9 x 7.4
  3 He stretched out his hand to the curtains   c 5.0 x 7.5

CVIII. 706 April 1904 THE STORY OF ADHELMAR *James Branch Cabell*
  1 He found Mélite alone [1]   c 4.8 x 7.2
  2 He sang for her as they sat in the gardens [1]   c 4.8 x 7.2
  3 He climbed the stairs slowly, for he was growing
      feeble [1]   c 4.7 x 7.2

CIX. 75 June 1904 THE CHARMING OF ESTERCEL   *Grace Rhys*
  1 Estercel   c 4.2 x 7.7
  2 "There is a charm," said the nurse at last   c 4.8 x 7.4
  3 Eileen slipped the ring into the nest   c 4.7 x 7.1

CIX. 327 Aug. 1904 THE SWORD OF AHAB   *James Edmund Dunning*
  1 The Battle of the Stairs   c 4.8 x 7.2
  2 The dark folk trooped to meet them on the shore [2] c 4.8 x 7.2
  3 Bertha, the much beloved   c 4.9 x 7.7
  4 The drawing of the sword [3]   c 4.9 x 7.5

CIX. 497 Sept. 1904 THE MAID OF LANDÉVENNEC *Justus Miles Forman*
  1 The rescue of Aziliçz   c 4.9 x 7.7
  2 Her head and shoulders hung over the space with-
      out   c 4.9 x 7.4
  3 "She tricked me, little maid"   c 4.9 x 7.5

CIX. 702 Oct. 1904 IN NECESSITY'S MORTAR   *James Branch Cabell*
  1 Catherine de Vaucelles, in her garden [1]   c 4.0 x 7.7
  2 "Villon—The singer Fate fashioned to her liking" [1] c 4.9 x 7.8
  3 "The King himself hauled me out of gaol" [1]   c 5.0 x 7.6

CIX. 831 Nov. 1904 NON-COMBATANTS   *Robert W. Chambers*
  1 The charge   c 4.9 x 7.3
  2 They brought in their dead and wounded on hay
      wagons   c 4.8 x 7.3

[1] Reproduced in "The Line of Love." James Branch Cabell, Harper, New York. 1905.
  [2] Reproduced with title "Demetrius Stood among Them," etc., in "The Soul of Melicent."
James Branch Cabell, Stokes, New York. 1913.
  [3] Reproduced with title "Demetrius Wrenched the Sword," etc., in "The Soul of Melicent."
James Branch Cabell, Stokes, New York. 1913.

3 "I thought of you, when I was falling," he said
vaguely   c 4.8 x 7.3

cx. 3 Dec. 1904 SAINT JOAN OF ARC   *Mark Twain*
   1 She believed that she had daily speech with angels [1] c 4.9 x 7.5
   2 The triumphal entry into Rheims [1]   c 4.9 x 7.4
   3 Guarded by rough English soldiers [1]   c 4.9 x 7.6
   4 A lithe, young, slender figure [1]   c 4.2 x 7.8

cx. 58 Dec. 1904 THE GOLD   *Mary E. Wilkins Freeman*
   1 Parson Rawson spoke to her with a pleasant
chiding   p 4.7 x 7.2
   2 Catherine Drake quickened her steps   p 4.7 x 7.3
                                        W. H. Clark, Sc.

cx. 257 Jan. 1905 MELICENT   *Warwick Deeping*
   1 Melicent stood motionless like a wild thing at gaze c 4.2 x 7.8
   2 A man lay prone there, half turned upon his face c 5.0 x 7.5
   3 Sir John shook his spear at the ladies who sneered c 5.0 x 7.5

cx. 335 Feb. 1905 THE GREAT LA SALLE   *Henry Loomis Nelson*
   1 La Salle christening the country "Louisiana" [2] c 4.9 x 7.2
   2 La Salle petitions the King for permission to explore
the Mississippi   c 4.9 x 7.3

cx. 344 Feb. 1905 SPECIAL MESSENGER   *Robert W. Chambers*
   1 She drew bridle, listening—there was no sound   p 4.7 x 7.2
   2 "Are you ever lonely here?" he enquired   p 4.7 x 7.1
                                        W. H. Clark, Sc.

cx. 570 March 1905 EDEN GATES   *Justus Miles Forman*
   1 "Come, come, your Future Majesty! Cheer up!"   c 4.8 x 7.2
   2 I knelt by the whispering, muttering old man   c 4.8 x 7.2

cx. 766 April 1905 "AN AMAZING BELIEF"   *Mrs. Henry Dudeney*
   1 They stood staring at the violent sky   p 4.7 x 7.1
                                        G. F. Smith, Sc.
   2 With a cry, Shallum flung up his arms and jumped p 4.7 x 7.1

---

[1] Reproduced in "Saint Joan of Arc." Mark Twain, Harper, New York. 1919.
[2] Reproduced in "Documentary Edition", Vol. III, "A History of the American People." Woodrow Wilson, Harper, New York. 1918.

cx. 900 May 1905 CARLOTTA   *Justus Miles Forman*
1 Crown Prince Karl, dead by his own hand   c 4.9 x 7.4
2 Carlotta—tall, white, queenly—a cluster of flowers
   in her arms   p 4.6 x 7.3
3 Her outstretched arms seemed to close upon something   p 4.7 x 7.1

cx. 957 May 1905 OLD IMMORTALITY   *Alice Brown*
1 Old Immortality   p 4.7 x 7.4
                          F. A. Pettit, Sc.

cxi. 339 Aug. 1905 THE FOX BRUSH   *James Branch Cabell*
1 "I loved the husk of a man"   c 4.9 x 7.4
2 Headpiece   c 4.9 x 2.6
3 So for a heart-beat she saw him [1]   c 4.9 x 7.4
4 He came to her—in his helmet a fox brush spangled
   with jewels   c 4.9 x 7.4
5 Headband on title page   p 4.7 x 1.3
6 Marginal decorations (used six times) [3]   p 5.1 x 8.1
7 Marginal decorations (used five times) [4] [2] [1]   p 5.1 x 8.1

cxi. 438 Sept. 1905 THE ISLAND OF ENCHANTMENT. I.
                           Justus Miles Forman
1 The doge sat alone in a great carven chair [5]   c 4.3 x 6.7
2 He laid the mantle over the girl's shoulders [5]   c 4.3 x 6.5

cxi. 682 Oct. 1905 THE ISLAND OF ENCHANTMENT. II.
                           Justus Miles Forman
1 "He lay awhile conscious of great comfort" [5]   c 4.3 x 6.5
2 "She hung drooping in the great chair of state" [5]   c 4.3 x 6.5

cxii. 3 Dec. 1905 THE FATE OF A TREASURE TOWN   *Howard Pyle*
1 The buccaneer was a picturesque fellow [6]   c 4.9 x 7.5

---

[1] Reproduced in "Chivalry." James Branch Cabell, Harper, New York. 1909.
[2] Reproduced in "Gailantry." James Branch Cabell, Harper, New York. 1907.
[3] Reproduced in "The Island of Enchantment." Justus Miles Forman, Harper, New York. 1905.
[4] Decorative headband reproduced in "The Buccaneers." Don C. Seitz, Harper, New York. 1912.
[5] Reproduced in "The Island of Enchantment." Justus Miles Forman, Harper, New York. 1905.
[6] Reproduced in black in "Adventures of Pirates and Sea Rovers." Howard Pyle and Others, Harper, New York. 1908.

2 An attack on a galleon [3] [1]   c 4.8 x 7.3
3 So the treasure was divided [3] [2]   c 7.4 x 4.9
4 Extorting tribute from the citizens   c 4.9 x 7.4
5 Title page, headband   p 4.8 x 1.5
6 Headband [4]   p 4.8 x 1.6
7 Initial A   p 0.7 x 0.7
8 Marginal decoration, left-hand page   p 5.2 x 8.0
9 Marginal decoration, right-hand page   p 5.2 x 8.0

CXII. 191 Jan. 1906 THE SESTINA   *James Branch Cabell*
    1 A neat and shrivelled gentleman sat at a desk [5]   c 4.9 x 7.3
    2 They were overtaken by Falmouth himself [5]   c 4.8 x 7.3

CXIII. 327 Aug. 1906 PICTURES FROM THACKERAY
    Beatrix and Esmond [6]   c 5.0 x 7.5

CXIV. 3 Dec. 1906 PICTURES FROM THACKERAY
    Becky Sharp and Lord Steyne [7]   c 4.9 x 7.6

CXIV. 399 Feb. 1907 A SENSE OF SCARLET   *Mrs. Henry Dudeney*
    1 A figure to provoke tears   c 4.8 x 7.5

CXIV. 497 March 1907 PICTURES FROM THACKERAY
    Pendennis [8]   c 4.0 x 7.7

CXIV. 675 April 1907 IN THE SECOND APRIL   *James Branch Cabell*
    1 "Who is the lucky miss, my little villain?" [9] [3]   c 4.9 x 7.3
    2 The duel between John Blumer and Cazaio [9] [3]   c 4.8 x 6.8

CXIV. 875 May 1907 IN THE SECOND APRIL   *James Branch Cabell*
    1 "The Bastille is not a very healthy place" [9]   c 4.8 x 7.3
    2 The death of Cazaio [9]   c 4.8 x 7.3

---

[1] Reproduced with title "Demetrius Sent Little Boats," etc., in "The Soul of Melicent." James Branch Cabell, Stokes, New York. 1913.
[2] Reproduced in black in "Adventures of Pirates and Sea Rovers." Howard Pyle and Others, Harper, New York. 1908.
[3] Reproduced in The Wilmington Society of the Fine Arts Catalogue, Wilmington. 1912.
[4] Reproduced in "The Buccaneers." Don C. Seitz, Harper, New York. 1912.
[5] Reproduced in "Chivalry." James Branch Cabell, Harper, New York. 1909.
[6] Reproduced in "Works of William Makepeace Thackeray," Vol. X. Harper, New York. 1910.
[7] Reproduced in "Works of William Makepeace Thackeray," Vol. I. Harper, New York. 1910.
[8] Reproduced in "Works of William Makepeace Thackeray," Vol. III. Harper, New York. 1910.
[9] Reproduced in "Gallantry." James Branch Cabell, Harper, New York. 1907.

cxv. 195 July 1907 THE NOBLE FAMILY OF BEAUPERTUYS
Stephen F. Whitman
1 The king glared down at her   c 4.9 x 7.4
2 Suddenly their comedy turned tragic   c 4.9 x 7.4

cxv. 327 Aug. 1907 THE RUBY OF KISHMOOR   *Howard Pyle*
1 "I am the daughter of that unfortunate Captain Keitt!" [1]   c 4.8 x 7.2
2 Headband   p 4.9 x 1.8
3 Initial T   c 0.7 x 0.7
4 Jonathan Rugg   c 3.0 x 6.6
5 The negress beckoned him to draw nearer [1]   c 3.0 x 6.5
6 The little gentleman with one eye [1]   c 2.0 x 3.2
7 With great amity the two walked off together [1]   c 3.0 x 5.6
8 The little gentleman in black emitted a piercing scream [1]   c 2.8 x 5.7
9 The man with the silver earrings   c 2.3 x 3.2
10 The stranger threw himself upon Jonathan with the fury of a madman [1]   c 3.2 x 4.1
11 The man with the broken nose [1]   c 2.2 x 2.9
12 The arms of his captor held him as in a vise [1]   c 3.0 x 4.7
13 The lady with the silver veil   c 2.3 x 3.0
14 Jonathan Rugg was married to Martha Dobbs the following year [1]   c 3.0 x 5.0
15 Captain Keitt [1]   c 4.8 x 7.5

cxv. 519 Sept. 1907 LINCOLN'S LAST DAY   *William H. Crook*
1 Abraham Lincoln [2]   c 4.9 x 7.3

cxvi. 16 Dec. 1907 THE CRUISE OF THE CARIBBEE *Thomas V. Briggs*
1 She became as famous for speed as her short career allowed   c 4.8 x 7.5
W. H. Clark, Sc.
2 Her captain was a Cuban   c 2.7 x 4.5
3 The cruiser piled on all sail   c 2.3 x 5.3
4 They have a so-called native king   c 2.3 x 5.2
5 They carried fruit and vegetables   c 3.5 x 4.0

[1] Reproduced in "The Ruby of Kishmoor." Howard Pyle, Harper, New York. 1908.
[2] Reproduced in "Lincoln and the Sleeping Sentinel." L. E. Chittenden, Harper, New York. 1909.

6 'Tween decks of the slaver   c 2.3 x 3.8
7 The rest were shot and thrown overboard   c 4.8 x 2.0
8 The mate elevated and sighted the gun   c 4.7 x 3.2
9 Lighters were soon alongside   c 2.3 x 4.7
10 She was a solid mass of flames   c 2.3 x 3.5

CXVI. 50 Dec. 1907 THE RAT-TRAP   *James Branch Cabell*
   1 Meregrett, daughter of Philippe the Bold [2] [1]   c 4.9 x 7.3
   2 Then sang Sire Edward [1]   c 4.9 x 7.4

CXVI. 177 Jan. 1908 A SIGN FROM HEAVEN   *Basil King*
   1 "Others have lived through greater woes than ours" c 4.7 x 8.0
   2 "Take care, my friend, take care" [2]   c 4.9 x 7.3

CXVI. 343 Feb. 1908 DONA VICTORIA   *Perceval Gibbon*
   1 The officers would be waiting until she should
     appear   c 4.4 x 7.9
   2 The passing of Dona Victoria   c 4.9 x 7.4

CXVI. 530 March 1908 THE CHOICES   *James Branch Cabell*
   1 Rosamund and Sir Gregory   c 4.8 x 7.5
   2 Queen Ysabeau in her carven chair [1]   c 4.8 x 7.2

CXVI. 677 April 1908 A PRINCESS OF KENT   *Marjorie Bowen*
   1 She arrayed herself in silence   c 4.5 x 7.8
   2 Horse and man plunged heavily after her   c 7.2 x 4.9

CXVI. 847 May 1908 THE SCABBARD   *James Branch Cabell*
   1 The coming of Lancaster [2] [1]   c 4.9 x 7.4
   2 Branwen   c 4.5 x 7.8

CXVII. 3 June 1908 PICTURES FROM THACKERAY
The Newcomes [3]   c 4.9 x 7.5

CXVII. 29 June 1908 THE MINSTREL   *Norman Duncan*
   1 The dark, smiling Salim, with his magic pack, was
     welcome   c 4.8 x 7.2

---

[1] Reproduced in "Chivalry." James Branch Cabell, Harper, New York. 1909.

[2] Reproduced in The Wilmington Society of the Fine Arts Catalogue, Wilmington. 1912.

[3] Reproduced in "Works of William Makepeace Thackeray," Vol. XII. Harper, New York. 1910.

CXVII. 383 Aug. 1908 EDRIC AND SYLVAINE   *Brian Hooker*
  1 Edric the singer [1]   c 4.9 x 7.7
  2 Illustrative border with title   c 4.9 x 7.9
  3 Illustrative border, left-hand page   c 4.8 x 7.8
  4 Illustrative border, right-hand page   c 4.8 x 7.8
  5 Illustrative border, left-hand page   c 4.8 x 7.8
  6 Illustrative border, right-hand page   c 4.8 x 7.8
  7 Illustrative border, left-hand page   c 4.8 x 7.8
  8 Illustrative border, right-hand page   c 4.8 x 7.8
  9 Illustrative border, left-hand page   c 4.8 x 7.8
 10 Illustrative border, right-hand page   c 4.8 x 7.8
 11 Illustrative border, left-hand page   c 4.8 x 7.8
 12 Illustrative border, right-hand page   c 4.8 x 7.8
 13 Illustrative border, left-hand page   c 4.8 x 7.8
 14 Illustrative border, right-hand page   c 4.8 x 7.8
 15 Illustrative border, left-hand page   c 4.8 x 7.8
 16 Illustrative border, right-hand page   c 4.8 x 7.8
 17 Tailpiece   c 3.2 x 1.7

CXVII. 541 Sept. 1908 MANASSEH   *Perceval Gibbon*
  1 "I will have him between these hands"   c 4.9 x 7.3
  2 In an instant those long fingers closed on the
    Governor   c 4.9 x 7.2

CXVII. 670 Oct. 1908 PENNSYLVANIA'S DEFIANCE OF THE
    UNITED STATES   *Hampton L. Carson*
  1 "The American captain and his mate boarded us" c 4.8 x 7.3
  2 Then the real fight began   c 4.9 x 7.3

CXVII. 859 Nov. 1908 THE ULTIMATE MASTER   *James Branch Cabell*
  1 Diana Sherley   c 4.2 x 7.9
  2 "Go, Madam, and leave the Prodigal among his
    husks"   c 4.9 x 7.2

CXVIII. 1 Dec. 1908 THE MYSTERIOUS CHEST   *Howard Pyle*
  1 Old Jacob Van Kleek had never favored our hero's
    visit   c 4.9 x 7.3
  2 Title page with decorations and initial U   c 4.8 x 6.0
  3 The skeletonlike stranger entered   c 3.0 x 4.7

[1] Reproduced in The Wilmington Society of the Fine Arts Catalogue, Wilmington. 1912.

[1] Reproduced in "Chivalry." James Branch Cabell, Harper, New York. 1909.

---

[1] Reproduced in "On Hazardous Service." William Gilmore Beymer, Harper, New York. 1912.
[2] Reproduced in The Wilmington Society of the Fine Arts Catalogue, Wilmington. 1912.

7 Marginal illustration   c 4.7 x 7.5
8 Marginal illustration   c 4.7 x 6.0
9 Vignette   c 3.4 x 4.5
10 Vignette   c 2.2 x 2.2
11 Headpiece   c 4.7 x 2.8
12 Tailpiece   p 4.5 x 4.5

cxx. 27 Dec. 1909 YOUNG   *William Gilmore Beymer*
  1 The nation is at war and must have men   p 4.7 x 7.0
  2 They awaited the order for the charge   p 6.9 x 4.6
                 W. H. Clark, Sc.

cxx. 197 Jan. 1910 SWANHILD   *Brian Hooker*
  1 "I grow old, having no son but Randver" [1]   c 4.7 x 7.0
  2 Thereafter she clung about Randver   c 4.7 x 7.0

cxx. 548 March 1910 THE WRECKER   *James B. Connolly*
  1 "I found him and he wasn't alone"   c 4.8 x 7.2
  2 "My boy wanted to do the divin', but 'twas me that
      went down"   c 4.8 x 7.2

cxx. 663 April 1910 THE INITIAL LETTER   *Marjorie Bowen*
  1 The whole world goes afield today   c 4.8 x 7.2
  2 Flaggingly the reed pen went up and down the
      vellum   c 4.9 x 7.3

cxx. 839 May 1910 "HOLY MR. HERBERT"   *Marjorie Bowen*
  1 She told him her adventures in a breath   c 4.8 x 7.2
  2 Writing on some loose sheets of paper that he held
      on his knee   c 4.8 x 7.2

cxxi. 32 June 1910 THE BLACK NIGHT   *James Hopper*
  1 "I have broken it," she wailed   c 4.8 x 7.2
  2 "And see that you watch well," he snarled   c 4.8 x 7.3
  3 "They questioned him with malevolent persistence" c 4.8 x 7.3

cxxi. 179 July 1910 "PAGE, A. B."   *Perceval Gibbon*
  1 The sea boiled over the wreckage in streaky white c 4.8 x 7.3
  2 Page was at the wheel, steering   c 4.8 x 7.3

---

[1] Reproduced in The Wilmington Society of the Fine Arts Catalogue, Wilmington. 1912.

CXXI. 327 Aug. 1910 YSOBEL DE CORVEAUX   *Brian Hooker*
1 There stood the Faery Prince   c 4.9 x 7.3
2 Title and marginal illustration   c 4.9 x 6.3
3 Marginal illustration, left-hand page   c 4.9 x 5.0
4 Marginal illustration, right-hand page   c 4.9 x 7.5
5 Marginal illustration, left-hand page   c 1.3 x 6.0
6 Marginal illustration, right-hand page   c 3.0 x 6.2
7 Marginal illustration, left-hand page   c 1.5 x 6.2
8 Marginal illustration, right-hand page   c 1.2 x 6.0
9 Marginal illustration, left-hand page   c 4.8 x 7.6
10 Marginal illustration, right-hand page   c 4.7 x 7.6
11 Marginal illustration, left-hand page   c 4.8 x 7.3
12 Marginal illustration, right-hand page   c 4.6 x 7.0
13 Headpiece   c 4.8 x 2.4

CXXII. 288 Jan. 1911 THE BUCCANEERS   *Don C. Seitz*
1 Which shall be Captain? [1]   c 4.8 x 7.3
Headband in black. Reprint from Harper's Magazine,
     Dec., 1905 [1]
Tailpiece. Reprint from Harper's Magazine, Aug., 1905 [1]

CXXII. 327 Feb. 1911 GENERAL LEE AS I KNEW HIM *A. R. H. Ranson*
1 General Lee on his famous charger "Traveler"   c 4.8 x 7.3
2 His army broke up and followed him, weeping and
     sobbing   c 4.9 x 7.3

CXXII. 524 March 1911 MAN AND DOG   *Laurence Housman*
1 So long as Gann would follow, his Master would
     lead   c 4.8 x 7.2
2 Man and staff sank into the peat mud   c 4.8 x 7.2

CXXII. 663 April 1911 THE SOUL OF MERVISAUNT
                                         James Branch Cabell
1 Jocelin, with many encomiums, displayed his
     emeralds   c 4.9 x 7.3
2 "I have loved you for a great while, fair Mervisaunt" c 4.8 x 7.2

CXXIII. 86 June 1911 MISS VAN LEW   *William Gilmore Beymer*
1 She was continually beset by spies   c 4.9 x 7.3
2 The secret room [2]   c 4.8 x 7.3

[1] Reproduced in "The Buccaneers." Don C. Seitz, Harper, New York. 1912.
[2] Reproduced in "On Hazardous Service." William Gilmore Beymer, Harper, New York. 1912.

CXXIII. 165 July 1911 PICTURES FROM THACKERAY
The Virginians [1]   c 4.8 x 7.5

CXXIII. 89 Sept. 1911 THE DEAD FINGER   *Howard Pyle*
  1 "Everything you wish for shall be yours"   c 4.8 x 7.2
  2 Marginal illustration with title   c 4.9 x 5.0
  3 So Beppo's first wish was fulfilled   c 3.3 x 3.0
  4 The two rode away together   c 3.0 x 2.8
  5 Beppo sat in the Notary's house talking about the
      will   c 3.5 x 5.4
  6 He saw a great coach approaching   c 3.0 x 5.5
  7 The grand duke gave him a golden chain   c 3.4 x 5.4
  8 He thrust the cobbler back against the door   c 4.8 x 7.2
  9 He was poor as ever   c 3.3 x 3.4

CXXIII. 610 Sept. 1911 SEA TOLLS   *Robert Welles Ritchie*
  1 The last of the "Naronic"   p 4.9 x 7.3

CXXIII. 829 Nov. 1911 THE PAINTED PITCHER   *Howard Pyle*
  1 Stefano and Serafina at the Well   c 4.8 x 7.2
  2 Vignette   c 4.9 x 6.5
  3 Montofacini, the Magician   c 1.0 x 4.0
  4 The shopman   c 1.0 x 3.4
  5 The bear would stand upon his hind legs and dance c 4.8 x 2.5
  6 Nicolo, the tallow chandler   c 2.0 x 3.9
  7 Serafina was leaning from the window   c 1.8 x 5.8
  8 Cassacinci and the runaway horse   c 4.8 x 2.1

CXXIV. 327 Feb. 1912 THE EVIL EYE   *Howard Pyle*
  1 Decorative title   c 4.8 x 6.2
  2 He was engaged to Caterina   c 1.7 x 5.5
  3 She pointed her finger at Caterina   c 1.3 x 3.8
  4 One of the horses fell dead in the field   c 2.5 x 5.5
  5 While she stood looking the cow died   c 3.0 x 5.0
  6 The vines were dying   c 1.5 x 5.3
  7 "The Evil Eye," he said   c 3.5 x 5.3
  8 Montofacini, the Magician   c 2.2 x 3.5
  9 "I am a ruined man"   p 1.5 x 4.2
  10 That night his straw stack caught fire   p 2.3 x 4.8
  11 He knew not what ailed her or what to do   c 4.8 x 7.2

[1] Reproduced in "Works of William Makepeace Thackeray," Vol. XVI. Harper, New York.
1910.

CXXIV. 599 March 1912 THE CRIME IN JEDIDIAH
PEEBLE'S HOUSE   *Muriel Campbell Dyar*
  1 He was lying on the library floor in the morning   c 4.8 x 7.2
  2 The traveller found the stone behind the hedge a
    resting-place   c 4.8 x 7.3

CXXIV. 883 May 1912 THE DIE OF FATE   *Howard Pyle*
  1 Nicolo and the Robber   p 4.8 x 7.2

CXXVII. 121 June 1913 HUNTFORD'S FAIR NIHILIST   *Howard Pyle*
  1 Herr Vollmer quietly stepped out into the street   p 4.7 x 7.2
  2 She began to talk to Huntford about himself   p 4.7 x 7.2
  3 The little man raced down the stairs and out into
    the street   p 4.7 x 7.2

HARPER'S ROUND TABLE

XVII. 506 March 24, 1896 TOM CHIST AND THE TREASURE BOX
                                        Howard Pyle
  1 Headband with title and initial T   p 5.9 x 2.0
  2 Such a wreck was a Godsend to the poor and
    needy settlers   p 6.1 x 1.3
  3 "And twenty one and twenty two" [1]   p 3.8 x 4.8
  4 The pirate captain looked impassively on   p 3.5 x 5.2
  5 Over the next rise he ran, and so on over the sliding,
    shifting ground, panting and gasping   p 5.8 x 2.4
  6 " 'Tis enough to make both rich men" [1]   p 3.7 x 5.3
  7 "I knew it, I knew it," exclaimed the great man   p 3.0 x 4.0

XVIII. 845 June 29, 1897 THE BUCCANEERS   *Howard Pyle*
  1 Headpiece with title   p 2.7 x 5.3
  2 He asked this figure of war to step aside for him [1] p 4.5 x 3.3
  3 The crowd scattered   p 3.8 x 4.7
  4 He leaped to the wheel [1]   p 4.0 x 3.4
  5 They would stand hours together [1]   p 3.0 x 5.0
  6 Tailpiece   p 4.8 x 2.0

[1] Reproduced in "Stolen Treasure." Howard Pyle, Harper, New York. 1907.

HARPER'S WEEKLY

XXIII. 649 Aug. 16, 1879 BREAKING THE NEWS
Full page   W 13.5 X 9.2

XXIV. 24 Jan. 10, 1880 THE OUTCAST'S RETURN
Full page   W 12.6 X 9.0
    Tonnard, Sc.

XXIV. 380 June 12, 1880 THE SONG OF THE WHIPPOORWILL
    Howard Pyle

1 Full page, poem inserted   W 9.2 X 12.5
    J. P. Davis, Sc.
2 Initial E   W 0.5 X 0.5
3 Initial B   W 0.4 X 0.5

XXIV. 440 July 10, 1880 THE FIRST PUBLIC READING OF
    THE DECLARATION OF INDEPENDENCE   *Eugene Lawrence*
Double page   W 19.8 X 13.4
    Smithwick & French, Sc.

XXIV. 488 July 31, 1880 THE CIRCUS
An Interrupted Performance
Double page   W 19.4 X 12.7
    F. Juengling, Sc.

XXIV. 724 Nov. 13, 1880 WOMEN AT THE POLLS IN NEW
    JERSEY IN THE GOOD OLD TIMES
Full page   W 13.3 X 8.7

XXIV. 828 Dec. 25, 1880 CHRISTMAS MORNING IN OLD
    NEW YORK
Double page   W 19.7 X 12.7
    Lagarde & Measom, Sc.

XXV. 24 Jan. 8, 1881 NEW YEAR'S DAY SEVENTY YEARS
    AGO
The Last Evening Caller. Full page   W 12.8 X 9.0

XXV. 136 Feb. 26, 1881 ST. VALENTINE'S DAY IN THE
    MORNING
Full page   W 9.0 X 12.7
    G. Kruell, Sc.

XXV. 164 March 12, 1881 A PRESIDENTIAL PROGRESS
Politics in the Olden Times—General Jackson,
    President-elect, on his way to Washington   W 13.3 X 9.1
    Smithwick & French, Sc.

XXV. 284 April 30, 1881 SHAD-FISHING ON THE LOWER
    DELAWARE AT NIGHT
Full page. The Last Haul before Dawn   W 12.2 X 9.0

xxv. 705 Oct. 22, 1881 The Surrender of Cornwallis
Double page [2] [1]   w 19.5 x 12.6

xxv. 747 Nov. 5, 1881 John Paul
   1 "He was doubtless a tramp"   w 2.3 x 4.6
   2 "Suppose you let me take care of this young lady
      in the future"   w 4.5 x 4.6
   3 "Thee has killed him?" timidly enquired the girl   w 4.5 x 5.6

xxv. 869 Dec. 24, 1881 The Christmas Tree   *Will Carleton*
   1 One page, title inserted, poem below   w 7.9 x 11.7

Exchange No Robbery   *M. Betham-Edwards*

xxvi. 97 Feb. 18, 1882
   1 "Holding forth the missive, he stood by, breath-
      less and speechless"   w 8.0 x 6.7
                                                    W. Zimmermann, Sc.

xxvi. 117 Feb. 25, 1882
   2 "Heart of gold! kindest of men!"   w 9.1 x 6.6

xxvi. 133 March 4, 1882
   3 "Hilda, airily mounting a high pair of steps, pro-
      ceeded to catalogue the various articles that she
      now dropped one by one into Grettel's wide-
      spread apron"   w 9.0 x 6.5

xxvi. 149 March 11, 1882
   4 "Glancing at the white-robed girlish figure before
      him, with evident admiration, he made a becom-
      ing obeisance"   w 9.0 x 6.8

xxvi. 165 March 18, 1882
   5 "They sat down and chatted in an easy, friendly
      fashion"   w 9.0 x 6.8
                                                    W. Zimmermann, Sc.

xxvi. 181 March 25, 1882
   6 "Then the Hofrath emerged from the balcony, and
      etiquette forbade a longer interview"   w 9.1 x 6.8

xxvi. 140 March 4, 1882 Washington's Birthday   *Howard Pyle*
   1 Full page, verses inserted   w 9.2 x 13.0

[1] Reproduced in "Harper's Ency. U. S History," Vol. X. Harper, New York. 1902.
[2] Reproduced in "Documentary Edition," Vol. I, "A History of the American People."
Woodrow Wilson, Harper, New York. 1918.

XXVI. 229 April 15, 1882 A Modern Puritan

Mrs. Zadel B. Gustafson

1 "The old man's face changed suddenly, and he
pressed his hand hard upon the arm of the hair
cloth sofa"   w 6.0 x 4.6
2 "Breaking from her companions with an excited
exclamation, Mlle. Bland grasped the old woman
by the wrists"   w 6.4 x 6.8

XXVI. 331 May 27, 1882 A Creamery

1 Arrivals at the creamery   w 9.1 x 2.6
2 Receiving milk   w 9.1 x 5.7
3 Making cheese   w 5.4 x 4.9
4 Early morning on the ferries   w 4.5 x 5.5

XXVI. 342 June 3, 1882 The Dead Stowaway   *Will Carleton*

The Dead Stowaway [1]   w 9.0 x 6.1

XXVI. 737 Nov. 25, 1882 The Sea-Gull's Song   *Howard Pyle*

1 Full page, verses inserted   w 9.0 x 11.2

XXVI. 778 Dec. 9, 1882 Christmas Time Two Hundred

Years Ago   *Howard Pyle*

1 Headpiece   w 1.1 x 1.9
2 Christmas Presents for the Squire   w 9.0 x 6.9
3 The Arrival at the Blue Boar Inn   w 4.5 x 1.5
4 The Stirrup Cup   w 4.4 x 3.0
5 The Mummers   w 5.8 x 5.0
6 The Snap Dragon   w 2.0 x 3.4
7 Bringing in the Yule Log   w 4.5 x 1.5
8 The Glee Singers   w 3.3 x 5.0
9 The Return from Church Christmas Morning   w 3.5 x 6.4
10 Christmas Pudding   w 2.0 x 2.5
11 The Contra-Dance   w 5.1 x 4.7
12 The Duel   w 9.2 x 5.8
13 The Elopement   w 4.4 x 1.9

[1] Reproduced with title "Battered and Bruised, Forever Abused, He Lay by the Moaning Sea"
in "City Ballads." Will Carleton, Harper, New York. 1886.

XXVII. 104 Feb. 17, 1883 A VALENTINE TO PHILLIS   *Unknown*
    Full page, verses inserted   w 8.1 x 14.4
                                                  W. Zimmermann, Sc.

XXVII. 169 March 17, 1883 A LOVE FEAST AMONG THE
        DUNKERS
    Full page   w 13.2 x 8.9
                                                  R. Stauenbaur, Sc.

XXVII. 185 March 24, 1883 THE MYSTERIOUS GUEST
    Full page. Scene in a Tavern on the Old Albany Post
        Road   w 12.6 x 9.0
                                                  Lagarde, Sc.

XXVII. 199 March 31, 1883 THE FIRST VISIT OF WILLIAM
        PENN TO AMERICA
    Double page. A Conference with the Colonists   w 19.0 x 12.8
                                                  Froment, Sc.

XXVII. 740 Nov. 24, 1883 "AUTUMN LEAVES"
    Full page   w 7.8 x 12.5
                                                  H. Claudius, Sc.

XXVII. 743 Nov. 24, 1883 THE EVACUATION 1783   *Eugene Lawrence*
    Evacuation Day One Hundred Years Ago—The
        Continental Army Marching Down the Old
        Bowery, New York, Nov. 25, 1783   w 18.9 x 13.8
    Double page

XXVII. 764 Dec. 1, 1883 YE TRUE STORY OF GRANNY
        GREENE OF SALEM TOWN   *Howard Pyle*
    1 Headpiece with title   w 4.3 x 2.0
    2 Initial S   w 0.7 x 0.7
    3 Vignette   w 3.5 x 4.2
    4 Granny Greene seeketh the Life of ye Hen   w 3.0 x 6.3
    5 Dame Charity Greene meeteth ye Strange Little
        Man   w 6.9 x 4.0
    6 Granny Greene Falleth into Ill Repute   w 9.2 x 6.8
    7 The Arrest   w 5.7 x 7.6
    8 Tailpiece   w 2.4 x 3.5

XXVII. 767 Dec. 1, 1883 WASHINGTON TAKING LEAVE OF
        HIS OFFICERS, DEC. 4, 1783
    Full page   w 13.2 x 8.9
                                                  R. Stauenbaur, Sc.

XXVII. 842 Dec. 29, 1883 "THE ANT AND THE GRASS-
HOPPER" *Æsop's Fables*
Full page W 9.1 X 11.4

XXVIII. 825 Dec. 15, 1884 MR. MERRIDEW'S GOLDPIECE
Virginia W. Johnson
Full page. "He seized and held the treasure near the
light" W 9.1 X 12.6

XXIX. 1 Jan. 3, 1885 THE STRANGE ADVENTURES OF
CARL SPICH *Howard Pyle*
  1 Headpiece with initial C W 2.4 X 4.8
  2 "Maybe the snow deadened his footsteps, maybe
    it was the Devil" W 9.1 X 6.6
  3 "The tall stranger with the club-foot stood before
    her" W 4.3 X 3.5
  4 "He stopped when he had come close to Carl" W 4.5 X 3.7

XXIX. 129 Feb. 28, 1885 MARKHAM'S BAYS *Kate Putnam Osgood*
  1 "I am going to run away with you" W 8.5 X 6.8
                          A. Negri, Sc.

XXIX. 819 Dec. 12, 1885 SQUIRE TRIPP'S OLD ARM CHAIR
Howard Pyle
  1 "She came close to him and laid her hand lovingly
    on his arm" W 9.2 X 6.8
  2 "The Squire went on as though he had not heard" W 9.2 X 6.6
  3 "He held his hammer poised for a moment" W 9.2 X 6.6
  4 "The fingers of the hand were clutched like a claw" W 9.3 X 6.7

THE ROSE OF PARADISE *Howard Pyle*
June 11, 1887, to July 30, 1887.

XXXI. 413 June 11, 1887
  1 "Mr. Longways looked up under his brows at me
    with a very curious leer"[1] W 9.2 X 8.0

XXXI. 437 June 18, 1887
  2 " 'Boat ahoy!' I cried out, and then levelled my
    pistol and fired"[1] W 9.1 X 6.6

---

[1] Reproduced in "The Rose of Paradise." Howard Pyle, Harper, New York. 1888.

xxxi. 453 June 25, 1887
    3 " 'Captain Mackra,' said he coldly, 'you were
      pleased to put upon me last night a gross and
      uncalled for insult!' " [1]   w 9.0 x 6.4

xxxi. 466 July 2, 1887
    4 "So soon as they saw me they fell to screaming,
      and clung to one another" [1]   w 9.2 x 6.4

xxxi. 485 July 9, 1887
    5 " 'I am Captain John Mackra,' said I, and I sat
      down upon the gunwale of the boat" [1]   w 9.1 x 5.9

xxxi. 501 July 16, 1887
    6 "I rose slowly from my chair, and stood with my
      hand leaning upon the table" [1]   w 9.2 x 5.8

xxxi. 518 July 23, 1887
    7 "The three fellows were brought aft to the quarter-
      deck, where Captain Croker stood, just below
      the rail of the deck above" [1]   w 9.1 x 5.9

xxxi. 534 July 30, 1887
    8 "There, in the corner, I beheld the famous pirate,
      Captain Edward England" [1]   w 9.2 x 6.3

xxxii. 231 March 31, 1888 THE GREAT SNOW STORM IN
        LEWES HARBOR   *Howard Pyle*
    Illustrated from photographs

xxxv. 689 Sept. 12, 1891 THE TWO CORNETS OF MONMOUTH
                                A. E. Watrous
    1 Headpiece   w 9.4 x 7.0
    2 "On sped the light chestnut, with the little officer
      bending almost to the saddle-bow"   w 7.8 x 11.2

xxxvi. 345 April 9, 1892 A TRANSFERRED ROMANCE   *Howard Pyle*
    1 Headpiece   p 8.4 x 6.2

xxxvi. 845 Sept. 3, 1892 A THREAD WITHOUT A KNOT   *Howard Pyle*
    1 Headpiece   p 8.6 x 4.5

[1] Reproduced in "The Rose of Paradise." Howard Pyle, Harper, New York. 1888.

XXXVI. 1188 Dec. 10, 1892 STOPPING THE CHRISTMAS STAGE
Double page   p 18.8 x 12.8

XXXVII. 589 June 24, 1893 STAMFORD'S SOPRANO   *Howard Pyle*
1 Headpiece   p 5.9 x 8.5

XXXVII. 1189 Dec. 16, 1893 THE PIRATES' CHRISTMAS
Scene in the Town Jail   c.p 18.8 x 11.3

THE PARASITE   *A. Conan Doyle*
        Nov. 10, 1894, to Dec. 1, 1894.

XXXVIII. 1061 Nov. 10, 1894
    1 " 'Austin,' she said, 'I have come to tell you our
        engagement is at an end' " [1]   p 8.4 x 10.2
                                                     Kurtz, Sc.

XXXVIII. 1085 Nov. 17, 1894
    2 "I was conscious only of her own eyes looking down
        at me, gray, deep, inscrutable" [1]   p 5.5 x 8.5

XXXVIII. 1109 Nov. 24, 1894
    3 "I stopped, for the woman's head had fallen back—
        she had fainted" [1]   p 5.7 x 8.3

XXXVIII. 1133 Dec. 1, 1894
    4 Illustration. No title [1]   p 5.5 x 8.4
                                                     Kurtz, Sc.

XXXVIII. 1189 Dec. 15, 1894 SAILORS AND LANDSMEN—
              A STORY OF 1812   *Howard Pyle*
    1 Headpiece with title   p 8.0 x 3.3
    2 Vignette   p 2.7 x 2.8
    3 Vignette   p 4.0 x 3.8
    4 Vignette   p 4.6 x 2.6
    5 Vignette   p 3.8 x 4.9
    6 Vignette   p 2.9 x 3.8
    7 Vignette   p 2.9 x 3.0
    8 Vignette   p 5.0 x 2.8
    9 Vignette   p 6.1 x 3.0
   10 Vignette   p 2.5 x 3.5

XXXIX. 1175 Dec. 14, 1895 AN UNWELCOME TOAST
Double page   p 19.3 x 12.8

[1] Reproduced in "The Parasite." A. Conan Doyle, Harper, New York. 1895.

XL. 1236 Dec. 19, 1896 The Ghost of Captain Brand *Howard Pyle*
1 Full page. "Captain Malyoe shot Captain Brand
through the head" [2] [1]   p 8.5 x 11.8
2 Headpiece (with title and initial B) [3] [1]   p 8.9 x 4.8
3 Initial B   p 0.4 x 0.4
4 Headpiece [1]   p 8.0 x 2.5
5 Headpiece [1]   p 8.0 x 2.5
6 Headpiece [3] [1]   p 8.0 x 2.5
7 Full page. "She would sit quite still, permitting
Barnaby to gaze" [1]   p 8.5 x 11.8
8 Headpiece [1]   p 8.0 x 2.5

XLI. 710 July 17, 1897 A Small School of Art   *Howard Pyle*
Illustrated with eight pictures by students of H. Pyle

XLI. 1250 Dec. 18, 1897 A True History of the Devil
at New Hope   *Howard Pyle*
1 Full page. "I've kept my ears open to all your
doings" [2]   c 8.5 x 12.9
2 I. How the Devil Haunted the Meeting-House [2] c.p 9.0 x 5.9
3 II. How the Devil Stole the Collector's Snuff Box c.p 6.2 x 3.1
4 III. The Strange Adventures of a Young Gentleman
of Quality   c.p 6.0 x 3.7
5 IV. A Romantic Episode in the Life of a Young
Lady   c.p 4.9 x 5.5
6 V. How the Devil was cast out of the Meeting-
House   c.p 6.0 x 3.3
7 Tailpiece   c.p 3.0 x 1.1

XLII. 184 Feb. 19, 1898 St. Valentine's Day   *Howard Pyle*
Illustrated by full-page picture by Miss Mhoon

XLII. 1217 Dec. 17, 1898 Small Game Better than None
Double page in color   c 12.4 x 18.7

XLIII. 20 Dec. 16, 1899 How the Buccaneers Kept Christmas
Double page in color   c 12.5 x 18.4

[1] Reproduced in "The Ghost of Captain Brand." Howard Pyle, edition of four copies, John W. Rogers, Wilmington. 1896.
[2] Reproduced in "Stolen Treasure." Howard Pyle, Harper, New York. 1907.
[3] Reproduced in "How to Draw." Leon Barritt, Harper, New York. 1904.

XLVIII. 3 Dec. 10, 1904 THE KING'S JEWEL *James Edmund Dunning*
    1 "Here is all I have to give thee—It is the King's ·
        Jewel"   c 7.4 x 10.7
    2 "I know thy heart, that thou dost love me well"   c 7.4 x 10.7
    3 "Not for myself do I seek this vengeance"   c 7.4 x 10.7

L. 1809 Dec. 15, 1906 HENRY MILLS ALDEN'S 70TH BIRTHDAY
    Tribute by Howard Pyle, picture entitled
    1 So may the future bring its wreath of roses and of
        bay to you.   p 4.2 x 6.4

LI. 203 Feb. 9, 1907 THE LANDING OF CARTERET IN NEW JERSEY
    Mural painting—Essex County Court-house,
    Newark, N. J.   p 10.7 x 4.4

HARPER'S YOUNG PEOPLE

I. 313 April 13, 1880 NANCY HANSEN'S PROJECT [1]   *Howard Pyle*
    1 Miss Nancy takes leave of the officer   w 6.3 x 5.3

OLD TIMES IN THE COLONIES   *Charles Carleton Coffin*

I. 572 Aug. 3, 1880
    1 Early settlers going to meeting [4] [2]   w 4.3 x 6.0
    2 Isaac Bradley carrying Joseph into the settlement [2]   w 4.5 x 6.4

I. 602 Aug. 17, 1880
    3 The escape of Hannah Dustin [3] [2]   w 6.5 x 4.5

I. 684 Sept. 21, 1880
    4 "Lieutenant Wyman, creeping up, put a bullet
        through him" [2]   w 6.6 x 4.4

I. 720 Oct. 5, 1880
    5 "Crack! crack! went the guns of the Indians" [6] [5] [2] w 4.5 x 6.5

[1] Published in book form in "Strange Stories of the Revolution." Harper, New York. 1907. Illustration not reproduced in book.

[2] Reproduced in "Old Times in the Colonies." Charles Carleton Coffin, Harper, New York. 1880.

[3] Reproduced with title "Hannah Dustin Escaping from the Indians" in "Harper's Ency. U. S. History," Vol. III. Harper, New York. 1902.

[4] Reproduced with title "Early Settlers in New England" in "Harper's Ency. U. S. History," Vol. VI. Harper, New York. 1902.

[5] Reproduced with title "Behind Trees and Gullies" in "Library of Universal Adventure by Sea and Land." Harper, New York. 1888.

[6] Reproduced with title "Stark Captured by Indians" in "Indian History for Young Folks." Francis S. Drake, Harper, New York. 1885.

I. 756 Oct. 19, 1880
    6 Cutting off a queue to bind a wound   w 4.5 x 5.2

THE STORY OF THE AMERICAN NAVY   *Benson J. Lossing*

I. 524 July 13, 1880
    1 Franklin on his way to France [1]   w 6.6 x 3.4

I. 545 July 20, 1880
    2 Battle between the "Bon Homme Richard" and
      the "Serapis"   w 5.5 x 3.4

I. 576 Aug. 3, 1880
    3 Decatur and his men boarding the gun-boat   w 5.4 x 3.3

II. 128 Dec. 21, 1880 A CHRISTMAS CAROL   *Howard Pyle*
    1 Illustrated verses   w 6.0 x 6.7

II. 338 March 29, 1881 THE MAGIC WAND   *Howard Pyle*
    1 "There's something in there"   w 6.3 x 6.4

II. 234 May 10, 1881 HOURS WITH THE OCTOGENARIANS
                                       Benson J. Lossing
    1 Paul Revere at Lexington [2]   w 6.3 x 6.5

II. 565 July 5, 1881 JEREMY BLACK'S FOURTH OF JULY   *Howard Pyle*
    1 "And blew as he'd not blown since he was born"   w 6.0 x 6.7

III. 121 Dec. 20, 1881 A PERFECT CHRISTMAS   *William O. Stoddard*
    1 "What a racket they made at the gate"   w 9.1 x 6.5
    2 "It seemed to lie sound asleep with a snow blanket
      all over its roof"   w 3.2 x 3.0
    3 "I'm Bijah"   w 4.6 x 5.9
    4 "Do you live with Santa Claus in his own house?" w 4.9 x 4.4
    5 "With a plate of mince-pie in his lap, and Bush,
      the big house dog, sitting beside him"   w 4.1 x 4.3
    6 "Grandfather came in with a backload of sleds"   w 6.6 x 4.8
    7 "He crawled forward, and looked down through
      the scuttle hole"   w 3.2 x 4.1

---

[1] Reproduced in "Harper's Ency. U. S. History," Vol. III. Harper, New York. 1902.
[2] Reproduced in "Harper's Ency. U. S. History," Vol. VII. Harper, New York. 1902.

IV. 85 Dec. 12, 1882 WILLIE'S CHRISTMAS   *Helen S. Conant*
  1 "Then Uncle Tom lifted her in his big, strong
     arms"   w 6.6 x 7.0

IV. 147 Jan. 9, 1883 MERRY ADVENTURES OF ROBIN HOOD
                           Howard Pyle
  1 Robin on his way to Nottingham   w 4.0 x 6.3

IV. 171 Jan. 16, 1883 MERRY ADVENTURES OF ROBIN HOOD
                           Howard Pyle
  1 Robin meets a fair lady   w 3.3 x 5.1
  2 Robin encounters John Little   w 3.3 x 5.1

IV. 685 Aug. 28, 1883 YE ROMANTIC ADVENTURES OF
        THREE TAILORS   *Howard Pyle*
  1 Page with title, illustrations and verse [1]   w 6.7 x 9.2

IV. 781 Oct. 9, 1883 TWO OPINIONS   *Howard Pyle*
  1 Page with title, illustrations and verse [1]   w 6.7 x 9.0

V. 45 Nov. 20, 1883 A VICTIM TO SCIENCE   *Howard Pyle*
  1 Page with title, illustrations and verse [1]   w 6.7 x 9.0

V. 108 Dec. 18, 1883 THE REVOLT OF THE HOLIDAYS *E. I. Stevenson*
  1 Headpiece with title [2]   w 6.6 x 3.6
  2 Fred [3]   w 1.1 x 2.7
  3 Dora—Dorothy [3]   w 2.1 x 2.6
  4 Thanksgiving Day [3]   w 2.8 x 4.1
  5 Enter Fourth of July [3]   w 2.7 x 4.6
  6 The Chorus of the Six Jolly Feeders [3]   w 6.5 x 2.4
  7 The Military Ballet Dance   w 3.3 x 1.5
  8 Easter and Saturday [3]   w 2.5 x 3.4
  9 Four Pages armed with spears attendant [3] w 4.0 x 3.2
  10 Enter New Year's Day [3]   w 2.3 x 3.7
  11 Santa Claus   w 3.2 x 2.6

V. 125 Dec. 25, 1883 A DISAPPOINTMENT   *Howard Pyle*
  1 Page with title, illustrations and verse [1]   w 6.6 x 9.1

---

[1] Reproduced in "Pepper & Salt." Howard Pyle, Harper, New York. 1886.
[2] Part of Headpiece and
[3] Reproduced in "Harper's Book of Little Plays." Harper, New York. 1910.

v. 205 Jan. 29, 1884 THE ACCIDENT OF BIRTH   *Howard Pyle*
  1 Page with title, illustrations and verse [1]   w 6.6 x 9.1

v. 301 March 11, 1884 A VERSE WITH A MORAL BUT NO NAME
                                                           Howard Pyle
  1 Page with title, illustrations and verse [1]   w 6.5 x 9.7

v. 295 March 11, 1884 FACING A GIANT   *David Ker*
  1 "I am the Grand Duke"   w 4.7 x 7.3

v. 365 April 8, 1884 A TALE OF A TUB   *Howard Pyle*
  1 Page with title, illustrations and verse [1]   w 6.6 x 9.0

v. 429 May 6, 1884 PRIDE IN DISTRESS   *Howard Pyle*
  1 Page with title, illustrations and verse [1]   w 6.6 x 9.3

v. 493 June 3, 1884 MORAL BLINDNESS   *Howard Pyle*
  1 Page with title, illustrations and verse [1]   w 6.6 x 9.2

v. 541 June 24, 1884 SERIOUS ADVICE   *Howard Pyle*
  1 Page with title, illustrations and verse   w 6.6 x 9.2

v. 589 July 15, 1884 THREE FORTUNES   *Howard Pyle*
  1 Page with title, illustrations and verse [1]   w 6.6 x 9.3

v. 580 July 15, 1884 THE ACCOMMODATING CIRCUMSTANCE. I.
                                                  Frank R. Stockton
  1 Headpiece with title   w 1.6 x 2.8
  2 An old woman and a young girl coming toward the
     castle   w 3.3 x 6.0
  3 Instantly there appeared before her a strange being w 3.2 x 6.0
  4 Blow ye horn for ye ferry man   w 3.2 x 5.8

v. 595 July 22, 1884 THE ACCOMMODATING CIRCUMSTANCE. II.
                                                  Frank R. Stockton
  1 Ye School for Men   w 3.4 x 5.8
  2 Then they began to pull   w 6.7 x 1.8
  3 Instantly there stood by her side a School Trustee w 4.6 x 7.0
  4 Fitting a long arrow to his bow, he sent it directly
     through the foremost horseman   w 4.9 x 3.0

---

[1] Reproduced in "Pepper & Salt." Howard Pyle, Harper, New York. 1886.

v. 619 July 29, 1884 THE ACCOMMODATING CIRCUMSTANCE. III.

Frank R. Stockton

1 They sat down under a tree in a quiet corner of
the palace grounds   w 4.3 x 5.0
2 To Zisk   w 2.0 x 3.8
3 To Zisk   w 3.2 x 2.8

v. 637 Aug. 5, 1884 YE SONG OF YE GOSSIPS   *Howard Pyle*
1 Page with title, illustrations and verse [1]   w 6.6 x 9.2

v. 685 Aug. 26, 1884 VENTURESOME BOLDNESS   *Howard Pyle*
1 Page with title, illustrations and verse [1]   w 6.6 x 9.2

v. 733 Sept. 16, 1884 YE SONG OF YE FOOLISH OLD WOMAN

Howard Pyle
1 Page with title, illustrations and verse [1]   w 6.6 x 9.2

v. 813 Oct. 21, 1884 YE SONG OF YE RAJAH AND YE FLY

Howard Pyle
1 Page with title, illustrations and verse [1]   w 6.6 x 9.2

VI. 13 Nov. 4, 1884 YE TWO WISHES   *Howard Pyle*
1 Page with title, illustrations and verse [1]   w 6.6 x 9.3

VI. 45 Nov. 18, 1884 SUPERFICIAL CULTURE   *Howard Pyle*
1 Page with title, illustrations and verse [1]   w 6.7 x 9.4

VI. 77 Dec. 2, 1884 PLAY AND EARNEST   *Howard Pyle*
1 Page with title, illustrations and verse [1]   w 6.6 x 9.2

VI. 107 Dec. 16, 1884 THE SWORD OF HILDEBRAND   *Sherwood Ryse*
1 Headpiece with initial   w 1.6 x 3.2
2 Vignette   w 4.8 x 6.0
3 Vignette   w 2.5 x 5.4
4 Vignette   w 4.6 x 6.2
5 Vignette   w 5.0 x 4.7
6 Vignette   w 6.7 x 8.8

VI. 141 Dec. 30, 1884 THE FORCE OF NEED   *Howard Pyle*
1 Page with title, illustrations and verse [1]   w 6.5 x 9.1

[1] Reproduced in "Pepper & Salt." Howard Pyle, Harper, New York. 1886.

VI. 189 Jan. 20, 1885 YE STORY OF A BLUE CHINA PLATE
Howard Pyle
   1 Page with title, illustrations and verse [1]   w 6.7 x 9.3

VI. 205 Jan. 27, 1885 YE SAD STORY CONCERNING ONE
       INNOCENT LITTLE LAMB AND FOUR WICKED
       WOLVES   *Howard Pyle*
   1 Page with title, illustrations and verse [1]   w 6.7 x 9.3

VI. 237 Feb. 10, 1885 OVERCONFIDENCE   *Howard Pyle*
   1 Page with title, illustrations and verse [1]   w 6.6 x 9.2

VI. 267 Feb. 24, 1885 HANS HECKLEMANN'S LUCK   *Howard Pyle*
   1 Initial and title [1]   w 6.6 x 2.0
   2 Hans Hecklemann [1]   w 1.6 x 2.9
   3 Catherine [1]   w 1.6 x 3.2
   4 Hans Hecklemann goes to the cottage of the Old
     Wise Woman in search of his Luck [1]   w 6.5 x 2.4
   5 Hans Hecklemann and the Old Wise Woman [1]   w 4.0 x 3.2
   6 Hans finds his Luck [1]   w 4.2 x 5.6
   7 Hans Hecklemann ploughs for Gold [1]   w 4.8 x 1.5

VI. 301 March 10, 1885 PROFESSION AND PRACTICE   *Howard Pyle*
   1 Page with title, illustrations and verse [1]   w 6.6 x 9.0

VI. 315 March 17, 1885 How DAME MARGERY TWIST SAW
       MORE THAN WAS GOOD FOR HER   *Howard Pyle*
   1 Initial and title [1]   w 6.7 x 2.6
   2 Dame Twist drinketh tea [1]   w 2.4 x 2.4
   3 The Little Man and the Great Horse [1]   w 3.3 x 6.6
   4 Dame Twist visits a Strange Patient [1]   w 2.4 x 2.2
   5 Dame Margery Twist goeth to see the merry doings
     at the fair [1]   w 6.7 x 2.1
   6 Dame Twist drives away the Little Folks [1]   w 3.2 x 5.8
   7 Dame Twist sees the Little Man in Green for the
     last time [1]   w 1.6 x 1.9

VI. 333 March 24, 1885 A NEWSPAPER PUFF   *Howard Pyle*
   1 Page with title, illustrations and verse [1]   w 6.6 x 9.3

[1] Reproduced in "Pepper & Salt." Howard Pyle, Harper, New York. 1886.

VI. 363 April 7, 1885 CLEVER PETER AND THE TWO BOTTLES
Howard Pyle

   1 Headpiece with title [1]   w 6.6 x 2.2
   2 Clever Peter and the Little Gentleman in Black [1]   w 2.5 x 2.8
   3 Clever Peter rides to the King's Palace upon his
     fine Horse [1]   w 6.6 x 2.2
   4 Peter eats with the King and Princess [1]   w 4.1 x 2.9
   5 Clever Peter and the Unlucky Bottle [1]   w 3.4 x 4.1
   6 Clever Peter opens the Unlucky Bottle for the
     King and the Princess [1]   w 6.7 x 2.4

VI. 397 April 21, 1885 FANCY AND FACT   *Howard Pyle*
   1 Page with title, illustrations and verse [1]   w 6.1 x 9.2

VI. 411 April 28, 1885 FARMER GRIGGS'S BOGGART   *Howard Pyle*
   1 Headpiece with title [1]   w 6.6 x 3.1
   2 Farmer Georgie Griggs [1]   w 2.4 x 2.4
   3 Dame Mally Griggs [1]   w 2.4 x 3.0
   4 Farmer Griggs and the Boggart [1]   w 2.4 x 3.0
   5 The Departure [1]   w 3.2 x 7.3
   6 Farmer Griggs and the Wise Man [1]   w 3.2 x 2.2
   7 The Boggart Rejoices [1]   w 2.5 x 3.2

VI. 459 May 19, 1885 THE SKILLFUL HUNTSMAN   *Howard Pyle*
   1 Headpiece with title and initial [1]   w 6.6 x 3.3
   2 Jacob's Mother and the Herr Mayor [1]   w 3.2 x 2.9
   3 Jacob and the Red One [1]   w 3.1 x 3.0
   4 Jacob shoots at [1]   w 2.1 x 2.7
   5 —the Magpie [1]   w 1.3 x 3.8
   6 Jacob and the Magic Plough [1]   w 4.1 x 2.0
   7 Jacob and the Red One go hunting together [1]   w 3.3 x 2.7
   8 Jacob and Gretchen get the best of the Red One
     and go home together happily [1]   w 6.7 x 1.7

VI. 587 July 14, 1885 CLAUS AND HIS WONDERFUL STAFF
Howard Pyle

   1 Headpiece with title [1]   w 6.6 x 3.2

[1] Reproduced in "Pepper & Salt." Howard Pyle, Harper, New York. 1886.

2 Claus and the White Snake [1]   w 2.4 x 2.3
3 Claus and the Master of Black Arts [1]   w 4.9 x 5.6
4 The Master is Angry [1]   w 4.2 x 4.0
5 Claus listens to the talk of the two ravens [1]   w 2.4 x 5.1
6 Claus and the Manikin [1]   w 4.1 x 3.5
7 Hans discovers Claus's Luck [1]   w 1.6 x 2.7

VI. 667 Aug. 18, 1885 THE APPLE OF CONTENTMENT   *Howard Pyle*
1 Headpiece with title [1]   w 6.6 x 2.7
2 The Little Man asks for his Cap [1]   w 3.3 x 2.7
3 Christine's Mother and Sisters wish for the Apple [1] w 2.4 x 2.8
4 Christine and the Apple [1]   w 3.2 x 2.8
5 The King talks with the Wise Man [1]   w 4.3 x 3.3
6 The King reaches for the Apple [1]   w 2.5 x 4.1
7 The King's Steward and Christine [1]   w 4.1 x 3.6
8 Christine gives the Apple to the King [1]   w 3.2 x 2.7

VI. 731 Sept. 15, 1885 THE BIRD IN THE LINDEN TREE   *Howard Pyle*
1 Headpiece with title [1]   w 6.4 x 3.4
2 Ye King [1]   w 1.6 x 3.2
3 Prince John [1]   w 1.6 x 2.7
4 The Prince aids the Old Woman [1]   w 3.2 x 2.7
5 The Great Ugly Troll finds the Prince by the fire [1] w 4.0 x 3.0
6 The Gooseherd and her Daughter meet the Princess at the Roadside [1]   w 6.6 x 2.6
7 The Prince looks through the Magic Key [1]   w 3.2 x 4.2
8 The Old King rejoices at his new Daughter-in-Law [1]   w 4.9 x 2.2

VI. 795 Oct. 13, 1885 THE SWAN MAIDEN   *Howard Pyle*
1 Headpiece with title [2]   w 6.6 x 3.0
2 The Swan carries the Prince away [2]   w 4.0 x 4.3
3 The Prince and the Old Witch with her three eyes [2] w 4.1 x 4.7
4 Ye Prince and Ye Swan Maiden [2]   w 2.4 x 4.5
5 The Witch and the woman of honey and barley meal [2]   w 3.3 x 2.6

VII. 3 Nov. 3, 1885 "THE BOOK OF BALBO"   *Sherwood Ryse*
1 Headpiece with initial   w 1.6 x 2.6

---

[1] Reproduced in "Pepper & Salt." Howard Pyle, Harper, New York. 1886.
[2] Reproduced in "The Wonder Clock." Howard Pyle, Harper, New York. 1888.

2 The Children are sent to the Asylum   w 4.8 x 4.0
3 The jolly red-faced Man comes to Town   w 4.1 x 3.4
4 Rambustius reads the Book of Balbo   w 4.8 x 4.3
5 The King finds his children   w 4.0 x 3.5

VII. 27 Nov. 10, 1885 How One Turned His Trouble
     to Some Account   *Howard Pyle*
1 Headpiece with title [1]   w 6.6 x 2.4
2 The Soldier and his Trouble [1]   w 3.8 x 3.8
3 The Soldier brings his Trouble before the King [1]   w 4.0 x 4.5
4 The three giants come to blows [1]   w 4.1 x 3.3
5 The Rich Man finds money and Trouble [1]   w 4.1 x 3.0

VII. 75 Dec. 1, 1885 How Boots Befooled the King   *Howard Pyle*
1 Headpiece with title [1]   w 6.6 x 3.7
2 Peter goes to befool the King [1]   w 2.5 x 4.4
3 Paul goes Home again [1]   w 3.2 x 5.5
4 The Old Woman breaks things [1]   w 3.2 x 4.7
5 The Councillor finds the Wisdom Sack [1]   w 3.1 x 4.8
6 Boots tricks the Princess into showing herself [1]   w 6.5 x 3.6

VII. 143 Dec. 29, 1885 How Three Went Out into Ye
     Wide World   *Howard Pyle*
1 Headpiece with title [1]   w 6.1 x 2.5
2 The Gray Goose meets the Sausage [1]   w 4.1 x 4.5
3 The Fox calls on the Cock [1]   w 4.0 x 4.0
4 The Fox calls on the Sausage [1]   w 4.9 x 4.5
5 The Fox's Wife makes his bed [1]   w 4.9 x 4.1

VII. 207 Jan. 26, 1886 The Princess Golden Hair and
     the Great Black Raven   *Howard Pyle*
1 Headpiece with title [1]   w 6.6 x 2.6
2 The King meets the Great Black Raven in the
     Forest [1]   w 4.1 x 4.8
3 The Princess drinks from the Golden Cup [1]   w 4.2 x 3.8
4 The Princess comes to Gruff's Door [1]   w 4.1 x 4.2
5 The Princess finds her dear Prince again [1]   w 4.0 x 4.7

[1] Reproduced in "The Wonder Clock." Howard Pyle, Harper, New York. 1888.

VII. 271 Feb. 23, 1886 THE CLEVER STUDENT AND THE
    MASTER OF BLACK ARTS   *Howard Pyle*
   1 Headpiece with title [1]   w 6.6 x 3.3
   2 The Princess walking beside the Sea [1]   w 4.1 x 3.6
   3 The Student and the Princess [1]   w 4.2 x 3.7
   4 The Master of Black Arts with a Hen [1]   w 4.1 x 3.8
   5 What happened to the Master [1]   w 3.8 x 4.0

VII. 335 March 23, 1886 PETERKIN AND THE LITTLE
    GRAY HARE   *Howard Pyle*
   1 Headpiece with title [1]   w 6.6 x 2.8
   2 Peterkin's brothers marvel at his fine trappings [1] w 4.1 x 4.2
   3 Peterkin makes off with the Giant's Goose [1]   w 4.0 x 4.9
   4 Peterkin brings the Silver Bell to the King [1] w 3.2 x 3.4
   5 Peterkin dressed as a lass, and the Giant [1]   w 4.0 x 3.8

VII. 415 April 27, 1886 HOW THE GOOD GIFTS WERE USED
    BY TWO   *Howard Pyle*
   1 Headpiece with title [1]   w 5.7 x 3.7
   2 Saint Nicholas at the Rich Man's Door [1]   w 4.0 x 4.2
   3 Saint Nicholas at the Poor Man's House [1]   w 4.0 x 3.6
   4 The Poor Man and St. Christopher [1]   w 4.0 x 4.2
   5 The Rich Man and the Two Saints [1]   w 4.8 x 3.0

VII. 479 May 25, 1886 MOTHER HILDEGARDE   *Howard Pyle*
   1 Headpiece with title [1]   w 5.7 x 2.5
   2 Mother Hildegarde and the Princess [1]   w 4.1 x 4.3
   3 The Princess peeped into the Jar [1]   w 4.1 x 4.3
   4 The Princess and the Pigeons [1]   w 4.1 x 4.3
   5 Mother Hildegarde carries away the Baby [1] w 4.0 x 4.2

VII. 551 June 29, 1886 MASTER JACOB   *Howard Pyle*
   1 Headpiece with title [1]   w 6.6 x 2.2
   2 Master Jacob brings his Pig to Market [1]   w 3.2 x 3.2
   3 Master Jacob goes to Town with his Goat [1] w 4.0 x 2.9
   4 The little tin horn has no effect [1]   w 3.2 x 3.0
   5 Master Jacob and the three Cronies meet in the
      Woods [1]   w 4.0 x 4.0

---

[1] Reproduced in "The Wonder Clock." Howard Pyle, Harper, New York. 1888.

VII. 623 July 27, 1886 HOW THREE LITTLE PIGS HAD
       THE BEST OF THE GREAT WICKED OGRE   *Howard Pyle*
  1 Headpiece with title [1]   w 6.0 x 3.0
  2 "Have you a roasted apple to put in my mouth?" [1] w 3.2 x 3.0
  3 "Do you find the hole?" asked the Little Pig [1] w 4.0 x 3.8
  4 "The Ogre shut his eyes and began to count" [1] w 4.0 x 2.8
  5 " 'Here comes the farmer and his men to see what
      all the stir is about' " [1]   w 4.8 x 3.5

VII. 695 Aug. 31, 1886 THE STAFF AND THE FIDDLE *Howard Pyle*
  1 Headpiece with title [1]   w 6.6 x 3.2
  2 "Give the poor old Woman a penny or two" [1] w 4.0 x 3.7
  3 " 'Rub-a-dub-dub!' says the Fiddler" [1]   w 4.0 x 3.8
  4 A Princess as pretty as a ripe Apple [1]   w 4.0 x 4.1
  5 "What do you want, Master?" [1]   w 4.0 x 3.7

VIII. 11 Nov. 2, 1886 THE SIMPLETON AND HIS LITTLE
       BLACK HEN   *Howard Pyle*
  1 Headpiece with title [1]   w 6.1 x 3.1
  2 Caspar and the cunning Landlord [1]   w 4.0 x 4.0
  3 Caspar finds the Gold in the Willow-Tree [1] w 4.0 x 3.1
  4 The Two Brothers and the Landlord divide the
      money [1]   w 4.0 x 2.1
  5 Caspar and the Three Rascals go to see the King [1] w 4.0 x 4.0

VIII. 75 Nov. 30, 1886 KING STORK   *Howard Pyle*
  1 Headpiece with title [1]   w 6.7 x 2.9
  2 The Drummer carries the Old Man across the
      River [1]   w 4.1 x 3.9
  3 The Princess starts for the Witch's House [1] w 4.1 x 4.2
  4 The Drummer with his Cap of Darkness in the
      Witch's House [1]   w 4.0 x 3.8
  5 The Drummer captures the one-eyed Raven [1] w 4.0 x 3.5

VIII. 143 Dec. 28, 1886 HOW THE PRINCESS'S PRIDE WAS
       BROKEN   *Howard Pyle*
  1 Headpiece with title [1]   w 6.6 x 3.1
  2 The Gooseherd plays with a Golden Ball [1] w 4.0 x 3.9
  3 The King peeps over the hedge [1]   w 4.1 x 4.0

[1] Reproduced in "The Wonder Clock." Howard Pyle, Harper, New York. 1888.

4 The Princess goes to Market with her Eggs [1]   w 4.0 x 3.2
5 King Florimel greets the Princess [1]   w 4.1 x 3.1

VIII. 150 Jan. 4, 1887 DAME BRIDGET'S PROPHECY   *Howard Pyle*
    1 Dame Bridget's Prophecy   w 6.8 x 6.2

VIII. 207 Jan. 25, 1887 HOW TWO WENT INTO PARTNERSHIP
    Howard Pyle
    1 Headpiece with title [1]   w 6.6 x 2.8
    2 The Great Red Fox at the Storehouse [1]   w 4.0 x 3.7
    3 "What are you doing here, Father Goat?" [1]   w 4.0 x 3.6
    4 " 'Which shall it be first—Sausages or Pudding?' " [1] w 4.0 x 4.3
    5 Uncle Bear and the Great Red Fox after Father
       John's Apples [1]   w 4.0 x 3.6

VIII. 287 March 1, 1887 BEARSKIN   *Howard Pyle*
    1 Headpiece with title [1]   w 6.5 x 3.0
    2 The basket with the baby in it drifted down the
       river [1]   w 4.0 x 4.1
    3 Bearskin and the Princess [1]   w 4.0 x 4.2
    4 The Princess wept and wept [1]   w 4.0 x 3.5
    5 Bearskin and the Swineherd had a fine feast
       together [1]   w 4.0 x 3.5

VIII. 309 March 15, 1887 HUGO GROTIUS AND HIS BOOK
       CHEST   *Mrs. M. C. Pyle*
    1 Hugo Grotius and his Book Chest   w 6.6 x 5.4

VIII. 335 March 22, 1887 COUSIN GREYLEGS, YE GREAT
       RED FOX AND GRANDFATHER MOLE   *Howard Pyle*
    1 Headpiece with title [1]   w 6.5 x 2.7
    2 "The Great Red Fox and Cousin Greylegs were
       great cronies" [1]   w 4.0 x 4.0
    3 Cousin Greylegs steals away with the bag of nails [1] w 4.0 x 4.0
    4 Brother Fox comes near tramping on the Mole's
       House [1]   w 4.0 x 2.8
    5 The Great Red Fox shut his teeth and grinned [1]   w 4.0 x 3.3

VIII. 399 April 19, 1887 WHICH IS BEST?   *Howard Pyle*
    1 Headpiece and title [1]   w 6.5 x 2.5

[1] Reproduced in "The Wonder Clock." Howard Pyle, Harper, New York. 1888.

2 So the Rich Man left him in his blindness [1]   w 4.0 x 4.1

3 He touched the lock with the little black stone [1]   w 4.0 x 3.6

4 The Poor Brother opens the chest [1]   w 3.9 x 4.3

5 The Rich Brother takes the diamond from the statue's hand [1]   w 3.9 x 4.3

VIII. 463 May 17, 1887 THE BEST THAT LIFE HAS TO GIVE

Howard Pyle

1 Headpiece with title [1]   w 6.6 x 2.4

2 " 'So you are stealing my pine cones,' said he" [1]   w 4.0 x 3.1

3 He snatched it and ran [1]   w 4.0 x 3.9

4 The Blacksmith carries the Golden Tree to the Queen [1]   w 4.0 x 4.1

5 And that was the end of the Dwarf [1]   w 4.0 x 4.3

VIII. 519 June 24, 1887 THE WATER OF LIFE   *Howard Pyle*

1 Headpiece with title [1]   w 6.6 x 3.2

2 A Stranger shows the King the portrait of a beautiful Princess [1]   w 4.0 x 4.3

3 The Faithful Servant is borne on the wings of the North Wind [1]   w 4.1 x 3.7

4 The King gives the Water of Life to the beautiful Princess [1]   w 4.0 x 3.7

5 The King goes to cut off the Faithful Servant's arm [1] w 4.0 x 4.0

VIII. 639 Aug. 2, 1887 THE STEPMOTHER   *Howard Pyle*

1 Headpiece with title [1]   w 6.6 x 2.5

2 The Stepdaughter follows the Golden Ball [1]   w 4.0 x 4.4

3 The King rescues the Maiden from a deep pit [1]   w 4.0 x 4.4

4 The Stepmother changes the Queen into a White Dove [1]   w 4.0 x 4.2

5 The King caresses the White Dove [1]   w 4.0 x 3.2

VIII. 719 Sept. 6, 1887 THE WHITE BIRD   *Howard Pyle*

1 Headpiece with title [1]   w 6.5 x 2.3

2 The door was opened by a poor man [1]   w 4.0 x 4.0

3 There sat three terrible giants [1]   w 4.0 x 4.0

4 The Prince takes the Sword of Brightness [1]   w 4.0 x 4.3

5 The White Bird recognizes the Prince [1]   w 4.0 x 4.3

---

1 Reproduced in "The Wonder Clock." Howard Pyle, Harper, New York. 1888.

VIII. 795 Oct. 11, 1887 ONE GOOD TURN DESERVES ANOTHER
Howard Pyle

1 Headpiece with title [1]   w 6.6 x 2.
2 The Fisher Lad catches a strange fish [1]   w 4.0 x 4.0
3 The Fisher Lad comes to the Gray Master's house [1] w 4.0 x 4.5
4 The Gray Master is caught in the stream and is
  swept away [1]   w 4.0 x 4.0
5 The Princess finds the Fisher Lad with the key of
  Wish-House [1]   w 4.0 x 4.3

IX. 595 June 26, 1888 THE THREE FORTUNES   *Howard Pyle*

1 Headpiece with title   w 6.2 x 2.
2 He was an old man no longer, but a Blessed Angel w 4.0 x 4.4
3 The Angel and the Youngest Brother said "Good-
  bye" and trudged away   w 4.1 x 3.
4 A great, ugly, poisonous snake crept out of a hole
  in the wall   w 4.1 x 4.2
5 They set before him a loaf of bread and a bowl
  of milk   w 4.1 x 4.

IX. 667 July 24, 1888 THE PRINCESS ON THE GLASS HILL *Howard Pyle*

1 Headpiece with title and initial   w 6.7 x 3.7
2 The Prince pours water into the barrel   w 4.2 x 4.2
3 The Prince bathes in the fountain   w 4.2 x 4.2
4 The Prince kills the Dragon   w 4.3 x 4.6
5 The Prince wins the Golden Apple and the Silver
  Pear   w 4.3 x 4.4

X. 735 Aug. 27, 1889 THAT WHICH IS DONE NEVER DIES
Howard Pyle

1 Headpiece with title   w 5.6 x 4.2
2 "A golden swan leaped into the air"   w 1.4 x 3.3
3 "As it sang it sang so sweetly and so sadly"   w 4.8 x 4.4
4 "The Princess sits in the window and sings"   w 3.2 x 4.1
5 "The King opened the closet door and brought
  forth the true bride"   w 6.0 x 3.
6 "There sprang from the midst of the smoke a
  beautiful bird"   w 6.1 x 2.9

---

[1] Reproduced in "The Wonder Clock." Howard Pyle, Harper, New York. 1888.

x. 885 Oct. 15, 1889 Ill-Luck and the Fiddler   *Howard Pyle*

  1 Headpiece with initial and title [1]   w 4.6 x 5.7
  2 Vignette [1]   w 4.4 x 4.7
  3 Vignette [1]   w 4.9 x 3.4
  4 Vignette [1]   w 4.6 x 2.4
  5 Vignette [1]   w 1.0 x 2.5
  6 Vignette [1]   w 2.5 x 2.5
  7 Vignette   w 1.3 x 2.4

xi. 11 Nov. 5, 1889 Wisdom's Wages and Folly's Pay

                                                     Howard Pyle

  1 Headpiece [1]   w 2.0 x 3.6
  2 Vignette [1]   w 0.9 x 0.2
  3 Vignette   w 0.9 x 1.2
  4 Vignette [1]   w 3.7 x 1.2
  5 Vignette [1]   w 3.2 x 3.5
  6 Vignette [1]   w 1.5 x 4.6
  7 Vignette [1]   w 5.9 x 2.4
  8 Vignette [1]   w 4.8 x 4.4

xi. 175 Jan. 7, 1890 The Salt of Life. I.   *Howard Pyle*

  1 Headpiece with title [1]   w 4.1 x 3.4
  2 "Away with you, and never let me see your face
       again" [1]   w 4.0 x 4.0
  3 "An old man looked down into the water" [1]   w 2.5 x 3.2
  4 "The Queen raised the veil and looked at the
       Prince" [1]   w 3.7 x 3.0
  5 "Away the boat went, swifter than the wind" [1]   w 3.2 x 3.5

xi. 191 Jan. 14, 1890 The Salt of Life. II.   *Howard Pyle*

  Headpiece with title same as in Jan. 7
  1 "Beat the statue with her steel-tipped whip" [1]   w 2.5 x 4.2
  2 "The raven spread his wings and flew" [1]   w 3.2 x 3.5
  3 "At last they dashed against one another" [1]   w 2.7 x 3.2
  4 "The statue became flesh and blood" [1]   w 1.5 x 2.7
  5 "He had a noble feast set for them" [1]   w 3.2 x 2.3

---

[1] Reproduced in "Twilight Land." Howard Pyle, Harper, New York. 1895.

XI. 275 Feb. 18, 1890 EMPTY BOTTLES   *Howard Pyle*
1 Headpiece with title [1]   w 3.7 x 2.7
2 "Making strange figures upon the table" [1]   w 2.3 x 3.6
3 " 'Now,' said the Master, 'take me by the belt' " [1] w 3.2 x 5.2
4 "He gazed and gazed until his heart melted within
   him" [1]   w 4.0 x 2.6
5 "The dragon leaped into the air" [1]   w 1.5 x 2.5
6 "He raised the dagger to strike" [1]   w 4.2 x 2.3

XI. 359 March 25, 1890 WHERE TO LAY THE BLAME   *Howard Pyle*
1 Headpiece with title [1]   w 6.6 x 3.5
2 "The old man began to utter strange spells" [1]   w 3.0 x 5.6
3 "He caught something that weighed heavily as
   lead" [1]   w 2.5 x 4.4
4 "They kissed one another" [1]   w 4.0 x 5.8
5 "The chief treasurer emptied a bag of money
   into the fur cap" [1]   w 3.2 x 3.8
6 "Down fell the fisherman" [1]   w 1.5 x 4.0

XI. 543 June 10, 1890 NOT A PIN TO CHOOSE. I.   *Howard Pyle*
1 Headpiece with title [1]   w 5.7 x 3.3
2 "He was like one bereft of wits" [1]   w 3.3 x 7.0
3 "A wise man stopped to enquire the cause of his
   sorrow" [1]   w 3.3 x 4.0
4 "A great crowd of horses laden with balls and
   bundles of rich stuffs" [1]   w 3.4 x 6.7
5 "There was a passageway yawning before him" [1] w 2.6 x 3.6

XI. 566 June 17, 1890 NOT A PIN TO CHOOSE. II.   *Howard Pyle*
1 "Out leaped a great hideous Genie" [1]   w 3.2 x 5.6
2 "Bread as white as snow, and a piece of cheese" [1] w 2.5 x 3.5
3 "Blazing with diamonds and rubies and emeralds" [1] w 2.5 x 3.1
4 "The Princess looked over the edge of the balcony" [1] w 2.4 x 4.2
5 " 'Sire,' said the Ambassador, 'I will answer now
   for my master' " [1]   w 4.9 x 3.3

XI. 660 July 29, 1890 WOMAN'S WIT   *Howard Pyle*
1 Headpiece with title [1]   w 3.2 x 3.8
2 "A box of adamant" [1]   w 1.6 x 2.8

[1] Reproduced in "Twilight Land." Howard Pyle, Harper, New York. 1895.

[84]

3 "The little man set him to work on the bench" [1]   w 2.3 x 2.3
4 "It was the King's daughter passing by" [1]   w 3.2 x 4.5
5 "The young man prostrated himself in the dust" [1] w 4.0 x 2.6
6 "Then prepare to die" [1]   w 2.1 x 2.8
7 Tailpiece [1]   w 2.0 x 2.3

XI. 770 Sept. 9, 1890 GOOD GIFTS AND A FOOL'S FOLLY
Howard Pyle

1 Headpiece with title [1]   w 3.3 x 3.2
2 "An old man with a beard as white as snow" [1]   w 3.2 x 4.0
3 "Away flew the carpet swifter than the wind" [1]   w 3.2 x 3.1
4 "Every day there was feasting and dancing and
   singing" [1]   w 4.0 x 4.1
5 "He balanced the earthen jar on his head" [1]   w 3.2 x 4.0
6 "Around and around they spun and whirled" [1]   w 4.0 x 3.7
7 "He lay there sighing and groaning" [1]   w 2.4 x 1.4

XI. 851 Oct. 14, 1890 ALL THINGS ARE AS FATE WILLS
Howard Pyle

1 Headpiece with title [1]   w 3.2 x 3.6
2 "Three men seized him" [1]   w 2.5 x 4.2
3 "The King and the beggar feasted" [1]   w 3.3 x 4.1
4 "He knocked upon the brazen gate" [1]   w 3.7 x 4.7
5 "The beggar crawled out" [1]   w 4.0 x 1.7
6 "He was seated upon a throne" [1]   w 3.3 x 4.4

XII. 31 Nov. 4, 1890 MUCH SHALL HAVE MORE AND
   LITTLE SHALL HAVE LESS   *Howard Pyle*
1 Headpiece with title [1]   w 1.5 x 4.6
2 "He spread the money out on the table" [1]   w 2.6 x 3.5
3 "Sat down by the road-side to eat his pie" [1]   w 2.5 x 4.4
4 "He met a poor woman coming home from market"[1] w 3.2 x 4.0
5 " 'Keep the bag of money for yourself,' said the
   King" [1]   w 3.7 x 3.5

XII. 138 Dec. 23, 1890 THE STOOL OF FORTUNE   *Howard Pyle*
1 Headpiece with title [1]   w 1.5 x 5.1
2 "If the shot had cracked the sky he could not have
   been more frightened" [1]   w 3.2 x 4.6

---

[1]Reproduced in "Twilight Land." Howard Pyle, Harper, New York. 1895.

3 "Away flew the stool"[1]   w 1.7 x 3.4
4 "The prettiest princess the sun ever shone upon"[1] w 4.4 x 2.2
5 "Riding in his gilded coach"[1]   w 4.1 x 3.0
6 "What are my lord's commands?"[1]   w 3.2 x 4.7
7 Tailpiece[1]   w 3.2 x 1.0

XII. 187 Jan. 13, 1891 THE FRUIT OF HAPPINESS   *Howard Pyle*
   1 Headpiece with title[1]   w 1.6 x 4.3
   2 "He came to the cross-roads and the stone cross"[1] w 3.2 x 4.3
   3 "He drew out his pipe, and began to play"[1]   w 4.0 x 2.3
   4 "In came the gang of thieves"[1]   w 4.2 x 4.3
   5 "All was a red blaze behind them"[1]   w 3.3 x 5.4
   6 "Went whirling over rocks and waterfalls"[1]   w 2.1 x 3.7

MEN OF IRON   *Howard Pyle*
   Jan. 20 to June 9, 1891.

XII. 193 Jan. 20, 1891
   The Flight from Falworth Castle[2]   p 6.6 x 8.6

XII. 220 Jan. 27, 1891
   "Myles as in a dream kneeled, and presented the
      letter"[2]   p 6.6 x 8.6

XII. 229 Feb. 3, 1891
   No title[2]   p 6.5 x 4.9

XII. 254 Feb. 10, 1891
   "At last they had the poor boy down"[2]   p 5.7 x 6.9

XII. 262 Feb. 17, 1891
   "Myles pushed the door further open"[2]   p 5.7 x 7.1

XII. 282 Feb. 24, 1891
   In the "Eyry"[2]   p 5.3 x 6.8

XII. 304 March 3, 1891
   "They bore him away to a bench at the far end of
      the room"[2]   p 6.7 x 8.7

[1] Reproduced in "Twilight Land." Howard Pyle, Harper, New York. 1895.
[2] Reproduced in "Men of Iron." Howard Pyle, Harper, New York. 1892.

XII. 326 March 10, 1891
   "But tell me, Robin Ingoldsby, dost know aught
   more of this matter?"[1]   p 8.5 x 6.5

XII. 334 March 17, 1891
   " 'Belike thou sought to take this lad's life,' said Sir
   James"[1]   p 4.8 x 6.3

XII. 355 March 24, 1891
   "Stories and jests recited by some strolling mummer
   or minstrel"[1]   p 6.5 x 4.9

XII. 372 March 31, 1891
   Myles entertains the Lady Anne and the Lady Alice
   with his adventures[1]   p 5.3 x 6.8

XII. 390 April 7, 1891
   "Myles found himself standing beside the bed"[1]   p 6.5 x 8.6

XII. 406 April 14, 1891
   The Earl of Mackworth receives King Henry IV.[1]   p 6.6 x 8.6

XII. 420 April 21, 1891
   "Lord George led him to where the King stood"[1]   p 6.7 x 8.7

XII. 437 April 28, 1891
   "There he watched and guarded while the others
   slept"[1]   p 5.6 x 8.6

XII. 453 May 5, 1891
   No title[1]   p 5.7 x 7.5

XII. 469 May 12, 1891
   No title[1]   p 5.3 x 6.8

XII. 484 May 19, 1891
   Prior Edward and Myles in the Priory garden[1]   p 6.4 x 8.4

XII. 500 May 26, 1891
   The Challenge[1]   p 8.5 x 6.5

XII. 517 June 2, 1891
   No title[1]   p 5.7 x 7.6

[1] Reproduced in "Men of Iron." Howard Pyle, Harper, New York. 1892.

XII. 532 June 9, 1891

"He held tightly to the saddle-bow of the fallen
man's horse" [1]   p 6.6 x 8.5

XIII. 137 Dec. 15, 1891 THE ENCHANTED ISLAND. I.   *Howard Pyle*
1 Headpiece with title [2]   w 4.0 x 1.3
2 "Selim the Fisherman finds a leaden box" [2]   w 2.5 x 4.7
3 "The old man rapped on the door three times" [2]   w 2.4 x 4.3
4 "There was feasting and merrymaking" [2]   w 4.2 x 4.7
5 "The men brought Selim up in front of the statue" [2] w 3.2 x 3.6

XIII. 141 Dec. 22, 1891 THE ENCHANTED ISLAND. II.
Headpiece same as previous number [2]
1 "Selim the Baker lands on the desert island" [2]   w 3.3 x 1.5
2 " 'Come with me,' said the little old man" [2]   w 2.5 x 3.7
3 "He called the wisest men of the island to him" [2] w 3.7 x 5.1
4 "Down she came from the pedestal where she
   stood" [2]   w 3.3 x 4.2
5 Tailpiece [2]   w 3.2 x 1.4

XIII. 373 March 29, 1892 THE TALISMAN OF SOLOMON. I.
                                                     Howard Pyle
1 "Zadok and his master" [2]   w 2.0 x 3.7
2 "An old man who had a curious necklace for sale" [2] w 2.4 x 3.7
3 "A vessel of brass full of money" [2]   w 2.4 x 3.3
4 "A great tall Demon" [2]   w 1.7 x 3.0
5 "He fell on his face and kissed the ground" [2]   w 3.3 x 3.4
6 "The Demon leaped from the earth" [2]   w 3.3 x 2.5

XIII. 395 April 5, 1892 THE TALISMAN OF SOLOMON. II. *Howard Pyle*
1 "A basin filled with jewels" [2]   w 2.5 x 3.3
2 "A palace of marble and gold" [2]   w 2.5 x 4.0
3 " 'I think everybody has gone mad,' said the
   young man" [2]   w 3.2 x 2.8
4 "They entered the vestibule of the palace" [2]   w 2.5 x 3.1
5 "The young man fell upon his knees" [2]   w 2.5 x 3.2

[1] Reproduced in "Men of Iron." Howard Pyle, Harper, New York. 1892.
[2] Reproduced in "Twilight Land." Howard Pyle, Harper, New York. 1895.

    6 "Drew a circle upon the ground with his finger
      tip" [1]   w 2.5 x 4.2

xiv. 7 Nov. 1, 1892 So It Is with Them All   *Howard Pyle*
    1 " 'This is my daughter,' said the merchant"   w 3.2 x 3.8
    2 "There sat an old woman at a wheel spinning" w 3.1 x 4.4
    3 "Thou art a wonder of wonders"   w 3.3 x 5.4
    4 "A dense cloud of blue smoke rose in the air" w 3.1 x 5.2
    5 " 'I am ready,' said the young man steadily"   w 3.0 x 4.3
    6 "Flew away swifter than the wind"   w 2.5 x 2.6

xv. 403 April 10, 1894 A Piece of Good Luck. I.   *Howard Pyle*
    1 Headpiece with title [1]   w 3.3 x 2.6
    2 "They danced around and around the chest" [1] w 3.3 x 5.8
    3 " 'What will you have?' said the Genius" [1]   w 3.2 x 5.6
    4 "Close your doors! close your doors! her Highness
      the Princess comes to ride" [1]   w 5.0 x 5.6
    5 "The Genius had flown with her through the air" [1] w 3.2 x 2.0

xv. 427 April 17, 1894 A Piece of Good Luck. II.   *Howard Pyle*
    1 "Next morning the Prime Minister looked like a
      shorn sheep" [1]   w 3.3 x 5.2
    2 "Jacob's magnificent court suit" [1]   w 2.4 x 4.4
    3 "As for the King, he could not believe his eyes
      when he saw it" [1]   w 4.0 x 5.5
    4 "Jacob and the King left in the desert by the
      Genius" [1]   w 3.3 x 3.3
    5 "The Genius snatched the Minister up and flew
      away with him" [1]   w 3.3 x 5.2

xv. 639 July 17, 1894 The Good of a Few Words. I. *Howard Pyle*
    1 Headband with title [1]   w 3.2 x 3.3
    2 "Feasting and drinking and junketing and merry-
      making" [1]   w 4.1 x 4.5
    3 " 'Look at yonder poor man,' said she to her
      nurse" [1]   w 2.5 x 4.0
    4 "The tall man in black knocked upon the gate" [1] w 2.5 x 4.1
    5 " 'Now,' said the King, 'now you are married' " [1] w 3.2 x 5.2
    6 "Then Beppo carried the Princess ashore" [1] w 2.5 x 4.2

[1] Reproduced in "Twilight Land." Howard Pyle, Harper, New York. 1895.

xv. 659 July 24, 1894 THE GOOD OF A FEW WORDS. II. *Howard Pyle*
1 "Again Sebastian served a feast" [1]   w 2.5 x 3.2
2 "Beppo offers the King milk" [1]   w 3.6 x 4.7
3 " 'Alas, my poor friend!' said he" [1]   w 2.3 x 3.4
4 "The King laid his hands on Beppo's shoulders" [1] w 4.1 x 5.7
5 " 'Do you not know me?' said she; 'I am the
    Queen' " [1]   w 4.1 x 5.2

THE LADIES' HOME JOURNAL

XIII. 1 March 1896 THE WEREWOLF   *Eugene Field*
1 "The werewolf skulked for a moment in the
    shadow of the yews, and Yseult plucked old
    Siegfried's spear from her girdle"   p 9.3 x 6.2
                                                A. M. Lindsay, Sc.
XIV. 15 Dec. 1896 LOVE AT VALLEY FORGE   *Sarah King Wiley*
1 "My dear," said General Washington, "Captain
    Prescott's behavior was inexcusable"   p 9.5 x 6.8

XIV. May 1897 COVER DESIGN IN COLORS   c 11.0 x 15.2

XVI. 13 Oct. 1899 THE LAST YEARS OF WASHINGTON'S
              LIFE   *William Perrine*
1 George and Martha Washington entertaining their
    friends on the lawn at Mount Vernon   p 9.0 x 5.0

McCLURE'S MAGAZINE

XIV. 109 Dec. 1899 THE MAN FOR THE HOUR   *James Barnes*
1 "He called on Franklin and received the necessary
    recognition"   p 5.0 x 3.4
2 "The good, aged Doctor, the appearance of whose
    rotund figure on the streets was the signal for the
    Parisians to doff their hats"   p 4.9 x 7.3
3 "At the same time he extended toward King Louis
    the precious Memorial"   p 5.0 x 7.4
4 The death of Colonel John Laurens   p 4.8 x 2.0

[1] Reproduced in "Twilight Land." Howard Pyle, Harper, New York. 1895.

xiv. Jan. 1900 Cover Design in Colors   c 6.0 x 8.9

xvi. 109 Dec. 1900 At the Turn of the Glass

Martha McCulloch Williams

     1 Headband   p 1.0 x 4.5
     2 Frontispiece   p 4.5 x 6.8
     3 Marginal decoration with poem enclosed   p 5.2 x 8.1

xvii. 307 Aug. 1901 The Chase of the Tide   *Norman Duncan*

     1 Uncle Sammy and Joe   p 4.2 x 7.8
     2 Headpiece with title   p 5.2 x 5.3
     3 Marginal illustration   p 5.0 x 8.1
     4 Vignette   p 2.3 x 4.1
     5 Illustration. No title   p 5.0 x 1.7
     6 "The Sea—he've cotched us"   p 4.2 x 7.7

xxvii. 641 Oct. 1906 The Second-Class Passenger

Perceval Gibbon

     1 "The tall man was lying at his feet, huddled
         hideously on the floor"   p 5.0 x 7.4
     2 Headband   p 4.9 x 1.8

xxviii. 44 Nov. 1906 The Hanging of Mary Dyer   *Basil King*

     1 "I have been reservéd for this—to free the land
         from spiritual tyranny"[1]   c 5.0 x 7.5
     2 " 'The Lord hath sent me here to die like Stephen
         at the feet of Saul' "[1]   c 5.0 x 7.5
     3 "At her appearing the multitude was hushed, awed
         by that air she wore"[1]   c 5.0 x 7.4

THE NEW YORK LEDGER

Jan. 11, 1890 Supplement, 4 pages

The Captain's Well   *John Greenleaf Whittier*

     1 Headpiece with title [2]   w 7.9 x 1.5
     2 Illustration [2]   w 8.8 x 5.9
                                          Henry Wolf, Sc.
     3 Illustration [2]   w 5.3 x 4.9
                                          R. G. Tietze, Sc.

[1] Reproduced in "Dulcibel." Henry Peterson, John C. Winston Co., Philadelphia. 1907.
[2] Reproduced in "The Captain's Well." John Greenleaf Whittier, New York Ledger. 1890.

4 Illustration [1] W 4.9 x 7.5
E. A. Clement, Sc.

5 Illustration [1] W 5.2 x 7.9
R. G. Tietze, Sc.

THE NORTHWESTERN MILLER

XXX. 10 Dec. 1890 BLUESKIN THE PIRATE *Howard Pyle*
1 "He lay silent and still, with his face half buried in
the sand" P 8.2 x 11.9

L. 29 Dec. 1900 CAPTAIN SCARFIELD *Howard Pyle*
1 "He struck once and again at the bald, narrow
forehead beneath him" P 7.5 x 11.0

OUR CONTINENT

UNDER GREEN APPLE BOUGHS *Helen Campbell*
I. 1 Feb. 15, 1882
"A child sunburned, and with many fluttering shreds
of raiment" [2] W 5.2 x 5.8
F. Juengling, Sc.

I. 17 Feb. 22, 1882
"She hadn't on anything but a little night-gown, the
same as if they'd snatched her out o' the berth,
with no time to dress her" [2] W 6.7 x 7.0
F. French, Sc.

I. 33 March 1, 1882
"They turned to the table where master and pupil
sat absorbed" [3] W 6.0 x 5.4
J. P. Davis, Sc.

I. 49 March 8, 1882
Sylvia's Troubles [2] W 4.5 x 4.1
F. French, Sc.

I. 65 March 15, 1882
"She wasn't no kin when I married her, but we have
lived together over thirty years" [4] W 5.4 x 4.6
J. P. Davis, Sc.

---

[1] Reproduced in "The Captain's Well." John Greenleaf Whittier, New York Ledger. 1890.
[2] Reproduced complete.
[3] One-half reproduced.
[4] Reproduced as two illustrations, in "Under Green Apple Boughs." Helen Campbell, Fords,
Howard & Hulbert, New York. 1882.

OUR CONTINENT—*Continued*

I. 81 March 22, 1882
    The fight in the fog [1]
                         w 5.4 x 5.7
                         F. French, Sc.

ST. NICHOLAS

IV. 261 Feb. 1877 THE CRAFTY FOX   *Howard Pyle*
   1 The Gosling states his opinion of the Cock   w 4.7 x 3.5
   2 The Gosling is punished   w 4.7 x 3.3

IV. 381 April 1877 THE FOX AND THE TABLET   *"P. Howard"*
   1 Heading   w 4.2 x 3.1

IV. 400 April 1877 *HANS GOTTENLIEB, THE FIDDLER *Howard Pyle*
   1 The Swineherd who knew curious things   w 3.6 x 5.1
   2 Gottenlieb's music works a charm   w 5.4 x 1.6

IV. 639 July 1877 PICTORIAL PUZZLE   *Howard Pyle*
   1 Heading   w 5.4 x 4.4

IV. 718 Sept. 1877 *DRUMMER FRITZ AND HIS EXPLOITS
                             Howard Pyle
Illustrations in silhouette:
   1 The King and his Prime Minister   w 3.4 x 1.8
   2 Fritz guides the Baron   w 1.5 x 1.9
   3 "I have brought you the Baron's head"   w 2.6 x 1.7
   4 The Princess and her Pigs   w 3.7 x 2.4
   5 "Poor Piggy led the way"   w 5.4 x 1.5
   6 The Royal Bodyguard   w 2.8 x 2.2
   7 Tailpiece   w 3.4 x 2.4

V. 187 Jan. 1878 THE STORK AND THE CRANE: A FABLE
                             Howard Pyle

V. 377 April 1878 How KITTY WAS LOST IN A TURKISH
     BAZAAR   *Sarah Keables Hunt*
   1 Kitty and the Turkish Merchant   w 5.0 x 5.5
                         R. A. Muller, Sc.

---

[1] Reproduced in "Under Green Apple Boughs." Helen Campbell, Fords, Howard & Hulbert, New York. 1882.
* Story republished without illustrations in "The Book of Laughter." G. P. Putnam's Sons, New York. 1911.

v. 407 April 1878 WISE CATHERINE AND THE KABOUTERMANNEKEN
Howard Pyle
    1 "A very little man seated in a very large chair"   w 3.4 x 3.0
    2 "He examined with astonishment and delight"   w 1.9 x 2.4
    3 "A page was appointed to escort it"   w 2.2 x 2.7
    4 "The king sat upon a chair of state, with a learned
       judge at each side"   w 3.3 x 3.0

v. 486 May 1878 THE STORY OF MAY-DAY   *Olive Thorne*
    1 An Old-time May Day in "Merrie England"   w 5.3 x 6.0

v. 562 June 1878 How WILLY-WOLLY WENT A-FISHING   *S. C. Stone*
    1 Silhouette   w 4.2 x 4.8
    2 Silhouette   w 4.0 x 6.0
    3 Silhouette   w 4.5 x 3.8

v. 743 Sept. 1878 THE FOX, THE MONKEY, AND THE PIG
Howard Pyle
    1 Illustration   w 5.4 x 3.2

vi. 250 Feb. 1879 ABOUT VIOLINS   *M. D. Ruff*
    1 "As good as new"   w 3.1 x 1.5

vi. 267 Feb. 1879 THE ORIGIN OF THE JUMPING-JACK   *I. L. Beman*
    1 Tailpiece   w 1.6 x 2.5

vi. 462 May 1879 THE GOURD AND THE OAK   *Howard Pyle*
    1 Heading   w 5.0 x 2.2

vi. 549 June 1879 How A COMET STRUCK THE EARTH
Edward C. Kemble
    1 The Home-made Press   w 4.0 x 1.9

vi. 533 June 1879 *ROBIN GOODFELLOW AND HIS FRIEND
    BLUETREE   *Howard Pyle*
    1 Bluetree declines Lord Diddledaddle's offer   w 2.6 x 2.7
    2 A Bowl of Milk for Robin Goodfellow   w 1.2 x 2.9
    3 A Great Black Bear came out of the Woods   w 3.6 x 2.7

---

* Story republished without illustrations in "The Book of Laughter." G. P. Putnam's Sons, New York. 1911.

VI. 745 Sept. 1879 GRETELEIN AND HER QUEER STOVE

Rosamund Dale Owen

    1 Gretelein and the Elf King   w 4.5 x 6.1

    2 Tailpiece   w 3.3 x 0.8

VII. 98 Dec. 1879 FABLES   *Howard Pyle*

    1 "A Person of Consequence, carefully fed and
        attended to"   w 5.4 x 3.0

VIII. 217 Jan. 1881 PHAETON ROGERS   *Rossiter Johnson*

    1 "Edmund Burton, you are a genius!"   w 4.7 x 3.9
                                                E. Hinemann, Sc.

    2 The Boys consult Jack-in-the-Box [1]   w 3.9 x 3.4
                                                E. Hinemann, Sc.

VIII. 331 Feb. 1881 A FABLE FROM DEACON GREEN   *Howard Pyle*

    1 Jupiter and the Philosopher   w 3.6 x 3.9

VIII. 379 March 1881 PHAETON ROGERS   *Rossiter Johnson*

    1 "One of the policemen produced a bull's-eye
        lantern"   w 4.6 x 4.3

    2 "The clown counted the money"   w 5.4 x 4.2

XX. 83 Dec. 1892 THE SOLDIERING OF BENIAH STIDHAM

Howard Pyle

    1 "They used to drill every evening"   w 5.0 x 7.5
                                             F. H. Wellington, Sc.

    2 Headpiece with title and initial W   p 4.9 x 4.4

    3 Vignette   p 3.7 x 2.3

    4 Vignette   p 1.6 x 1.9

    5 Vignette   p 2.7 x 2.4

    6 Vignette   p 2.5 x 1.6

    7 Vignette   p 1.1 x 2.1

    8 Vignette   p 2.6 x 2.3

    9 Vignette   p 4.0 x 1.7

    10 Vignette   p 1.0 x 1.4

---

[1] Reproduced in "Phaeton Rogers." Rossiter Johnson, Scribner's, New York. 1909.

JACK BALLISTER'S FORTUNES   *Howard Pyle*
        April, 1894, to Sept., 1895.

XXI. 497 April 1894
    Uncle and Nephew—"Well, Jacky, you shall have that
        hundred pounds, you shall"   p 5.4 x 7.9

XXI. 617 May 1894
    " 'He'll come to by and by; he's only stunned a trifle,'
        said the Captain"[1]   p 5.0 x 7.6

XXI. 712 June 1894
    " 'Now then, Gentlemen, how much do you bid for
        this boy?' said the auctioneer"[1]   p 5.0 x 7.5
                                                          Kurtz, Sc.
XXI. 801 July 1894
    " 'Speak up, boy,—speak up,' said the gentleman"[1] p 5.0 x 7.7

XXI. 845 Aug. 1894
    "Mr. Parker stood looking at his visitor with his
        usual calm reserve"[1]   p 7.6 x 5.0

XXI. 997 Sept. 1894
    " 'I don't want to be anybody's servant, lady, and
        wouldn't if I could help it' "[1]   p 5.0 x 7.6

XXI. 1032 Oct. 1894
    "He picked up the bird and held it out at arm's
        length"[1]   p 5.0 x 7.6

XXII. 30 Nov. 1894
    "He led Jack up to a man who sat on a barrel"[1]   p 5.0 x 7.6

XXII. 128 Dec. 1894
    "Jack followed the Captain and the young lady up
        the crooked path to the house"[1]   p 5.0 x 7.7

XXII. 225 Jan. 1895
    "They found her still sitting in the same place"[1] p 5.0 x 7.6

XXII. 313 Feb. 1895
    Governor Spottiswood visits Colonel Parker   p 5.0 x 7.7

[1] Reproduced in "Jack Ballister's Fortunes." Howard Pyle, Century Co., New York. 1895.

xxii. 375 March 1895
Jack and Dred rescue Eleanor—The Start [1]   p 5.0 x 7.6

xxii. 488 April 1895
The pirates fire upon the fugitives [1]   p 5.0 x 7.6
                                                        Kurtz, Sc.

xxii. 561 May 1895 No illustrations

xxii. 649 June 1895
"Colonel Parker reached out and laid his hand upon
    Jack's shoulder. 'Ay,' said he, ' 'tis a good, honest
    face' " [1]   p 5.0 x 7.6

xxii. 732 July 1895
Blackbeard's last fight [1]   p 5.0 x 7.6

xxii. 857 Aug. 1895 No illustrations

xxii. 903 Sept. 1895
" 'Then I will come,' said he" [1]   p 5.0 x 7.6

THE STORY OF KING ARTHUR AND HIS KNIGHTS   *Howard Pyle*
    Nov., 1902, to Oct., 1903.

xxv. 5 Nov. 1902
  1 Title with illustrated initial T [2]   p 5.4 x 0.8
  2 The Enchanter Merlin [2]   p 5.4 x 6.3
  3 Headpiece [2]   p 5.5 x 2.4
  4 Illustrated initial A   p 1.3 x 1.3
  5 Title with illustrated initial H   p 5.3 x 0.8
  6 How one clad all in black did a wonder before King
      Leodegrance of Camilard   p 5.3 x 6.4
  7 Sir Kay overthroweth his Enemies. (With title) [2]   p 5.4 x 3.6
  8 Illustrated initial I   p 1.3 x 1.3
  9 Title with illustrated initial S [2]   p 5.4 x 0.8
  10 Sir Kay breaketh his sword at ye Tournament [2]   p 5.4 x 6.2

---

[1] Reproduced in "Jack Ballister's Fortunes." Howard Pyle, Century Co., New York. 1895.
[2] Reproduced in "The Story of King Arthur and His Knights." Howard Pyle, Scribner, New York. 1903.

xxv. 102 Dec. 1902

  1 Headpiece [1]   p 5.4 x 3.1
  2 Title with illustrated initial S [1]   p 5.2 x 0.8
  3 Sir Kay showeth the mystic Sword unto Sir Ector [1]   p 5.3 x 6.2
  4 Title with illustrated initial K   p 5.2 x 0.8
  5 King Leodegrance cometh to the assay of the Sword   p 5.2 x 6.2

xxv. 208 Jan. 1903

  1 Title with illustrated initial H [1]   p 5.4 x 0.8
  2 How Arthur drew forth ye Sword [1]   p 5.4 x 6.4
  3 Headpiece [1]   p 5.4 x 2.2
  4 Title with illustrated initial K [1]   p 5.4 x 0.8
  5 King Arthur of Britain [1]   p 5.3 x 6.1

xxv. 328 Feb. 1903

  1 Initial S   p 1.3 x 1.2
  2 Title with illustrated initial I [1]   p 5.2 x 0.8
  3 In the Valley of Delight [1]   p 5.2 x 6.2
  4 Title with illustrated initial T [1]   p 4.8 x 0.8
  5 The Battle with the Sable Knight [1]   p 4.8 x 6.3

xxv. 396 March 1903

  1 The Winning of a Sword and a Queen [1]   p 5.4 x 3.4
  2 Title with illustrated initial E [1]   p 5.2 x 0.8
  3 Excalibur the Sword [1]   p 4.8 x 6.1
  4 Title with illustrated initial T [1]   p 4.0 x 0.7
  5 The Lady Guinevere [1]   p 4.0 x 4.5
  6 Title with illustrated initial T [1]   p 5.2 x 1.0
  7 Two Knights do Battle before Camilard [1]   p 5.5 x 6.5

xxv. 518 April 1903

  1 Headpiece [1]   p 4.7 x 4.0
  2 Title with illustrated initial T [1]   p 5.5 x 1.0
  3 The White Champion meets two Knights at the Mill [1]   p 5.5 x 6.2
  4 Title with illustrated initial F [1]   p 5.5 x 1.0
  5 Four Knights serve the Gardener Lad [1]   p 5.5 x 6.4

[1] Reproduced in "The Story of King Arthur and His Knights." Howard Pyle, Scribner, New York. 1903.

xxv. 617 May 1903

1 Headpiece [1]	p 5.4 x 3.1
2 Title with illustrated initial T [1]	p 4.0 x 0.7
3 The Gardener Lad takes off his Cap [1]	p 4.0 x 4.4
4 Title with illustrated initial K [1]	p 5.5 x 0.9
5 King Arthur meets the Lady Guinevere [1]	p 5.5 x 6.6

xxv. 697 June 1903

1 Headpiece [1]	p 5.4 x 3.7
2 Title with illustrated initial S [1]	p 4.0 x 0.7
3 Sir Pellias encounters the Sorrowful Lady in Arroy [1]	p 4.0 x 0.7
4 Title with illustrated initial S [1]	p 4.0 x 0.7
5 Sir Pellias, the Gentle Knight [1]	p 4.0 x 4.5

xxv. 793 July 1903

1 Headpiece [1]	p 5.4 x 3.1
2 Title with illustrated initial P [1]	p 4.0 x 0.6
3 Parcenet covers Sir Pellias with a cloak [1]	p 4.0 x 4.5
4 Title with illustrated initial T [1]	p 4.0 x 0.6
5 The Lady of the Lake sits by the Fountain in Arroy [1]	p 4.0 x 4.7

xxv. 908 Aug. 1903

1 Headpiece [1]	p 5.5 x 3.5
2 Title with illustrated initial S [1]	p 4.0 x 0.7
3 Sir Gawaine sups with ye Lady Ettard [1]	p 4.0 x 4.7
4 Title with illustrated initial T [1]	p 4.0 x 0.7
5 The Lady of the Lake finds Sir Pellias wounded [1]	p 4.0 x 4.2

xxv. 984 Sept. 1903

1 Headpiece	p 5.5 x 2.9
2 Title with illustrated initial S	p 4.0 x 0.7
3 Sir Percival of Gales	p 4.0 x 4.2
4 Title with illustrated initial S	p 4.0 x 0.7
5 Sir Percival and Sir Pellinore ride together	p 4.0 x 4.0

[1] Reproduced in "The Story of King Arthur and His Knights." Howard Pyle, Scribner, New York. 1903.

xxv. 1097 Oct. 1903
1 Headpiece [1]   p 5.5 x 3.3
2 Title with illustrated initial S   p 4.0 x 0.7
3 Sir Percival overcometh ye Enchantress Vivien   p 4.0 x 4.5
4 Title with illustrated initial S   p 4.0 x 0.7
5 Sir Kay interrupts ye meditations of Sir Percival   p 4.0 x 4.6
6 Title with illustrated initial T   p 4.0 x 0.7
7 The Lady Yvette the Fair   p 4.0 x 4.3

SCRIBNER'S MAGAZINE

I. 3 Jan. 1887 THE SIEGE AND COMMUNE OF PARIS *E. B. Washburne*
1 Gambetta Proclaiming the Republic of France [2]   w 4.4 x 5.8
                                                      F. French, Sc.

I. 162 Feb. 1887 THE SIEGE AND COMMUNE OF PARIS
                                            E. B. Washburne
1 Looking into the Prussian Lines from the Château
  de la Muette   w 4.7 x 5.0

II. 666 Dec. 1887 TARPEIA   *Louise Imogen Guiney*
1 "Then faced her the leonine chief"   w 4.7 x 6.8
                                              Johnson, Sc.

IN THE VALLEY   *Harold Frederic*
      Sept., 1889, to July, 1890.

VI. 284 Sept. 1889
1 "A moment later there was a great hammering on
  the oak door" [3]
                                              w 4.8 x 7.2
                                              F. Juengling, Sc.
2 "Five red-coated soldiers on horseback, with another cloaked to the eyes. . . . Clustering about
  these, a motley score of poor people, young and
  old" [4]
                                              w 7.0 x 4.8
                                              F. Juengling, Sc.

---

[1] Reproduced in "The Story of King Arthur and His Knights." Howard Pyle, Scribner, New York. 1903.

[2] Reproduced in "Recollections of a Minister to France." E. B. Washburne, Charles Scribner's Sons, New York. 1889.

[3] Reproduced in "The Art of the American Wood Engraver." Philip G. Hamerton, Scribner, New York. 1894.

[4] Reproduced in "In the Valley." Harold Frederic, Scribner, New York. 1890.

VI. 431 Oct. 1889

  1 Within sound of the shouting waters [1]   w 5.0 x 7.2
F. Juengling, Sc.

  2 "We men-folk thought the music as sweet as that
    of the Cherubim" [1]   w 7.4 x 4.9
F. Juengling, Sc.

VI. 573 Nov. 1889

  1 "This is Enoch Wade, gentlemen," said the Baro-
    net [1]   w 7.2 x 4.8
G. Kruell, Sc.

  2 "Good-by, big brother," she said softly [1]   w 5.0 x 7.2
F. Juengling, Sc.

VI. 663 Dec. 1889

  1 "He told them, when we chanced to sit around the
    fires of an evening, most remarkable stories of
    field and forest" [1]   w 7.0 x 4.7
H. M. Peckwell, Sc.

  2 "At sight of me the good soul gave a guttural ex-
    clamation, and stared at me open-mouthed"   w 7.1 x 4.7
Wm. Miller, Sc.

VII. 73 Jan. 1890

  1 "The negro boy, arms whirling wide in the air, shot
    over the side of the cliff" [1]   w 4.9 x 7.1
F. Juengling, Sc.

  2 "The blow—the whole crushing series of blows—
    had fallen" [1]   w 4.8 x 7.0
F. Juengling, Sc.

VII. 221 Feb. 1890

  1 "She was silent for a moment, her eyes seeking the
    floor"   w 4.7 x 6.8
H. Wolf, Sc.

  2 "The dignified sober figure of Abraham Ten Broeck
    appeared in our wrathful circle" [1]   w 7.0 x 4.8
F. Juengling, Sc.

VII. 318 March 1890

  1 "While his eyes still glowed fiery wrath, the trem-
    bling lips became piteous in their inability to
    form words" [1]   w 4.7 x 6.9

  2 "Then a great mashing blow on my face ended my
    fight"   w 6.8 x 4.7
F. Juengling, Sc.

---

[1] Reproduced in "In the Valley." Harold Frederic, Scribner, New York. 1890.

VII. 497 April 1890

    1 " 'Who are you? and off with your hat!' I said to
the man sharply" [2]   w 6.7 x 4.6
                                                           R. G. Tietze, Sc.

    2 "Is your hanging-party ready?" he said [2]   w 4.7 x 7.0

VII. 587 May 1890

    1 "I turned the sheet over and over in my hands,
re-reading lines here and there" [2]   w 6.9 x 4.7
    2 " 'I wish to God we were well out of this all,' he
said, almost gloomily" [2]   w 4.7 x 6.9

VII. 757 June 1890

    1 "There, half stretched on the wet blood-stained
grass, lay Philip Cross" [2]   w 4.7 x 6.9
                                                               G. Kruell, Sc.

VIII. 81 July 1890

    1 "My hatred of him seemed suddenly to have taken
to itself wings" [1] [2]   w 6.8 x 4.7
                                                        H. M. Peckwell, Sc.

VIII. 1 Dec. 1890 THE PARDON OF STE. ANNE D'AURAY

                                                    William P. Northrup

    1 Breton Peasants at a Wayside Cross   w 4.2 x 6.2
                                                               H. Wolf, Sc.

VIII. 692 Dec. 1890 A PASTORAL WITHOUT WORDS   *Howard Pyle*

    1 Title—Full page   w 3.2 x 5.5
    2 A Pastoral without words. (With sub-title) [3]   w 4.8 x 6.9
                                                       S. G. Putnam, Sc.

    3 Verse I.   w 3.4 x 5.0
    4 Illustration [3]   w 5.0 x 6.0
                                                         Thomas H. Heard, Sc.

    5 Verse II.   w 3.5 x 5.5
    6 Illustration [3]   w 5.0 x 7.1
                                                         R. G. Tietze, Sc.

    7 Verse III.   w 3.4 x 4.8
    8 Illustration [3]   w 5.0 x 7.1
                                                         H. M. Peckwell, Sc.

---

[1] Reproduced in "American Illustrators." F. Hopkinson Smith, Scribner, New York. 1892.

[2] Reproduced in "In the Valley." Harold Frederic, Scribner, New York. 1890.

[3] Reproduced in "The Art of the American Wood Engraver." Philip G. Hamerton, Scribner, New York. 1894.

---

[1] Reproduced in "The Art of the American Wood Engraver." Philip G. Hamerton, Scribner New York. 1894.

[2] Reproduced in "American Illustrators." F. Hopkinson Smith, Scribner, New York. 1892.

[3] Reproduced in "The First Christmas Tree." Henry Van Dyke, Scribner, New York. 1897.

[4] Reproduced in "The Blue Flower." Henry Van Dyke, Scribner, New York. 1902.

[5] Reproduced in "History of the United States." E. Benjamin Andrews, Scribner, New York 1895.

[6] Reproduced in "History of the United States." Wilbur F. Gordy, Scribner, New York. 1904.

[1] Reproduced in "The History of the Last Quarter Century in the United States." E. Benjamin Andrews, Scribner, New York. 1896.

[1] Reproduced in "The Story of the Revolution." Henry Cabot Lodge, Scribner, New York. 1898.

[2] Reproduced in "A History of the United States." Wilbur F. Gordy, Scribner, New York. 1904.

[3] Reproduced in "Stories of Later American History." Wilbur F. Gordy, Scribner, New York. 1915.

---

[1] Reproduced in "The Story of the Revolution." Henry Cabot Lodge, Scribner, New York. 1898.
  [3] Reproduced in "A History of the United States." Wilbur F. Gordy, Scribner, New York. 1904.
  [2] Reproduced in "Stories of Later American History." Wilbur F. Gordy, Scribner, New York. 1915.

A STORY OF THREE STATES   *Alfred Mathews*
XXXI. 408 April 1902
    Queen Ester inciting the Indians to attack the settlers
        at Wyoming   c 4.7 x 7.1

XXXI. 558 May 1902
    The Connecticut Settlers entering the Western Re-
        serve [1]   c 7.1 x 4.7

XXXII. 147 Aug. 1902 SINBAD ON BURRATOR   *A. T. Quiller-Couch*
  1 We started to run back to the raft for our lives   c 4.7 x 7.2
  2 The boat and I went by him with a rush   c 4.7 x 7.2
  3 Headband with title and initial S   c 4.6 x 4.3
  4 I began to play   c 4.7 x 7.3
  5 I sat at her feet while she drilled the island language
     into me   c 4.7 x 7.2
  6 "If I catch you here again you'll need someone to
     sew you up"   c 4.7 x 7.1
  7 I clutched at his ankle   c 4.7 x 7.2

XXXIII. 96 Jan. 1903 THE STORY OF A GREAT-GRANDFATHER
                                                    George Hibbard
  1 "There is a time to fight and that time has now
     come"   p 4.7 x 7.2

XXXIII. 423 April 1903 THE NATURAL BORN PREACHER
                                                    Nelson Lloyd
  1 "Humility is the fountain of all virtue"   p 4.7 x 7.4

SCRIBNER'S MONTHLY

XII. 446 July 1876 THE MAGIC PILL   *Howard Pyle*
  1 " 'Ah me!' said the Parson, 'I wish I were young' " w 3.0 x 2.8
  2 "Alas! he had turned to a terrible boy"   w 2.4 x 2.3

XIII. 359 Jan. 1877 PAPA HOORN'S TULIP   *R. V. C. Meyers*
  Illustrations in silhouette:

---

[1] Reproduced in "A History of the United States." Wilbur F. Gordy, Charles Scribner's
Sons, New York. 1904.

xv. 825 April 1878 AMONG THE THOUSAND ISLANDS   *Howard Pyle*
  1 Spearing Eels in Eel Bay [1]   w 3.6 x 4.3
  2 French Canadian   w 2.2 x 3.1
  3 Ruins of Old Fort, Carleton's Island [1]   w 3.7 x 3.9
                                R. A. Muller, Sc.
  4 Catching Muskallonge [1]   w 3.9 x 5.4
  5 Camping Out [1]   w 5.0 x 4.0
                                R. A. Muller, Sc.
  6 Billy Patterson   w 1.3 x 3.8
  7 Joseph Gladd   w 1.6 x 3.5
  8 McCue   w 2.4 x 3.2
  9 Cooking a Camp Dinner [1]   w 3.4 x 4.6
 10 George Campbell   w 1.7 x 3.1

xvi. 192 June 1878 THE STORY OF LESKEN   *Anna Eichberg*
  Illustrations in silhouette:
  1 Young deLesken   w 2.3 x 4.0
  2 Mistress Betty   w 2.3 x 2.4
  3 Dietrich examines the disaster from a distance w 3.4 x 2.8
  4 "He kissed the little hand"   w 5.0 x 3.0
  5 Kobus and his pupil   w 3.4 x 3.0
  6 Jan's courtship   w 2.5 x 2.3
  7 DeLesken entertaining   w 3.5 x 3.1
  8 Kobus brings news to Mynheer Jan   w 5.1 x 2.6
  9 Jan returns   w 2.3 x 3.2
 10 Tailpiece   w 2.3 x 2.5

TRUTH (NEW YORK)

xviii. 69 March 1899
  Stained Glass Window, Colonial Club, New York c 3.5 x 5.9

WIDE AWAKE

xxii. 61 Dec. 1885 A CYCLE OF CHILDREN   *Elbridge S. Brooks*
  1 Prince Charles sprang to his side: "If he goes, so
    do I!" [2]   w 5.6 x 4.0
                                G. L. Cowee, Sc.

[1] Reproduced in "Sports with Gun and Rod." Alfred M. Mayer, The Century Co., New York. 1883.
[2] Reproduced in "Storied Holidays." Elbridge S. Brooks, Lothrop, Boston. 1887.

XXII. 107 Jan. 1886

Was this . . . King Henry's self? Margery dropped
to her knee [1]   w 5.4 x 3.9
                                                   G. L. Cowee, Sc.

XXII. 179 Feb. 1886

Young William Penn meets the disapproval of his
Father, the admiral [2] [1]   w 5.0 x 3.7
                                                   G. L. Cowee, Sc.

XXII. 255 March 1886

On the great terrace of Donegal Castle [1]   w 4.7 x 3.7
                                                   G. L. Cowee, Sc.

XXII. 320 April 1886

"To sea in a bowl!" exclaimed the puzzled Pembroke [1] w 5.1 x 3.7
                                                   G. L. Cowee, Sc.

XXII. 385 May 1886

The Young Emperor's Entrance to the Circus
Maximus [3] [1]   w 5.1 x 3.7
                                                   G. L. Cowee, Sc.

XXIII. 60 June 1886

"The dark and shadowy outline of a man" [1]   w 4.6 x 3.7
                                                   G. L. Cowee, Sc.

XXIII. 129 July 1886

"A great day this, my young friend," said Mr. John
Adams of Massachusetts [1]   w 4.6 x 3.7
                                                   G. L. Cowee, Sc.

XXIII. 192 Aug. 1886

" 'Tis an unfair race, O master," cried Ephialtes [1] w 4.5 x 3.7
                                                   G. L. Cowee, Sc.

XXIII. 243 Sept. 1886

"Come hither, lads," she said [1]   w 4.6 x 3.7
                                                   G. L. Cowee, Sc.

XXIII. 315 Oct. 1886

Surprised by the Hero of Seventy Fights—The Good
Lord James of Douglas [1]   w 4.5 x 3.8
                                                   G. L. Cowee, Sc.

---

[1] Reproduced in "Storied Holidays." Elbridge S. Brooks, Lothrop, Boston. 1887.

[2] Reproduced in "The True Story of the United States." Elbridge S. Brooks, Lothrop, Boston. 1891.

[3] Reproduced in "Great Men's Sons." Elbridge S. Brooks, G. P. Putnam's Sons, New York. 1895.

[1] Reproduced with title "He would not take an unfair advantage" in "The True Story of George Washington." Elbridge S. Brooks, Lothrop, Boston. 1895.
[2] Reproduced in "The Star Bearer." Edmund Clarence Stedman, Lothrop, Boston. 1888.
* Story published in "School and Playground." Howard Pyle and Others, D. Lothrop Company, Boston. 1891.

Books by HOWARD PYLE

Including Books Which Contain Writings
by Other Authors

1882

The / Elocutionist's Annual / Number 10 / Comprising / New and Popular Readings Recitations / Declamations Dialogues / Tableaux, etc. / (rule) / Edited by Mrs. J. W. Shoemaker / Vice-President of the National School of Elocution aṅd Oratory / (rule) / Philadelphia / National School of Elocution and Oratory / 1882

12mo. Cloth and paper.
Contains: TILGHMAN'S RIDE, by Howard Pyle, without illustrations.
First published in *Harper's Monthly*, Nov., 1881, together with two illustrations by Howard Pyle.
Copyright, No. 16406, Oct. 3, 1882.

1883

The / Merry Adventures / of / Robin Hood / of Great Renown, in Nottinghamshire. / Written and Illustrated / By Howard Pyle. / (rule) / (ornamental monogram) / ===== / New York: / Printed by Charles Scribner's Sons at / No. 743 & 745 Broadway, and sold by same / (rule) / MDCCCLXXXIII.

8vo. Collation: Half title in ornament (I); frontispiece (IV); title in ornamental border (V); copyright (1883) (VI); preface (VII, VIII); table of contents (IX–XVI); list of illustrations (XVII–XX); second frontispiece (XXII); prologue (1–10); illustration (12); text (13–296).
Size of leaf trimmed 7 x 9.5 inches.
Issued in full leather. Front and back cover stamped with ornamental design and in center: The / Merry / Adventures / of / Robin Hood / Howard Pyle
Label on back stamped in gold: (double rule) / Adventures of / Robin Hood / Pyle / (double rule) / (at bottom) 1883
This book was issued in England bearing on title page the name of publishers: Sampson, Low, Marston, Searle and Rivington, London, 1883. Not previously published in periodicals.
Copyright, No. 9138, May 17, 1883. Deposited Oct. 29, 1883.

Contains twenty-three illustrations and twenty-eight decorations, head and tailpiece, and ten illustrated initials, or a total of sixty-one illustrations, etc., by Howard Pyle, not previously published, as follows:

p I	Sub-title (in circle)	w 1.8 x 1.8
IV	Frontispiece—The Merry Friar carrieth Robin across the Water	w 4.7 x 6.6
V	Title page (ornamented)	w 5.1 x 7.2
(VII)	Headband	w 4.6 x 1.3
VIII	Tailpiece	w 1.9 x 1.5
IX	Headband, Table of Contents	w 4.7 x 1.0
(XVII)	Headband, List of Illustrations	w 4.8 x 1.2
XX	Tailpiece	w 2.3 x 1.4
XXII	Robin Hood meeteth the tall Stranger on the Bridge [1]	w 5.0 x 7.1
I	Headpiece, Young Robin goes to the Shooting Match	w 4.7 x 2.3
I	Illustrated initial I	w 1.3 x 1.3
10	Tailpiece	w 3.3 x 1.5
(12)	Robin and the Tinker at the Blue Boar Inn	w 4.7 x 6.6
(13)	Headpiece, The Sheriff of Nottingham plotting against Robin sends a messenger to Lincoln	w 4.7 x 1.7
(13)	Illustrated initial N	w 1.1 x 1.1
(24)	The Sheriff of Nottingham cometh before the King at London	w 4.7 x 6.6
(39)	The Aged Palmer gives Young David of Doncaster news of Will Stutely	w 5.1 x 7.2
44	Tailpiece	w 2.6 x 1.8
(46)	Robin turns butcher and sells his meat in Nottingham	w 4.7 x 6.6
(47)	Headpiece—Robin buys the Butcher's Meat	w 5.1 x 1.1
(47)	Illustrated initial N	w 1.2 x 1.2
(62)	Little John overcomes Eric o' Lincoln [1]	w 4.7 x 6.7
(72)	The Mighty Fight betwixt Little John and the Cook	w 4.7 x 6.6
(78)	The stout bout between Little John and Arthur à Bland	w 4.7 x 6.6
(79)	Headpiece—Little John knoweth not which Road to take	w 4.7 x 1.7
(79)	Illustrated initial I	w 1.4 x 1.3

[1] Reproduced in "Some Merry Adventures of Robin Hood." Howard Pyle, Charles Scribner's Sons, New York. 1902.

(289) Illustrated initial A   w 1.3 x 1.3
 296 Tailpiece   w 4.6 x 2.3
      Front cover design, stamped   w 6.9 x 9.7
      Back design, stamped   w 1.9 x 9.7

"The Merry Adventures of Robin Hood" was commenced in *Harper's Young People*, Jan. 9 and Jan. 16, 1883, and part of the "Prologue" printed together with three illustrations. These illustrations, however, were not used in the book.

1883

Sport / With Gun and Rod / in / American Woods and Waters / Edited by / Alfred M. Mayer / Professor in / The Stevens Institute of Technology / (cut) / New York / The Century Co.

4to. Cloth.
Contains, pp. 573–596, AMONG THE THOUSAND ISLANDS, by Howard Pyle, with five illustrations by Howard Pyle. Both the article and illustrations were first published in *Scribner's Monthly*, April, 1878.
Copyright, No. 18099, Oct. 3, 1883.

1885

Within the Capes / By / Howard Pyle / New York / Charles Scribner's Sons / 1885

16mo. Collation: Half title (i); title (iii); copyright (1885) and imprint (iv); dedication (v); sub-title (vii); text (1–266); ten pages of book lists by publishers.
Size of leaf trimmed 4.7 x 7 inches. Figured end papers.
Issued in full cloth. Front cover and back stamped with rectangular ornamental designs and lettering stamped on side: Within / the Capes * * * / Howard / Pyle / Back stamped in gold: Within / the / Capes / and in black: (rule) Howard / Pyle / Scribners /
Contains no illustrations.
Not previously published in periodicals.
Copyright, No. 10086, May 4, 1885. Deposited May 11, 1885.

1886

Pepper & Salt, / or / Seasoning for Young Folk. / Prepared
by / Howard Pyle / (rule) / Harper and Brothers / Printers
and Publishers. / New York. / MDCCCLXXXVI.

4to. Collation: Half title (engraved) (I); frontispiece (IV); title
(printed in black over ornamental design in red) (V); copyright (1885)
(VI); preface (VII, VIII); table of contents (IX, X); list of illustrations
(XI-XIII); sub-title (XIV); text (1-121); two pages publishers' book
lists.

Size of leaf trimmed 8.4 x 11.1 inches.

Issued in full cloth. Front cover stamped in red and gold with
ornamental design: Pepper / and Salt / H P (monogram) / or Seasoning / for Young Folk. Back cover: Ornamental design in black and
gold. Back stamped in black and gold: * Pep- / per / & / Salt /
(ornament) / Harpers.

Copyright, No. 22087, Oct. 21, 1885. Deposited Oct. 31, 1885.

The following table of contents shows stories in prose in capitals;
those in verse in lower-case. The date of first printing in *Harper's
Young People* is shown at right.

Contains twenty-four full page text and illustrations, and fifty-eight headpieces and illustrations of less than page by Howard Pyle, first published in *Harper's Young People;* also one illustration and fifteen decorations, or a total of sixteen illustrations, etc., by Howard Pyle not previously published, as follows:

	Design for front cover book	w 6.4 x 9.7
	Design for back cover book	w 6.0 x 6.5
p(III)	Half title	w 1.9 x 3.3
(IV)	Frontispiece—This is the way that one in Cap and Motley stops for a while along the stony Path of Life to make you laugh	w 6.6 x 9.5
(V)	Title page, in red	w 6.6 x 9.2
(VII)	Headpiece, Preface	w 6.5 x 2.6
(VIII)	Tailpiece	w 2.8 x 2.0
(IX)	Headpiece, Table of Contents	w 6.6 x 2.0
x	Tailpiece	w 3.7 x 2.7
(XI)	Headpiece, List of Illustrations	w 6.6 x 1.9
XIII	Tailpiece	w 4.8 x 2.5
22	Tailpiece, How Hans was caught	w 1.5 x 2.5
23	Decoration	w 2.7 x 2.2
(39)	Decoration	w 2.1 x 2.5
(55)	Decoration	w 2.7 x 3.5
(99)	Decoration	w 2.2 x 0.7

1888

The / Wonder / Clock / or / Four & Twenty Marvel- /
lous Tales. being one for / each hour of the day; / written
& illustrated / By / Howard Pyle. / Embellished with
Verses by / Katharine Pyle. / (rule) / New York, printed
by / Harper & Brothers, 1888.

8vo. Collation: Half title (i); frontispiece (ii); title (as above in
center of decoration) (iii); copyright (1887) (iv); preface (v, vi);
table of contents (vii, viii); list of illustrations (ix–xiv); text (1–319).
Size of leaf trimmed 7.0 x 9.7 inches.

Issued in half leather, cloth sides. Front cover stamped in gold
(ornamental work above and below): The Wonder Clock / By Howard
Pyle. Stamped on back in gold in box rules: The / Wonder / Clock /
(rule) / Pyle / Harpers

This book was issued in England bearing on the title page the name
of publishers: Osgood McIlvane & Co., London, 1888.

Copyright, No. 16200, June 23, 1887. Deposited Oct. 19, 1887.

Two series of "Clock" verses, 1 to 12, together with decorations
each covering a page, are by Katharine Pyle.

The following table of contents shows the "Clock" verses of Katharine Pyle, with decorations, in capitals; the stories by Howard Pyle are
in lower-case. The date of first printing in *Harper's Young People*
is shown at right.

ONE O'CLOCK	Mar. 16, 1886
Bearskin	Mar. 1, 1887
TWO O'CLOCK	Mar. 23, 1886
The Water of Life	June 14, 1887
* THREE O'CLOCK	Mar. 30, 1886
How One Turned his Trouble to Some Account	Nov. 10, 1885
FOUR O'CLOCK	Apl. 6, 1886
How Three went out into the Wide World	Dec. 29, 1885
* FIVE O'CLOCK	Apl. 13, 1886
The Clever Student and the Master of Black Arts	Feb. 23, 1886
SIX O'CLOCK	May 4, 1886
The Princess Golden Hair and the Great Black Raven	Jan. 26, 1886

* The decorations in book are different from those first published in *Harper's Young People.*

Contains ninety-six illustrations and twenty-four headpieces by Howard Pyle, first published in *Harper's Young People* on dates shown in list. It should be noted that the titles of illustrations in the book (which are shown with an illustrated initial and heading above the illustration) are different from the titles of the same illustrations in *Harper's Young People*.

In addition the book contains: front cover decoration, one frontispiece, one title page, three headpieces, nine decorations, twenty-five illustrated initials and seventy headings with illustrated initials, or a total of one hundred and ten illustrations, etc., by Howard Pyle, not previously published, as follows:

Front cover decoration	w 5.3 x 5.7
p (I) Half title	w 1.8 x 1.6
(II) Frontispiece [1]	w 4.8 x 6.8
(III) Title page	w 4.8 x 7.0
(v) Headpiece—Preface	w 4.8 x 1.9
(v) Initial I	w 0.9 x 0.9
(VII) Headpiece—Table of Contents	w 4.8 x 1.8
VIII Tailpiece	w 2.9 x 1.7
(IX) Headpiece—List of Illustrations	w 4.8 x 1.8
XIV Tailpiece	w 2.9 x 1.6
(3) Illustrated initial I	w 1.2 x 1.2
(5) Illustrated initial T with heading	w 4.7 x 1.3
(9) Illustrated initial B with heading	w 4.7 x 1.0
(17) Illustrated initial O	w 1.2 x 1.2
(19) Illustrated initial T with heading	w 4.7 x 0.9
(21) Illustrated initial T with heading	w 4.7 x 1.0
(25) Illustrated initial T with heading	w 4.7 x 1.2
(29) Illustrated initial T	w 1.3 x 1.3
(31) Illustrated initial T with heading	w 4.7 x 1.0
(33) Illustrated initial H with heading	w 4.7 x 1.2
(41) Illustrated initial T	w 1.2 x 1.2
(43) Illustrated initial T with heading	w 4.8 x 1.7
(45) Illustrated initial T with heading	w 4.8 x 1.5
(51) Illustrated initial T	w 1.2 x 1.2
(53) Illustrated initial A with heading	w 4.8 x 1.0
(55) Illustrated initial T with heading	w 4.8 x 1.2
57 Illustrated initial T with heading	w 4.8 x 1.2

[1] Reproduced in "Pen Drawing and Pen Draughtsmen." MacMillan, New York. 1889.

p (307) Illustrated initial T   w 1.2 x 1.2
  (311) Illustrated initial T with heading   w 4.7 x 1.2
  (315) Illustrated initial T with heading   w 4.8 x 1.0
  (317) Illustrated initial T with heading   w 4.8 x 0.9
  (318) Tailpiece   w 1.6 x 1.6

1888

The Rose of Paradise / Being a detailed account of certain
adventures that / happened to Captain John Mackra, in
connection / with the famous pirate, Edward England, in
/ the year 1720, off the Island of Juanna / in the Mozam-
bique Channel; writ / by himself, and now for the / first
time published / By Howard Pyle / Author of / "Pepper
and Salt" "The Wonder Clock" Etc. / Illustrated / New
York / Harper and Brothers, Franklin Square / 1888

12mo. Collation: Frontispiece; title (I); copyright (1887) (II);
dedication (III); list of illustrations (v); text (I-231).
Size of leaf trimmed 4.7 x 7.2 inches.
Issued in full cloth. Stamped in gold at top front cover: The Rose
of Paradise. Back stamped in gold: The Rose / of / Paradise / (rule)
/ Howard Pyle. / Illustrated / Harper & Brothers
Copyright, No. 22459, Sept. 3, 1887. Deposited Oct. 1, 1887.

The story and eight illustrations by Howard Pyle previously
published in *Harper's Weekly*, June 11th to July 30th, 1887.

1888

Otto / Of the Silver Hand / Written and Illustrated by /
Howard Pyle / New York / Charles Scribner's Sons / 1888

8vo. Square. Collation: Publishers' advertisement; half title (I);
frontispiece (IV); title (V); copyright (1888) (VI); contents (VII-IX);
list of illustrations (XI-XIII); foreword (1, 2); text (3-170); illustration (171); afterword (173); sixteen pages of publishers' lists in back.
Size of leaf trimmed 6.5 x 8.9 inches.
Issued in cloth sides and leather back. Front cover stamped in red
gilt and black: Otto of the / Silver Hand / (seal) / By / Howard Pyle.

Back stamped in gilt: Otto / of the / Silver / Hand / Howard Pyle. / Scribners

Not previously published in periodicals.

This book was issued in England bearing on the title page the name of the publishers: Sampson, Low, Marston, Searle and Rivington, London, 1888.

Copyright, No. 31083, Nov. 1, 1888. Deposited Nov. 12, 1888.

Contains twenty-six illustrations, thirty-six decorations, headpieces and tailpieces and sixteen initials, or a total of seventy-eight illustrations, etc., by Howard Pyle, not previously published, as follows:

Decoration, front cover	w 4.6 x 8.2
p (I) Half title	w 2.3 x 2.7
(IV) Frontispiece, In the Belfry	w 4.6 x 6.0
(VII) Headpiece, Contents	w 4.6 x 1.8
IX Line tailpiece	w 3.1 x 1.0
(XI) Headpiece, List of Illustrations	w 4.6 x 1.6
XIII Line tailpiece	w 2.5 x 1.1
(I) Headpiece, Foreword	w 4.4 x 2.0
(I) Illustrated initial B	w 1.0 x 1.0
2 Line tailpiece	w 2.9 x 1.0
(3) Headpiece, Chapter I	w 4.8 x 2.8
(3) Illustrated initial U	w 1.0 x 1.0
(5) There they sat, just as little children of the town might sit upon their father's doorstep	w 4.4 x 5.9
10 Tailpiece	w 2.5 x 1.7
(11) Headpiece, Chapter II	w 4.5 x 2.8
(11) Illustrated initial B	w 1.0 x 1.0
(15) Away they rode with clashing hoofs and ringing armor	w 4.5 x 6.0
19 Tailpiece	w 1.8 x 1.8
(20) Headpiece, Chapter III	w 4.5 x 2.8
(20) Illustrated initial B	w 1.0 x 1.0
(23) No one was within but old Ursela, who sat crooning over a fire	w 4.5 x 6.0
26 Tailpiece	w 2.0 x 1.4
(27) Headpiece, Chapter IV	w 4.6 x 2.3
(27) Illustrated initial W	w 1.0 x 1.0

[128]

Contains also on advertising pages reprints of four illustrations from "The Merry Adventures of Robin Hood," Howard Pyle, Scribner's, 1883, pp. 1, 79, 187, 219.

Contains also on advertising pages reprint of one illustration from "The Story of Siegfried," James Baldwin, Scribner's, p. 63.

1891

* * The Buccaneers / and Marooners of / America / * * *
* * * * * * / Being an Account of the / Famous Adventures and / Daring Deeds of Certain / Notorious Freebooters / of the Spanish Main / A New Illustrated Edition
/ Edited by Howard Pyle / London: T. Fisher Unwin
New / York: MacMillan & Co. MDCCCXCI.

12mo. Collation: Title of series (1); list of series (2); frontispiece;
title (3); contents (5–11); list of illustrations (13); introduction (by
Howard Pyle) (15–41); translator's preface to first edition (43–48);
text (49–403).

Size of leaf trimmed 5.2 x 8 inches.

Issued in full cloth. Front cover stamped in black with ornamental
design: The Adventure Series / T. Fisher Unwin, Paternoster Square
/ London 1890. Also in gilt in black ruled box: The Buccaneers / &
Marooners / of America. Back cover stamped in black with publishers'
emblem. Back stamped in black and gold: Adventure / Series / The
/ Buccaneers / and / Marooners / of / America / Edited by / Howard
Pyle / MacMillan & Co.

Contains, pp. 15 to 41, introduction by Howard Pyle; also picture
used as frontispiece with title "Morgan Recruiting for the attack on
Porto Bello," by Howard Pyle; was first published in *Harper's
Monthly*, August, 1887, illustrating "Buccaneers and Marooners of
the Spanish Main," by Howard Pyle, with the title "Henry Morgan
recruiting for the Attack."

1891

School / and Playground / By / Howard Pyle / and Others
/ Illustrated / Boston / D. Lothrop Company / Washington Street opposite Bromfield.

16mo. Cloth.

Contains, pp. 9 to 32, "Lambkin: Was He a Hero or a Prig?" by
Howard Pyle; no illustrations.

First published in Chautauqua Young Folks' Reading Union supplement to *Wide Awake*, Dec., 1889.

Copyright, No. 32260, Sept. 11, 1891.

Men of Iron / By / Howard Pyle / Author of / "The Wonder Clock" "Pepper and Salt" / "The Rose of Paradise" Etc. / Illustrated / (publishers' seal) / New York / Harper & Brothers, Franklin Square / 1892

8vo. Collation: Frontispiece; title (I); copyright (1891); dedication (III); list of illustrations (v, VI); text (1–328).

Size of leaf trimmed 5.5 x 8.4 inches.

Issued in full cloth. Front cover stamped in black and silver with coat of arms and below in black: Men of Iron. Back stamped in gold: (ornament) / Men / of / Iron / (ornament) / Howard Pyle / and at bottom: Harpers.

The story and twenty-one illustrations by Howard Pyle first published in *Harper's Young People*, Jan. 20 to June 9, 1891.

Contains also decoration not previously published, as follows:
Front cover decoration   4.8 x 6.8

This book was issued in England, bearing on the title page the name of the publishers: Osgood McIlvane & Co., London, 1892.

Copyright, No. 33018, Sept. 16, 1891. Deposited Oct. 29, 1891.

1892

A Modern Aladdin / or, / The Wonderful Adventures / of Oliver Munier / An Extravaganza in Four Acts / By Howard Pyle / Author of "Pepper and Salt" Etc. / Illustrated. / New York / Harper & Brothers, Franklin Square / 1892

12mo. Collation: Frontispiece (II); title (III); copyright (1891) (IV); list of illustrations (v, VI); half title (1); text (3–205); (publishers' lists, two pages).

Size of leaf 4.7 x 7.2 inches.

Issued in full cloth. On front cover surrounded by ornamental design in red and gold: A Modern Aladdin. Back stamped in gold: (ornament) / A Modern / Aladdin / (ornament) / Howard Pyle / (ornament) / Harpers.

Copyright, No. 39484, Nov. 3, 1891. Deposited Nov. 14, 1891.

The story and thirty-two illustrations by Howard Pyle were first published in *Harper's Bazar*, May 23 to June 11, 1881.

Contains also one illustration by Howard Pyle not previously published, as follows:

p 130 "Enter Oliver and Mademoiselle Celeste" p 1.8 x 3.8

1895

The Story of / Jack Ballister's Fortunes / By / Howard Pyle / * / Being the Narrative of the Adventures / of a Young Gentleman of Good Fam- / ily, who was Kidnapped in the Year 1719 / and carried to the Plantations of the / Continent of Virginia, where he fell / in with that Famous Pirate Captain / Edward Teach, or Blackbeard: of his / Escape from the Pirates and the Rescue / of a Young Lady from out their hands / (seal) / New York / The Century Co. / 1895

8vo. Collation: Half title (I); frontispiece (IV); title (V); copyright (1894, 1895) and imprint (VI); contents (VII, VIII); list of illustrations (IX); half title (XI); text (1–420).

Size of leaf trimmed 5.7 x 8.1 inches.

Issued in full cloth. Front cover and back cover stamped ornamentally in red and black: Jack Ballister's / Fortunes. / (seal) / Pyle. Back stamped in black and red with ornamental designs: Jack / Ballister's / Fortunes / (rule) / Pyle / The / Century Co.

This book was issued in England bearing on the title page the name of publishers: Osgood McIlvane & Co., London, 1897.

Copyright, No. 47489, Sept. 18, 1895. Deposited Sept. 20, 1895.

The story and fourteen illustrations by Howard Pyle first published in *St. Nicholas*, April, 1894, to Sept., 1895.

One illustration in magazine Feb., 1895, not reproduced in book.

1895

The Garden / Behind the Moon / A Real Story of the / Moon Angel / Written and Illustrated by / Howard Pyle / (ornament) / Printed and Published by / Charles Scrib- ner's Sons / New York, MDCCCXCV.

[132]

8vo. Square. Collation: Frontispiece; title (1) (first, second, sixth and eighth lines in red); copyright (1895) (II); dedication (III); contents (v, vi); illustrations (vii); foreword (1–4); text (5–192).
Size of leaf trimmed 6.0 x 8.2 inches.
Issued in full cloth. Front cover stamped ornamentally in gold and color: The Garden / Behind the / Moon. Back stamped in gold: The / Garden / Behind the / Moon / * / Pyle. / (ornament) Scribners
This book was issued in England bearing on the title page the name of publishers: Lawrence and Bullen / London 1895
Not previously published in periodicals.

Copyright, No. 51412, Oct. 10, 1895. Deposited Oct. 12, 1895.

Ten illustrations, twenty-two headpieces, one tailpiece and one cover decoration, or a total of thirty-four illustrations, etc., by Howard Pyle not previously published, as follows:

Front cover and back decorations		7.0 x 7.0
Frontispiece, In the garden behind the moon		p 4.5 x 6.0
p v	Headband, Contents	p 3.7 x 0.8
vii	Headband, Illustrations	p 3.7 x 0.8
1	Headpiece, Foreword	p 3.7 x 2.1
4	Tailpiece	p 0.8 x 1.3
5	Headpiece	p 3.7 x 2.2
9	Headband	p 3.7 x 0.7
13	Headband	p 3.7 x 0.7
21	Headband	p 3.7 x 0.7
(25)	David looked up into Hans Krout's face	p 4.5 x 6.0
31	Headband	p 3.7 x 8.0
(41)	Suddenly a half-door opened and there stood a little man	p 4.5 x 6.0
44	Headband	p 3.7 x 0.8
(57)	David sat down on the wooden bench and took up a big blue star	p 4.5 x 6.0
61	Headband	p 3.7 x 0.7
(69)	He was standing at an open window	p 4.5 x 6.0
(77)	"Where did you come from, little boy?" she said	p 4.5 x 6.0
84	Headband	p 3.7 x 0.8
91	Headband	p 3.7 x 0.8
103	Headband	p 3.7 x 0.8
112	Headband	p 3.7 x 0.7

p126	Headband	p 3.7 x 0.7
(133)	Quick as a flash, David leaped out and upon it	p 4.5 x 6.0
135	Headpiece	p 3.7 x 0.8
139	Headpiece	p 3.7 x 0.8
148	Headpiece	p 3.7 x 0.7
(153)	Fast flew the black winged horse	p 4.5 x 6.0
159	Headpiece	p 3.7 x 0.8
(163)	The giant fell crashing upon the stones	p 4.5 x 6.0
172	Headband	p 3.7 x 0.7
177	Headband	p 3.7 x 0.7
186	Headband	p 3.7 x 0.7
(189)	She placed her hands on his shoulders	p 4.5 x 6.0

1895

Twilight Land / By / Howard Pyle / Author of / "The Wonder Clock" "Pepper and Salt" / "Men of Iron" etc. / Illustrated / (publishers' seal) / New York / Harper & Brothers Publishers / 1895

8vo. Collation: Frontispiece; title (two initials and publishers' seal in red) (I); copyright (1894), book list of publishers (II); dedication (III); table of contents (V, VI); introduction (I–4); text (5–438); (two pages book lists).

Size of leaf trimmed 5.6 x 8.4 inches.

Issued in cloth sides and leather back. Front cover ornamental stamping in black and red, and in ruled box in gilt: Twilight / Land / By / Howard Pyle. Stamped on back in gold: (ornament) / Twilight / Land / Pyle / (ornament) / Harpers

This book was issued in England bearing on the title page the name of the publishers: Osgood McIlvane & Co. / London 1895

Copyright, No. 49782, Oct. 25, 1894. Deposited Dec. 5, 1894.

The following table of contents shows the date originally published in *Harper's Young People* and number of illustrations.

The Stool of Fortune	Dec. 23, 1890	7 illustrations
The Talisman of Solomon. I.	Mar. 29, 1892	6 illustrations
The Talisman of Solomon. II.	Apl. 5, 1892	6 illustrations
Ill Luck and the Fiddler	Oct. 15, 1889	6 illustrations
Empty Bottles	Feb. 18, 1890	6 illustrations

Good Gifts and a Fool's Folly	Sep. 9, 1890	7 illustrations
The Good of a Few Words. I.	July 17, 1894	6 illustrations
The Good of a Few Words. II.	July 24, 1894	5 illustrations
Woman's Wit	July 29, 1890	7 illustrations
A Piece of Good Luck. I.	Apl. 10, 1894	5 illustrations
A Piece of Good Luck. II.	Apl. 17, 1894	5 illustrations
The Fruit of Happiness	Jan. 13, 1891	6 illustrations
Not a Pin to Choose. I.	June 10, 1890	5 illustrations
Not a Pin to Choose. II.	June 17, 1890	5 illustrations
Much shall have more and little shall have less	Nov. 4, 1890	5 illustrations
Wisdom's Wages and Folly's Pay	Nov. 5, 1889	7 illustrations
The Enchanted Island. I.	Dec. 15, 1891	5 illustrations
The Enchanted Island. II.	Dec. 22, 1891	5 illustrations
All Things are as Fate wills	Oct. 14, 1890	6 illustrations
Where to Lay the Blame	Mar. 25, 1890	6 illustrations
The Salt of Life. I.	Jan. 7, 1890	5 illustrations
The Salt of Life. II.	Jan. 14, 1890	5 illustrations

The stories and one hundred and twenty-six illustrations by Howard
Pyle first published in *Harper's Young People* as shown in the list.
In addition the book contains one illustration, four decorations, or a
total of five illustrations by Howard Pyle not previously published,
as follows:

Front cover decoration	4.1 x 7.8
Frontispiece—Ita Primo Ita Semper	p 3.5 x 5.5
Dedication to daughter Phoebe—Ornamental	p 3.5 x 5.1
Headpiece, Table of Contents	p 3.4 x 1.5
Headpiece, Introduction	p 3.5 x 1.4

1896

The Ghost / of / Captain Brand: / Or, a true / Account /
of the / Most remarkable Appearance / of that renowned
Freebooter off the Harbor / of New York, / And the last
time ever he was beheld by / the Eyes of a Living Man. /
Being a Narrative of certain / Extraordinary Adventures
that befell Barnaby True, Esq., / of the Town of New
York in the Year 1750, or thereabouts. / ——— / Written

originally by Howard Pyle, for Harper's Weekly Christ / mas Number. Now first imprinted in this form for the pleasure / of those friends of the Author, whose names appear below. / ———— / Wilmington: / Printed for Anne Poole Pyle, Thomas F. Bayard, Henry A. duPont, / and J. Henry Harper, by John M. Rogers, on Orange / Street, opposite the Old Malt House. / 1896.

Edition 4 copies on uncut paper.

8vo. Collation: Copyright (1896) (I); title (III); preface (V–XVIII); text (1–73).

Issued in full leather with clasps.

On back, paper label: Capt / Brand

Size of leaf uncut 7.0 x 9.0 inches.

The story and seven illustrations first published in *Harper's Weekly*, Dec. 19, 1896.

1897

A / Catalogue of Drawings / Illustrating the Life of / Gen. Washington, / and of / Colonial Life. / Together with a few other Examples / of work done for the Public Prints, / By Howard Pyle. / (rule) / Exhibited for the Pleasure of such as choose / to view them, at the Drexel Institute of / Art, Science and Industry, upon the Sixth / of February next. / (rule) / Philadelphia / MDCCCXCVII.

Issued with paper covers.

Edition of 50 copies on handmade paper.

4to. Collation: Title (front cover); imprint; preface (1–4); frontispiece; text (5–28); copyright (1897).

Size of leaf uncut 7.6 x 10.5 inches.

Preface and descriptions of drawings written by Howard Pyle.

Contains three illustrations by Howard Pyle first published in *Harper's Monthly*, July (1) and Sept., 1896 (1), and *The Century*, Feb., 1897 (1).

Copyright, No. 8680, Feb. 1, 1897. Deposited Feb. 1, 1897.

1897

A / Catalogue of Drawings / Illustrating the Life of / Gen. Washington, / and of / Colonial Life. / Together with a few other examples / of work done for the Public Prints,

/ By Howard Pyle. / (rule) / Exhibited originally at the
Drexel Institute of / Art, Science and Industry, in Phila-
delphia, / Now again put upon exhibition at the St. /
Botolph Club of Boston, upon the Twenty- / seventh of
February next. / (rule) / Wilmington: / Printed for the
St. Botolph Club, by John M. / Rogers, on Orange Street
opposite / the Old Malt House. / 1897

Issued with paper covers.

Edition of 50 copies on handmade paper.

4to. Collation: Title (I); copyright (1897) (II); preface to a second
edition (III–v); half title (vI); preface (1–4); frontispiece; text (5–28).

Size of leaf uncut 7.6 x 10.5 inches.

Front cover: A / Catalogue / of / Illustrations / (cut) / By Howard
Pyle. / (rule) / Exhibited by the St. Botolph Club / for the Enter-
tainment of its Friends. / at No. 2 Newbury Street, in Boston /
(rule) / Preface and descriptions written by Howard Pyle.

Contains three illustrations by Howard Pyle first published in
Harper's Monthly, July (1) and Sept., 1896 (1), and *The Century*,
Feb., 1897 (1).

This catalogue is same as the one used at Drexel Institute, Philadelphia, Feb. 6, 1897, with following exceptions:

Cover.

Title page.

Preface to second edition by Howard Pyle.

1898

The Divinity of Labor. / ——— / An Address delivered
by / Howard Pyle, / At the Commencement Exercises of /
Delaware College, June 16, 1897 / ——— / The John M.
Rogers Press, / Wilmington, Del. / 1898

8vo. Collation: Title (1); address to graduates (3–11).

Size of leaf trimmed 6.0 x 9.0 inches.

Paper cover with title as above on front.

No illustrations.

The / Price of Blood / (two lines) / An Extravaganza of
New York Life in 1807 / Written in Five Chapters and
Illustrated by / Howard Pyle / (two lines) / (ornament in
red) / Boston From the Publishing House of / Richard G.
Badger & Co. / 157 Tremont Street / MDCCCXCIX.

12mo. Square. Collation: Half title (1); frontispiece in colors; title
(enclosed in double box rules and ornamental border in red) (3);
copyright (1899) (4); contents (5); illustrations (7); introduction (9–
13); text (15–98); imprint (99).
Size of leaf trimmed 5.9 x 8.0 inches.
Issued with board covers. Front cover printed in black and red.
Picture on upper half of cover, and on lower half: The Price of Blood /
written and Illustrated by / Howard Pyle. Back cover ornament in
center.
Copyright, No. 33216, May 17, 1899. Deposited Sept. 15, 1899.

The story first published in *Collier's Weekly*, Dec. 17, 1898, together
with seven illustrations, including one on cover by Howard Pyle.

First / Year Book / (ornament) / The / Bibliophile /
Society / (ornament) / Boston MCMII / Issued / for Members only

8vo. Collation: Half title (I); society engraved title page (III);
officers (V); council (VI); incorporation certificate (VII); seal of society
(VIII); note (IX); title (designed and drawn by H. Pyle) (X); copy-
right (1902); frontispiece, The Bibliophile, by H. Pyle; text (1–61).
Size of leaf 7.4 x 9.1 inches, printed on handmade paper.
Issued with board sides. Back lettered in gold: The Bibliophile
Year Book.
8vo. Board. Edition 500 copies.
Contains, pp. 17–21, "Concerning the Art of Illustration," by
Howard Pyle.
Also illustration and title page by Howard Pyle not previously
published, as follows:

Title page

Frontispiece, "The Bibliophile" [2] [1]

3.5 x 6.5

4.0 x 6.3

1902

Some / Merry Adventures / of / Robin Hood / of Great Renown in Nottinghamshire / Written and Illustrated by / Howard Pyle / Charles Scribner's Sons / New York / Chicago / Boston

12mo. Cloth.

Contains, pp. v–vii, preface by Howard Pyle dated Wilmington, April 29, 1902.

A curtailed edition of The Merry Adventures of Robin Hood published by Charles Scribner's Sons, 1883.

Contains four illustrations by Howard Pyle, reproduced from the original edition of 1883 on pages 137, xxii, 62 and 91.

Copyright, No. 33317, May 19, 1902. Deposited May 23, 1902.

1903

Rejected of Men / A Story of To-day / By / Howard Pyle / (publishers' seal) / New York and London / Harper & Brothers Publishers / 1903

12mo. Collation: Title (first line in red, all surrounded by double boxed rules) (i); copyright (1903) (ii); contents (iii); proem (v–viii); half title (ix); text (1–269); two pages publishers' list.

Size of leaf trimmed 4.7 x 7.3 inches.

Issued full cloth. Lettered on side in gold: * / Rejected of Men / * / By Howard Pyle (surrounded by stamped rule border in black). Back is lettered in gold: (3 rules in black) Rejected / of / Men / (rule) / Howard / Pyle / Harpers / (3 rules in black).

No illustrations. Story not published in periodicals.

Copyright, No. A59141, May 8, 1903. Deposited June 19, 1903.

[1] Reproduced in "Portfolio of Etchings," by W. H. W. Bicknell, Bibliophile Society, Boston, 1903.

[2] Reproduced on bookplate of Willard S. Morse. 1916.

1903

The Story of / King Arthur / and his Knights. / Written and Illustrated / by / Howard Pyle. / (double rule) / New York: / Charles Scribner's Sons / 1903

8vo. Collation: Frontispiece (II); title (in center of illustrated page) (III); copyright (1903) (published Nov., 1903), imprint (IV); foreword (V, VI); contents (VII–XII); list of illustrations (XIII–XVI); half title (XVII); illustration (XVIII); text (1–313).

Size of leaf trimmed 6.7 x 9.2 inches.

Issued full cloth. Front cover stamped in red and gold with coat of arms. Back stamped in gold: The Story of / King / Arthur / and his / Knights / (rule) / H. Pyle. / Scribners / (back stamped with ornamental design in red and black).

This book was issued in England bearing on the title page the name of the publishers: George Newnes, Ltd. / London 1903
Copyright, No. 72935, Nov. 18, 1903. Deposited Nov. 19, 1903.

First published in *St. Nicholas*, Nov., Dec., 1902; Jan., Feb., Mar., April, May, June, July, Aug., Sept., Oct., 1903.

Contains thirty-one illustrations (twenty of which have illustrated initials and titles) first published in *St. Nicholas*.

Also ten illustrations (nine of which have illustrated initials and titles), two title pages and twelve tailpieces and front cover and back decorations, or a total of thirty-five illustrations, etc., by Howard Pyle not previously published, as follows:

Front cover		4.5 x 6.0
Back decorations		1.7 x 1.3
p (III)	Title page	p 5.0 x 7.0
VI	Tailpiece	p 2.0 x 1.6
XII	Tailpiece	p 2.7 x 0.8
XVI	Tailpiece	p 2.8 x 1.3
XVII	Ornamental sub-title (used also p. 149)	p 4.5 x 6.4
XVIII	Illustrated initial U with heading	p 4.8 x 0.9
XVIII	Uther-Pendragon	p 4.8 x 5.5
5	Tailpiece	p 3.4 x 1.6
38	Tailpiece	p 2.1 x 0.6
76	Tailpiece	p 2.5 x 1.3
98	Tailpiece (used also p. 147)	p 2.5 x 1.3

1905

The Story of / the Champions / of the / Round Table /
Written and Illustrated / By / Howard Pyle. / (double
rule) / New York: / Charles Scribner's Sons / 1905

8vo. Collation: Publishers' book list; frontispiece; title (in center of
illustrated page) (III); copyright (1905) (published Oct., 1905), imprint (IV); foreword (V, VI); contents (VII–XIII); list of illustrations
(XV–XVIII); text (2–329).

Size of leaf trimmed 6.7 x 9.2 inches.

Issued in full cloth. Front cover stamped in red and gold with
coat of arms. Back stamped in gold: The Story of / The / Champions
/ of the / Round Table / (rule) / H. Pyle. / Scribners (back stamped
in ornamental design in red and black).

This book was issued in England bearing on the title page the name of the publishers: George Newnes, Ltd., / London 1905

Not previously published in periodicals.

Copyright, No. A129144, Oct. 19, 1905. Deposited Oct. 19, 1905.

Title page with same border as used in The Story of King Arthur and his Knights, 1903.

Contains thirty-one full page illustrations, thirty-one illustrated initials with headings, ten headpieces and eleven tailpieces and front and back cover decorations, or a total of eighty-five illustrations, etc., by Howard Pyle not previously published, as follows:

Front cover	Coat of arms	4.5 x 6.0
Back decorations		1.7 x 1.3
p (II) Frontispiece	Illustrated initial S with heading	p 4.7 x 0.8
(II) Frontispiece	Sir Launcelot of the Lake	p 4.7 x 5.3
(III) Title page	(see above)	
(v) Foreword	Headpiece	p 4.7 x 2.1
VI	Tailpiece	p 3.0 x 1.4
(VII) Contents	Headpiece	p 4.7 x 3.5
XIII	Tailpiece	p 2.7 x 2.0
(xv) Illustrations	Headpiece	p 4.8 x 2.5
(XVIII)	Tailpiece	p 3.4 x 2.1
p (2) Illustrated initial T with heading		p 4.7 x 1.0
(2) The Lady Nymue beareth away Launcelot into the Lake		p 4.7 x 5.5
(3) Headpiece		p 4.8 x 2.7
10 Tailpiece		p 2.1 x 1.1
(12) Illustrated initial S with heading		p 4.8 x 0.8
(12) Sir Launcelot greets Queen Guinevere		p 4.8 x 5.5
(13) Headpiece		p 4.8 x 2.6
(26) Illustrated initial S with heading		p 4.1 x 0.9
(26) Sir Lionel of Britain		p 4.8 x 5.3
(34) Illustrated initial Q with heading		p 4.8 x 0.7
(34) Queen Morgana appears unto Sir Launcelot		p 4.8 x 5.2
(44) Illustrated initial S with heading		p 4.7 x 0.7
(44) Sir Launcelot doeth battle with Sir Turquine		p 4.7 x 5.3
(54) Illustrated initial S with heading		p 4.8 x 0.8
(54) Sir Launcelot sits with Sir Hilaire and Croisette		p 4.8 x 5.4
(64) Illustrated initial S with heading		p 4.8 x 0.7

[143]

(230) Sir Kay and the Forest Madman	p 4.8 x 5.5
(242) Illustrated initial S with heading	p 4.8 x 0.7
(242) Sir Tristram leaps into ye Sea	p 4.8 x 5.4
(252) Illustrated initial K with heading	p 4.8 x 0.7
(252) King Mark broods mischief	p 4.8 x 5.4
258 Tailpiece	p 2.3 x 1.1
(260) Illustrated initial S with heading	p 4.8 x 0.8
(260) Sir Percival of Gales	p 4.8 x 5.0
(261) Headpiece	p 4.8 x 2.5
(268) Illustrated initial T with heading	p 4.8 x 0.9
(268) The Lady Yvette the Fair	p 4.8 x 5.0
(280) Illustrated initial S with heading	p 4.8 x 0.9
(280) Sir Percival and Sir Lamorack ride together	p 4.8 x 4.8
(290) Illustrated initial S with heading	p 4.8 x 0.8
(290) Sir Percival overcometh ye Enchantress Vivien	p 4.8 x 5.5
(304) Illustrated initial T with heading	p 4.8 x 0.7
(304) The Demoiselle Blanchefleur	p 4.8 x 5.4
(316) Illustrated initial S with heading	p 4.8 x 0.8
(316) Sir Kay interrupts ye meditations of Sir Percival	p 4.7 x 5.5
328 Tailpiece	p 2.7 x 1.2

1907

Strange Stories / of the / Revolution / By / Howard Pyle,
Winthrop Packard / Molly Elliot Seawell / and others /
Illustrated / (publishers' seal) / New York and London /
Harper & Brothers Publishers / MCMVII.

16mo. Collation: Publishers' book list; frontispiece; title (surrounded by ornamental boxed rules) (I); copyright (various dates) (published April, 1907) (II); contents (III, IV); illustrations (V); introduction (VII–IX); half title (XI); text (1–221).

Size of leaf trimmed 4.6 x 6.9 inches.

Issued in full cloth. Front cover stamped in colors: Strange / Stories / of the / Revolution / (cut). Back stamped in black: Strange / Stories / of the / Revolution / Harpers

Contains, pp. 55–71, "Nancy Hansen's Project," by Howard Pyle. No illustrations.

The story first published in *Harper's Young People*, April 13, 1880, together with one illustration by Howard Pyle.

Copyright, No. A167815, Feb. 6, 1907. Deposited April 11, 1907.

1907

Stolen / Treasure / By / Howard Pyle / Author of / "Men of Iron" "Twilight Land" / "The Wonder Clock" "Pepper and Salt" / Illustrated by / the Author /(publishers' seal) / New York and London / Harper & Brothers Publishers / MCMVII.

12mo. Collation: Frontispiece; title (surrounded by border and printed in red and black) (1); copyright (1907) (II); contents (III); illustrations (v); half title (1); text (3–254).
Size of leaf trimmed 4.8 x 7.8 inches.
Issued in full cloth. Front cover stamped in black with ornamental border: Stolen Treasure / Howard Pyle and in center inlaid picture. Stamped on back: Stolen / Treasure /(cut)/ Howard / Pyle / Harpers
Copyright, No. A173769, April 12, 1907. Deposited May 9, 1907.

Contains four stories by Howard Pyle and nine illustrations first published as follows:

With the Buccaneers	*Harper's Round Table*	
	June 29, 1897	3 illustrations
Tom Chist and the Treasure Box	*Harper's Round Table*	
	Mar. 24, 1896	2 illustrations
The Ghost of Captain Brand	*Harper's Weekly*	
	Dec. 19, 1896	1 illustration
The Devil at New Hope	*Harper's Weekly*	
	Dec. 18, 1897	2 illustrations
On cover of book—insert picture in colors being part of illustration with title "Buried Treasure" in	*Harper's Magazine*	
	Dec., 1902	1 illustration

1907

Shapes that / Haunt the Dusk / Harper's Novelettes / (rule) / Edited by / William Dean Howells / and / Henry Mills Alden / (publishers' seal) / Harper & Brothers Publishers / New York and London / 1907

16mo. Collation: Title (surrounded by boxed rules and printed in red and black) (I); copyright notice (1907) (II); list of authors (III); introduction (v–vII); text (I–301).

Size of leaf trimmed on top only 4.3 x 6.8 inches.

Bound in full cloth. Stamped on back in gold ornamental design with letters color of cloth: Shapes / That / Haunt / the / Dusk, and in gold: Harper's / Novel- / ettes / Harpers

Contains, pp. 63–125, "In Tenebras," by Howard Pyle. No illustrations.

First published in *Harper's Monthly*, Feb., 1894.

Copyright, No. A166573, June 22, 1907. Deposited June 14, 1907.

1907

The Story of / Sir Launcelot / and his / Companions / By / Howard Pyle. / (rules) / New York: / Charles Scribner's Sons / 1907

8vo. Collation: Book lists (II); frontispiece; title (in center of illustration) (III); copyright (1907) (published Oct., 1907) and imprint (IV); foreword (v, vI); contents (vII–xIV); list of illustrations (xv–xvIII); prologue (3–8); introduction, part I (9); illustration (10); text (11–332); illustration (334); conclusion (335–340).

Size of leaf trimmed 6.7 x 9.2 inches.

Issued in full cloth. Front cover stamped in black, red and gold with coat of arms. Back stamped in gold: The Story of / Sir / Launcelot / and His / Companions / (rule) / H. Pyle / Scribners / (back stamped with ornamental design in red and black).

This book was issued in England bearing on the title page the name of the publishers: Chapman & Hall / London 1907

Not previously published in periodicals.

Copyright, No. A190354, Oct. 23, 1907. Deposited Oct. 25, 1907.

Title page with same border as used in The Story of King Arthur and his Knights, 1903, and The Story of the Champions of the Round Table, 1905.

Contains thirty illustrations, eleven headpieces, thirty initials, eight tailpieces and front and back cover decorations, or a total of eighty-one illustrations, etc., by Howard Pyle, not previously published as follows:

[147]

1908

Adventures of / Pirates and Sea-Rovers / (rule) / By / Howard Pyle, Rear-Admiral J. H. Upshur, / Paul Hull, Reginald Gourlay / and others / Illustrated / (publishers' seal) / (rule) / New York and London / Harper & Brothers Publishers / MCMVIII.

12mo. Collation: Frontispiece; title (boxed with border) (I); publishers' book lists, copyright (1908) (published April, 1908) (II); contents (III–V); illustrations (VII); introduction (IX–XI); sub-title (I); text (3–212).

Size of leaf trimmed 5.8 x 6.9 inches.

Bound in full cloth. Front cover stamped in black and red ornamental with cut at top and: Adventures / of Pirates and / Sea-Rovers. Back stamped in black: Adventures / of / Pirates / and / Sea-Rovers / (ornament) / Harpers.

Contains, pp. 3–14, "The Buccaneers—Wolves of the Spanish Main," by Howard Pyle.

Contains, pp. 15–40, "The Fate of a Treasure Town," by Howard Pyle.

These two stories were first published in "The Fate of a Treasure Town," Howard Pyle, *Harper's Magazine*, Dec., 1905.

Copyright, No. A201794, Mch. 17, 1908. Deposited June 10, 1908.

Contains four illustrations by Howard Pyle first published in *Harper's Monthly*, Jan., 1883 (2), and *Harper's Magazine*, Dec., 1905 (2).

1908

The Ruby of / Kishmoor / (ornament) / By / Howard Pyle / With Illustrations / By the Author / (publishers' seal) / New York and London / Harper & Brothers Publishers / MCMVIII.

8vo. Collation: Frontispiece (in colors); title (surrounded by yellow border in black rules) (I); copyright (1908) (published Oct., 1908) (II); contents (III); illustrations (v); sub-title (VII); text (1–73); epilogue (74).

Size of leaf uncut 5.7 x 8.7 inches.

Issued in full cloth. Front cover stamped in gilt, dark green, white and brown with ornamental design and in gilt: The Ruby / of / Kishmoor / Howard Pyle. Back stamped in gilt: The / Ruby / of / Kish- / moor / ——— / Pyle (ornament in dark green and white) / Harpers

The story and ten illustrations first published in *Harper's Magazine*, Aug., 1907.

This book was issued in England bearing on the title page the name of the publishers: Harper & Brothers / London 1908

Copyright, No. A215949, Sept. 2, 1908. Deposited Oct. 29, 1908.

1910

The Story of / the Grail / and the / Passing of Arthur. / by / Howard Pyle. / (double rules) / New York: / Charles Scribner's Sons / 1910

8vo. Collation: Book lists (II); frontispiece (IV); title (in center of illustration) (v); copyright (1910) (published September, 1910) (VI); foreword (VII, VIII); contents (IX–XIV); list of illustrations (XV–XVIII); illustration (2); prologue (3–6); text (7–256); conclusion (257, 258).

Size of leaf trimmed 6.7 x 9.2 inches.

Issued in full cloth. Front cover stamped in black, red and gold with coat of arms. Back stamped in gold: The Story of / The Grail / and / The Passing / of Arthur / (rule) / H. Pyle. / Scribners (back stamped with ornamental design in red and black).

This book was issued in England bearing on the title page the name of the publishers: Bickers & Son / London 1910

Not previously published in periodicals.

Copyright, No. A273065, Sept. 24, 1910. Deposited Sept. 29, 1910.

Title page with same border as used in

The Story of King Arthur and his Knights	1903
The Story of the Champions of the Round Table	1905
The Story of Sir Launcelot and his Companions	1907

Contains twenty-five full page illustrations, seven headpieces and six tailpieces, twenty-five illustrated initials with headings and front and back cover decorations, or a total of sixty-five illustrations, etc., by Howard Pyle not previously published, as follows:

Front cover	Coat of arms	4.4 x 6.3
Back	Decorations	1.7 x 1.3
p (iv) Frontispiece	Illustrated initial S with heading	p 4.8 x 1.0
(iv) Frontispiece	Sir Galahad of the Grail	p 4.8 x 5.8
(v) Title	(see above)	
(vii) Foreword	Headpiece	p 5.0 x 2.3
viii	Tailpiece	p 2.1 x 1.0
(ix) Contents	Headpiece	p 5.0 x 2.2
xiv	Tailpiece	p 1.5 x 0.9
(xv) Illustrations	Headpiece	p 5.0 x 2.3
xviii	Tailpiece	p 1.7 x 1.2
p (2) Illustrated initial S with heading		p 4.9 x 0.9
(2) Sir Geraint, Son of Erbin		p 4.9 x 5.3
(3) Headpiece		p 5.0 x 2.2
6 Tailpiece		p 3.0 x 1.2
(8) Illustrated initial E with heading		p 4.9 x 0.8
(8) Enid and Geraint in the garden		p 4.9 x 6.0
(9) Headpiece		p 5.0 x 2.4
(16) Illustrated initial S with heading		p 4.9 x 0.8
(16) Sir Geraint and the Knight of the Sparrowhawk		p 4.9 x 5.8
(25) Illustrated initial S with heading		p 4.9 x 0.7
(25) Sir Geraint lies asleep		p 4.9 x 5.7
(38) Illustrated initial E with heading		p 4.9 x 0.9
(38) Enid talks with the Earl		p 4.9 x 5.9
(48) Illustrated initial E with heading		p 4.9 x 0.8

(236) The Passing of Arthur	p 4.9 x 5.9
(348) Illustrated initial T with heading	p 4.9 x 0.7
348 The Passing of Guinevere	p 4.9 x 5.8
358 Tailpiece	p 1.7 x 1.1

1910

The Merry Adventures of Robin Hood / By / Howard Pyle / ——— / Prologue * * * Page 2 / Part First / Robin Hood and the Tinker * * * Page 20 / The Shooting Match at Nottingham * * Page 40 / Will Stutely rescued by his Good Com / panions * * * Page 57 / Printed by Permission of / Charles Scribners Sons Publishers / Copyright 1883 / The Howe Memorial Press / Perkins Institution and / Massachusetts School / for the Blind / Boston 1910

Folio. Eight volumes.
The story embossed in Braille type for the use of the blind.

1911

The Book of Laughter / Selections from / Bret Harte—Howard Pyle—Joel Chandler / Harris—John Habberton—Frank R. / Stockton, and Others / Edited by / Katherine N. Birdsall / and / George Haven Putnam / Illustrated / G. P. Putnam's / Sons / The Knickerbocker Press / New York and London

12mo. Cloth.
Contains the following stories by Howard Pyle first published in *St. Nicholas Magazine* on dates given. None of the illustrations published in *St. Nicholas* with the stories are reproduced.

p 262	Hans Gottenlieb, The Fiddler	April 1877
33	Robin Goodfellow and His Friend Bluetree	June 1879
134	Drummer Fritz and His Exploits	Sept. 1877

These are the earliest writings of Howard Pyle to be published in book form.

Books by Other Authors
Containing Illustrations by
Howard Pyle

1879

Eclectic Educational Series / ——— / McGuffey's / Fifth / Eclectic Reader / ——— / Revised Edition / ——— / (cut) / Van Antwerp, Bragg & Co. / Cincinnati-New York

16mo. Cloth sides. Leather back.

Contains two illustrations by Howard Pyle not previously published, as follows:

p 105   Illustration. No title   w 3.5 x 5.0
Illustrating "The Town Pump," by Nathaniel Hawthorne.

p 249   Illustration. No title   w 3.4 x 4.7
Illustrating "Squeers's Method," by Charles Dickens.

This is the first book published containing illustrations by Howard Pyle.

Copyright, No. 8125, June 18, 1879.

1879

Eclectic Educational Series / ——— / McGuffey's / Sixth / Eclectic Reader / ——— / Revised Edition / ——— / (cut) / Van Antwerp, Bragg & Co. / Cincinnati-New York

16mo. Cloth. Leather back.

Contains one illustration by Howard Pyle not previously published, as follows:

p 240   The Quack   w 3.5 x 5.2
                                         J. P. Davis, Sc.

Copyright, No. 17977, Dec. 31, 1879. Deposited Dec. 31, 1879.

1880

ART IN AMERICA, by S. G. W. Benjamin. Harper & Brothers, New York, 1880.

8vo. Cloth.

Contains one illustration by Howard Pyle. First published in *Harper's Monthly*, Sept., 1879.

1881

OLD TIMES IN THE COLONIES, by Charles Carleton Coffin.
Harper & Brothers, New York, 1881.

8vo. Cloth.
Contains eight illustrations by Howard Pyle, first published in
Harper's Monthly, Dec., 1879 (3), *Harper's Young People*, Aug. 3
(2), Aug. 17, Sept. 21, Oct. 5, 1880.

1881

Yankee Doodle / an / Old Friend in a / New Drefs. /
Pictured by / Howard Pyle / New York / Printed by
Dodd, Mead / and Company, at No. 755 / Broadway.
MDCCCLXXXI / Copyright 1881 by Dodd, Mead & Com-
pany

4to. Square. Board covers.
Contains thirty-two illustrations and decorations by Howard Pyle
not previously published, as follows:

1	Cover decoration in color	w 8.0 x 9.6
1	Title page in black, decorations in blue	w 8.0 x 9.0
8	Full page illustrations in colors	w 8.0 x 9.0
21	Pages, text in black, decorations in blue	w 8.0 x 9.0
1	Design on back cover	w 1.8 x 2.0

Copyright, No. 15784, Oct. 13, 1881. Deposited Oct. 13, 1881.

1881

PHAETON ROGERS, by Rossiter Johnson. Charles Scribner's
Sons, New York, 1881.

12mo. Cloth.
Contains one illustration by Howard Pyle, first published in *St.
Nicholas*, Jan., 1881.

1881

(Front Cover) The / Lady of / Shalott / By A. Tennyson
/ (First Page) Dodd / Mead & / Company / Publishers /
New York / Decorated by / Howard Pyle

8vo. Square. Cloth.
Contains forty-five illustrations and decorations by Howard Pyle
not previously published, as follows:

1	Title page	w 5.9 x 7.0
4	Sub-title pages	w 5.9 x 7.0
19	Full page illustrations and text	w 5.9 x 7.0
11	Full page illustrations	w 5.9 x 7.0
10	Pages with decorations only	w 5.9 x 7.0

Copyright, No. 18488, Nov. 29, 1881. Deposited Nov. 29, 1881.

1881

HARPER'S POPULAR CYCLOPAEDIA OF UNITED STATES HIS-
TORY, by Benson J. Lossing, LL.D. Harper & Brothers,
New York, 1881.

8vo. Cloth.
Two volumes.
Vol. I, p. 687, contains one illustration by Howard Pyle first pub-
lished in *Harper's Monthly*, Nov., 1879.

1882

Farm Ballads. / By Will Carleton. / Illustrated / (cut) /
New York: / Harper & Brothers, Publishers, / Franklin
Square

8vo. Square.
Contains two illustrations by Howard Pyle not previously published, as follows:

p 103	"The clang of the Yankee Reaper, on Salisbury Plain!"	w 4.4 x 6.8
123	"The sweet love-planted Christmas Tree"	w 4.5 x 6.8

Copyright, No. 10583, June 27, 1882. Deposited July 27, 1882.

1882

The / Story of Siegfried / By / James Baldwin / Illustrated
by Howard Pyle / New York / Charles Scribner's Sons /
1882

12mo. Cloth.
Contains six illustrations by Howard Pyle not previously published, as follows:

Frontispiece	The Forging of Balmung	w 3.4 x 5.2 Frank French, Sc.
p 62	The Death of Fafnir	w 3.4 x 5.2 J. P. Davis, Sc.
94	The Awakening of Brunhild	w 5.2 x 3.4 E. Clement, Sc.
180	The Trial of Strength	w 5.2 x 3.4 John Karst, Sc.
256	The Quarrel of the Queens	w 5.2 x 3.4 John Karst, Sc.
282	The Death of Siegfried	w 5.2 x 3.4 E. Clement, Sc.

Copyright, No. 12107, July 22, 1882. Deposited Oct. 11, 1882.

1882

The Chronicle of the Drum / By William Makepeace Thackeray / (cut) / New York / Charles Scribner's Sons / 1882

8vo. Cloth.
Contains three illustrations by Howard Pyle not previously published, as follows:

Frontispiece	"Ho, Drummer! quick, silence yon Capet"	w 5.0 x 7.2 F. French, Sc.
p 33	"Awful, and proud, and erect"	w 4.4 x 6.4 F. French, Sc.
38	"She looked from the bars of her prison"	w 4.3 x 6.2 E. Clement, Sc.

Copyright, No. 17837, Nov. 18, 1881. Deposited Nov. 25, 1881.

1882

UNDER GREEN APPLE BOUGHS, by Helen Campbell. Fords, Howard, & Hulbert, New York, 1882.

16mo. Cloth.
Contains seven illustrations by Howard Pyle, first published in *Our Continent*, Feb. 15 to March 22, 1882.
One illustration is only part of the original, and two of the illustrations are made from one original picture.

1883

New England Bygones / By / E. H. Arr. / (Ellen H. Rollins) / New Edition, Enlarged and Illustrated. /———/ Introduction by Gail Hamilton. /——— / Philadelphia: / J. B. Lippincott & Co. / 1883

8vo. Square.
Contains two illustrations by Howard Pyle not previously published, as follows:

p 114	Grandfather and Little Benny	w 3.5 x 4.0
		Wm. Miller, Sc.
173	The Beloved Pastor	w 3.9 x 3.9
		F. French, Sc.

First edition published in 1880 was not illustrated.
Copyright, No. 16503, Oct. 5, 1882. Deposited Nov. 9, 1882.

1883

The Reader the Focus of Language-Training / ——— / Swinton's / Fifth Reader / and / Speaker / ——— / Copyright 1883 by / Ivison, Blakeman, Taylor, and Company / Publishers / New York and Chicago.

12mo. Cloth.
Contains two illustrations by Howard Pyle not previously published, as follows:

p 76	Illustrating: Knickerbocker Life in New York [1]	w 3.5 x 4.1
		J. Karst, Sc.
148	Illustrating: Gradgrind's Idea of Education	w 3.5 x 4.0
		J. Karst, Sc.

Copyright, No. 4305, Mar. 8, 1883. Deposited April 21, 1883.

1883

Building the Nation / Events in the / History of the United States / from the Revolution to the Beginning of / the War between the States / By / Charles Carleton Coffin

---

[1] Reproduced in "A School History of the United States." William Swinton, American Book Co., New York. 1893.

/Author of / "The Boys of '76" "The Story of Liberty"
"Old Times in the Colonies" Etc. / Illustrated / New
York / Harper & Brothers, Franklin Square / 1883

8vo. Cloth.

Contains twelve illustrations by Howard Pyle, first published in
Harper's Monthly, Nov. (4), Dec. (2), 1879; Apl. (1), May (2), 1880;
Jan. (1), Mch. (2), 1881.

Also three illustrations by Howard Pyle not previously published,
as follows:

Frontispiece	Inaugural Procession	w 4.4 x 7.0
p 109	A Kentucky Wedding	w 6.9 x 4.4
114	Scene in the Theatre in Philadelphia 1794 [1]	w 4.4 x 3.4 Ketsch, Sc.

Copyright, No. 18116, Oct. 28, 1882. Deposited Nov. 27, 1882.

1884

A History / of the / United States of America / Preceded
by a Narrative / of / The Discovery and Settlement of /
North America / and of the Events which led to the Independence of / the Thirteen English Colonies / for the use of
Schools and Academies / By / Horace E. Scudder / with
maps and illustrations / Sheldon & Company / New York
and Chicago

12mo. Cloth.

Contains four illustrations by Howard Pyle not previously published, as follows:

p 58	Dutch and Indians trading	w 3.5 x 3.0 F. H. Wellington, Sc.
87	Roger Williams in exile	w 3.5 x 3.5 G. P. Williams, Sc.
262	The Indian and the Pioneer	w 3.5 x 3.5 Henry Marsh, Sc
349	Whitman starting for Washington	w 3.5 x 3.5 Henry Marsh, Sc.

Copyright, No. 9433, May 9, 1884. Deposited Aug. 18, 1884.

[1] Reproduced in "Harper's Ency. U. S. History," Vol. IV. Harper & Brothers, New York.
1902.

1884

Art / Year / Book / 1884 / American Art / Prepared and Published by the / New England Institute / Boston Mass U S A (title page decorated design)

4to. Boards.
Edition of 100 copies.
Contains one sub-title page by Howard Pyle not previously published, as follows:

Title   "Notes: Descriptive and Biographic."
Decoration   w 5.9 x 7.9

Copyright, No. 19502, Sept. 27, 1884. Deposited Sept. 27, 1884.

1885

Illustrated Poems / of / Oliver Wendell Holmes / With illustrations by / George Randolph Barse, Frederic Crowninshield, Frances Houston, William / Formby Halsall, Helen Maria Hinds, Francis Coates Jones, Hugh Bolton / Jones, George Willoughby Maynard, Charles Elliott Mills, John Francis / Murphy, Howard Pyle, Louis Ritter, William Henry Shelton, / William Thomas Smedley, Sidney Lawton Smith, Isaac H. / Stiefel, Charles John Taylor, William L. Taylor, / Ross Turner, Frederic Porter Vinton / (publishers' monogram) / Boston / Houghton, Mifflin and Company / New York: 11 East Seventeenth Street / The Riverside Press, Cambridge / 1885

4to. Cloth.
Contains four illustrations by Howard Pyle not previously published, as follows:

p 48 Headpiece, An Incident   w 4.1 x 3.1
49 The Embarkation   w 4.2 x 3.0
50 "Blazing and clanging from thicket and wall"   w 4.2 x 3.0
60 "For they all thought he was dying, as they gathered round him crying"   w 4.5 x 3.3

Copyright, No. 20195, Oct. 7, 1884. Deposited Nov. 8, 1884.

1885

INDIAN HISTORY FOR YOUNG FOLKS, by Francis S. Drake. Harper & Brothers, New York, 1885.

8vo. Cloth.
Contains three illustrations by Howard Pyle first published in *Harper's Monthly*, March, 1883, June, 1883, *Harper's Young People*, Oct. 5, 1880.

1886

A LARGER HISTORY OF THE UNITED STATES OF AMERICA, by Thomas Wentworth Higginson. Harper & Brothers, New York, 1886.

8vo. Cloth.
Contains twenty illustrations by Howard Pyle first published in *Harper's Monthly*, Jan. (2), Mch. (4), Apl. (2), June (2), July (3), Aug. (2), and Oct. (2), 1883; Jan. (2), Feb., 1884.

1886

CITY BALLADS, by Will Carleton. Harper & Brothers, New York, 1886.

8vo. Cloth.
Contains one illustration by Howard Pyle first published in *Harper's Weekly*, June 3, 1882.

1886

The Reader the Focus of Language-Training / Swinton's / Advanced / Third Reader / ———— / Ivison, Blakeman Taylor and Company / Publishers / New York and Chicago

16mo. Cloth sides. Leather back.
Contains one illustration by Howard Pyle not previously published, as follows:

p 97   Illustrating "The Peddler's Pack"   w 3.5 x 4.6
Copyright, No. 829, Jan. 9, 1886. Deposited Mar. 4, 1886.

1886

The / Inca Princess / An Historical Romance. / By / The Author of "Sir Rae," "Iris," "Onti Ora," Etc. / ———— / Illustrated from paintings by / Church, Chase, Davidson, Fredericks, Pyle, Schell, and Smedley. / ———— / Philadelphia: / J. B. Lippincott Company. / London: 15 Russell St., Covent Garden. / 1886

8vo. Cloth. Large paper edition. Uncut.

Contains one illustration by Howard Pyle not previously published, as follows:

p 52	"Her native songs for him she sung"	w 4.0 x 6.0
	Copyright, No. 20780, Oct. 3, 1885. Deposited Dec. 21, 1885.	Wellington, Sc.

1886

A History of New York from / The Beginning of the World to the end of / the Dutch Dynasty; containing, among many / surprising and curious matters, The Unutter- / able ponderings of Walter the Doubter, / The Disastrous Projects of William the / Testy, and the Chivalric Achievements of / Peter the Headstrong—The Three Dutch / Governors of New Amsterdam; being the / Only Authentic History of the Times that / ever hath been or ever will be Published / By Diedrich Knickerbocker / ———— / (2 line quotation) / ———— / A New Edition, containing unpublished corrections of the / Author, with illustrations by Geo. H. Boughton, Will / H. Drake, and Howard Pyle, and Etchings by Henry C. / Eno and F. Raubicheck, in two volumes. —— Volume / (club seal) / New York / Printed for the Grolier Club / MDCCCLXXXVI.

8vo. Boards. Edition of 175 copies.

Contains three decorations by Howard Pyle not previously published, as follows:

Vol. I	p 33	Headband[1]	w 3.4 x 1.3
	33	Initial A[1]	w 1.0 x 1.0
	89	Tailpiece[1]	w 2.1 x 1.4

[1] Reproduced in "Transactions of the Grolier Society," Part II. New York. 1894.

1887

The / Closing Scene. / By / Thomas Buchanan Read /
——— / Illustrated / ——— / Philadelphia: / J. B.
Lippincott Company. / 1887

8vo. Square. Cloth.
Contains five illustrations by Howard Pyle not previously published, as follows:

p 35   Sat, like a Fate, and watched the flying thread   w 4.2 x 4.8
                                                        S. G. Putnam, Sc.

  37   She heard the stir of his black mantle trailing in the
         dust   w 4.1 x 4.7
                                                         C. H. Reed, Sc.

  39   While yet her cheek was bright with summer bloom w 4.1 x 4.8
                                                           F. French, Sc.

  43   Breathed through her lips a sad and tremulous tune w 4.1 x 4.8
                                                         E. Heineman, Sc.

  45   Death and Winter closed the autumn scene   w 4.1 x 4.8
                                                      F. H. Wellington, Sc.

Copyright, No. 13304, June 8, 1886. Deposited July 24, 1886.

1887

A Story / of / The Golden Age / By / James Baldwin /
Author of "The Story of Siegfried," Etc. / Illustrated by
Howard Pyle / New York / Charles Scribner's Sons / 1887

12mo. Cloth.
Contains twelve illustrations by Howard Pyle not previously published, as follows:

Frontispiece   Pyrrhus Finds Philoctetes in a Cave   p 3.7 x 4.6
         p 8   Odysseus and His Mother [1]   p 3.7 x 4.7
          42   Apollo Slaying the Python   p 3.8 x 4.8
          74   Meleager Refuses to Help in Defence of the
                 City   p 5.2 x 3.4
          98   The Silver Footed Thetis Rising from the
                 Waves [1]   p 3.7 x 4.7
         116   The Swineherd Telling His Story to Odys-
                 seus [1]   p 4.4 x 3.5

———
[1] Reproduced in "Odysseus, the Hero of Ithaca." Mary E. Burt, Charles Scribner's Sons,
New York. 1898.

Copyright, No. 20374, Aug. 10, 1887. Deposited Oct. 27, 1887.

1887

Storied Holidays / A Cycle of / Historic Red-Letter Days / By / Elbridge S. Brooks / Author of / Historic Boys / In Leisler's Times / Chivalric Days / In No-Man's Land / and Others / Boston: D. Lothrop Company / Franklin and Hawley Streets

12mo. Cloth.

Contains eleven illustrations by Howard Pyle, first published in *Wide Awake*, Dec., 1885, to Oct., 1886.

Also one illustration by Howard Pyle not previously published, as follows:

p 252   The Boys present the Salmagundi to Heer Governor Stuyvesant   w 4.5 x 3.7

                                                   G. L. Cowee, Sc.

Copyright, No. 25617, Oct. 5, 1887. Deposited Oct. 9, 1887.

1888

THE STAR BEARER, by Edmund Clarence Stedman. D. Lothrop Company, Boston, 1888.

4to. Paper covers.

Contains one illustration and three border decorations by Howard Pyle, first published in *Wide Awake*, Dec., 1887.

1888

OLD HOMESTEAD POEMS, by Wallace Bruce. Harper & Brothers, New York, 1888.

[1] Reproduced in "Odysseus, the Hero of Ithaca." Mary E. Burt, Charles Scribner's Sons, New York. 1898.

8vo. Cloth.

Contains one illustration by Howard Pyle, first published in *Harper's Monthly*, Oct., 1883.

1888

Harper's Educational Series / ——— / Harper's / Fourth Reader / In two parts / New York / Harper & Brothers, Franklin Square

12mo. Cloth.

Contains one illustration by Howard Pyle not previously published, as follows:

* p 216   Washington, the Young Surveyor   w 3.5 x 5.0
Copyright, No. 8458, Mar. 12, 1888. Deposited Nov. 15, 1888.   H. Wolf, Sc.

1888

LIBRARY OF UNIVERSAL ADVENTURE BY SEA AND LAND. Edited by William Dean Howells and Thomas Sargeant Perry. Harper & Brothers, New York, 1888.

8vo. Cloth.

Contains one illustration by Howard Pyle, first published in *Harper's Young People*, Oct. 5, 1880.

1889

PEN DRAWING AND PEN DRAUGHTSMEN, by Joseph Pennell. MacMillan & Co., London and New York, 1889.

Folio. Cloth binding.

Contains, pp. 208, 209, article on Howard Pyle with illustration, first published as frontispiece in The Wonder Clock, Howard Pyle, Harper & Bros., N. Y., 1888.

1889

RECOLLECTIONS OF A MINISTER TO FRANCE, by E. B. Washburne, LL.D. Charles Scribner's Sons, New York, 1889.

8vo. Cloth. Two volumes.

Vol. I contains one illustration by Howard Pyle, first published in *Scribner's Magazine*, Jan., 1887.

* Reproduced in "Founders of Our Country." F. E. Coe, American Book Company. 1912.

1890

YOUMA: The Story of a West Indian Slave, by Lafcadio
Hearn. Harper & Brothers, New York, 1890.

12mo. Cloth.
Contains one illustration by Howard Pyle, first published in *Harper's
Monthly*, Jan., 1890.

1890

IN THE VALLEY, by Harold Frederic. Charles Scribner's
Sons, New York, 1890.

12mo. Cloth.
Contains sixteen illustrations by Howard Pyle, first published in
Scribner's Magazine, Sept., Oct. (2), Nov. (2), Dec., 1889; Jan. (2),
Feb., Mar., Apl. (2), May (2), June and July, 1890.

1890

THE CAPTAIN'S WELL, by John Greenleaf Whittier. New
York Ledger, New York, 1900.

12mo. Board.
A reduced size of the original publication in *New York Ledger* now
published in book form.
Contains four illustrations and one headpiece by Howard Pyle,
first published in *New York Ledger* Supplement, Jan. 11, 1890.

1891

FLUTE AND VIOLIN, and Other Kentucky Tales and
Romances, by James Lane Allen. Harper & Brothers,
New York, 1891.

12mo. Cloth.
Contains seventeen illustrations by Howard Pyle, first published in
Harper's Monthly, Dec., 1890.

1891

THE TRUE STORY OF THE UNITED STATES OF AMERICA, by Elbridge S. Brooks. D. Lothrop Company, Boston, 1891.

8vo. Square. Cloth.
Contains one illustration by Howard Pyle, being part of illustration first published in *Wide Awake*, Feb., 1886, and later in Storied Holidays, Brooks, D. Lothrop & Co., Boston, 1887.

1892

Vol. I. Works of John Greenleaf Whittier
The Poetical Works of / John Greenleaf Whittier / In Four Volumes / Volume I / Narrative and Legendary Poems / (cut) / Boston and New York / Houghton, Mifflin and Company / The Riverside Press, Cambridge

8vo. Cloth sides, vellum back.
Artists' Edition, limited to 750 copies.
Contains one illustration by Howard Pyle not previously published, as follows:

p 104   "The Sachem's Daughter"   p 5.2 x 3.5
Copyright, No. 32672, Aug. 8, 1892. Deposited Aug 12, 1892.

1892

Vol. II. Works of John Greenleaf Whittier
The Poetical Works of / John Greenleaf Whittier / In Four Volumes / Volume II / Poems of Nature, Poems Subjective / and Reminiscent, Religious Poems / (cut) / Boston and New York / Houghton, Mifflin and Company / The Riverside Press, Cambridge

8vo. Cloth sides, vellum back.
Artists' Edition, limited to 750 copies.
Contains one illustration by Howard Pyle not previously published, as follows:

p 315   "The Vision of Echard"   p 3.5 x 5.3
Copyright, No. 32673, Aug. 8, 1892. Deposited Aug. 12, 1892.

1892

The One Hoss Shay / With its Companion Poems / How the Old Horse Won the Bet / & / The Broomstick Train / By Oliver Wendell Holmes / With Illustrations by / Howard Pyle / (publishers' seal) / Boston and New York / Houghton, Mifflin and Company / The Riverside Press, Cambridge / MDCCCXCII.

12mo. Leather.

Contains fourteen full page illustrations, forty-four small illustrations, eight half-titles, tailpiece and headings, a total of sixty-six illustrations and decorations by Howard Pyle not previously published, as follows:

Frontispiece, Ye Deacon		p 2.0 x 3.5
p 4	Headpiece, Preface	p 2.8 x 0.8
7	Tailpiece	p 1.3 x 0.4
8	Headpiece, Illustrations	p 2.7 x 1.3
10	Tailpiece	p 1.2 x 0.4
11	Half title, The Deacon's Masterpiece	p 2.4 x 3.4
12	The Deacon's Masterpiece	p 2.6 x 1.3
14	"A chaise breaks down but doesn't wear out" [1]	p 2.6 x 4.4
16	"The Deacon inquired of the village folk"	p 2.7 x 3.4
18	"Naow she'll dew"	p 2.4 x 2.4
19	"She was a wonder, and nothing less" [1]	p 2.6 x 4.3
20	"Deacon and deaconess dropped away"	p 2.5 x 2.6
21	Eighteen Hundred	p 2.4 x 1.3
21	Fifty-five	p 2.1 x 1.1
22	"Its hundredth year"	p 2.6 x 2.2
23	"A general flavor of mild decay"	p 2.5 x 2.7
24	"In another hour it will be worn out"	p 2.3 x 1.1
25	"The parson takes a drive"	p 2.5 x 2.4
26	"All at once the horses stood still"	p 2.4 x 2.6
27	"The something decidedly like a spill"	p 2.6 x 4.4
28	"Just as bubbles do when they burst"	p 2.5 x 1.3
29	"End of the wonderful one-hoss-shay"	p 2.5 x 1.9
30	Half title, How the Old Horse Won the Bet	p 2.3 x 3.2
31	"The famous trotting ground"	p 2.5 x 1.6

[1] Reproduced in "Modern Illustration." Joseph Pennell, George Bell & Son, London.

[172]

p 78	"You can hear the black cat's purr"	p 2.6 x 1.6
79	"Catch a gleam from her wicked eye"	p 2.6 x 4.4
80	Tailpiece	p 1.4 x 2.1

Copyright, No. 35402, Oct. 2, 1891. Deposited Oct. 3, 1891.

1892

AMERICAN ILLUSTRATORS, by F. Hopkinson Smith. In Five Parts / Charles Scribner's Sons / New York, 1892.

Folio. Five parts enclosed in board portfolio.

Edition of 1,000 copies.

Part one contains a Goupelgravure 7.1 x 10.3, "A Wounded Enemy," by Howard Pyle, first published in *Scribner's*, July, 1890, also in "In the Valley," Harold Frederic, Charles Scribner's Sons, New York, 1890.

Part three contains portrait of Howard Pyle, and reproductions of three illustrations by Howard Pyle, from *Scribner's*, Dec., 1891, and one illustration from *Scribner's*, Dec., 1890.

1892

Vol. XII. Works of Oliver Wendell Holmes
The Poetical Works / of / Oliver Wendell Holmes / In Two Volumes / Volume I / Earlier Poems, Songs in Many Keys / Poems of the Class of '29, Etc. / (cut) / Boston and New York / Houghton, Mifflin and Company / The Riverside Press, Cambridge

8vo. Cloth sides, vellum back.

Limited edition of 750 copies.

Contains two illustrations by Howard Pyle not previously published, as follows:

| p 4 | The Last Leaf | p 3.3 x 4.9 |
| 420 | The One Hoss Shay | p 5.0 x 3.3 |

Copyright, No. 46458, Nov. 14, 1892. Deposited May 29, 1893.

1892

Vol. XIII. Works of Oliver Wendell Holmes
The Poetical Works / of / Oliver Wendell Holmes / In Two
Volumes / Volume II / Songs of Many Seasons, Bunker
Hill Battle / The Iron Gate, Before the / Curfew, Etc. /
(cut) / Boston and New York / Houghton, Mifflin and
Company / The Riverside Press, Cambridge

8vo. Cloth sides, vellum back.
Limited edition of 750 copies.
Contains three illustrations by Howard Pyle not previously published, as follows:

p 48	Dorothy Q	p 3.2 x 4.9
58	The Boston Tea Party	p 3.2 x 4.7
154	Grandmother's Story of Bunker Hill Battle	p 3.1 x 4.8

Copyright, No. 46459, Nov. 14, 1892. Deposited May 29, 1893.

1893

A Tour Around New York and My Summer Acre, by
John Flavel Mines, LL.D. Harper & Brothers, New York,
1893.

8vo. Cloth.
Contains two illustrations by Howard Pyle, first published in
Harper's Monthly, April, 1889.

1893

Abraham Lincoln, by Charles Carleton Coffin. Harper
& Brothers, New York, 1893.

8vo. Square. Cloth.
Contains two illustrations by Howard Pyle, first published in
Harper's Monthly, June, 1887.

1893

Dorothy Q / Together with / A Ballad of the Boston Tea
Party / & / Grandmother's Story of Bunker Hill Battle /

By Oliver Wendell Holmes / With Illustrations by /
Howard Pyle / (cut) / Cambridge / Printed at the Riverside Press / MDCCCXCIII.

12mo. Vellum.
Edition 250 copies.
Contains sixty-four full page illustrations, etc., and thirty-one
decorations, head and tailpieces, a total of ninety-five illustrations,
etc., by Howard Pyle not previously published, as follows:

Frontispiece	Dorothy Q	p 2.8 x 4.6
p 13	Half title, Dorothy Q	p 2.0 x 3.4
14	Painting the picture	p 2.5 x 4.1
15	"Girlish bust, but womanly air"	p 2.5 x 1.4
17	"Hint and promise of stately mien"	p 2.0 x 4.0
18	"The youthful sire"	p 2.1 x 3.6
21	"Soft as the breath of a maiden's Yes"	p 2.2 x 4.1
22	"Lady and lover"	p 2.2 x 4.0
26	"The Boston teapot bubbled"	p 2.5 x 4.3
27	Half title, A Ballad of the Boston Tea-Party	p 2.0 x 3.1
28	A cup of tea	p 1.6 x 3.3
31	"Many a six foot grenadier, etc."	p 2.6 x 4.2
32	"Her tearful memories treasured"	p 2.5 x 4.1
35	"Behold the guests advancing"	p 2.5 x 4.1
36	"The lively barber"	p 2.0 x 3.7
39	"The truant tapster"	p 2.5 x 4.1
40	"The cooper's boys"	p 2.5 x 4.2
43	"The lusty young Fort Hillers"	p 2.5 x 4.1
44	"The Tories seize the omen"	p 2.3 x 4.1
47	"The Mohawk band is swarming"	p 2.5 x 4.2
48	"So gracious, sweet, and purring"	p 2.5 x 3.6
51	"The quiet dame"	p 2.5 x 4.0
52	An old North-Ender	p 2.5 x 3.8
54	Tailpiece	p 2.1 x 3.1
56	Watching the battle from the steeple	p 2.5 x 4.1
57	Half title—Grandmother's Story	p 2.1 x 3.5
58	The Grandmother	p 2.5 x 3.5
59	Half title	p 2.6 x 4.1
61	"Lord Percy's hunted soldiers"	p 2.5 x 4.0
62	"Says Grandma, 'What's the matter?'"	p 2.5 x 4.1

[176]

1893

A / School History / of the / United States / By / William Swinton / Author of "History of the Army of the Poto- mac," "Outlines / of the World's History," "First Lesson in Our / Country's History" / Being / A Revision and Rewriting of Swinton's "Condensed / School History of the United States" / New York * Cincinnati * Chicago / American Book Company

[177]

16mo. Cloth.
Contains, p. 141, Household Scene in New Amsterdam. Previously published in Swinton's Fifth Reader, Ivison, Blakeman, Taylor & Co., New York, 1883.

The picture on p. 64, "Landing of the Pilgrims," is drawn very poorly after Pyle's picture, "The Landing of the Pilgrims," illustrating "An English Nation," *Harper's Monthly*, April, 1883.

Contains one illustration by Howard Pyle not previously published, as follows:

p 36   Balboa discovering the Pacific   p 3.6 x 4.0
                                                                J. Karst, Sc.

Copyright, No. 26463, June 2, 1893. Deposited July 10, 1893.

1893

GILES COREY, YEOMAN, by Mary E. Wilkins. Harper & Brothers, New York, 1893.

24mo. Cloth.
Contains four illustrations by Howard Pyle, first published in *Harper's Monthly*, June, 1892.

1894

IN OLD NEW YORK, by Thomas A. Janvier. Harper & Brothers, New York, 1894.

12mo. Cloth.
Contains six illustrations by Howard Pyle, first published in *Harper's Monthly*, May (3) and June, 1893 (3).

1894

TRANSACTIONS OF THE GROLIER CLUB OF THE CITY OF NEW YORK, Part II, The Grolier Club, New York, 1894.

8vo. Boards.
Edition of 750 copies.
Contains three illustrations by Howard Pyle from History of New York, Diedrich Knickerbocker, The Grolier Club, New York, 1886.

1894

THE ART OF THE AMERICAN WOOD ENGRAVER, by Philip Gilbert Hamerton, LL.D. To accompany the collection of Forty hand-printed proofs. Charles Scribner's Sons, New York, 1894.

16mo. Half morocco.
100 copies autographed by author and publisher.

The Art of the American / Wood Engraver / * / Forty India proofs / To accompany the Text of / Philip Gilbert Hamerton / * / New York / Charles Scribner's Sons / 1894

Folio. Half morocco.
Contains eight illustrations by Howard Pyle, printed on India paper, each signed by the engraver; first published in *Scribner's Magazine*, Sept., 1889, Dec., 1890 (6), May, 1893.

1894

Swinton's Primary United States / ———— / First Lessons / in / Our Country's History / By William Swinton / Author of "School History of the United States" "Outlines / of the World's History" "History of the / Army of the Potomac" / Revised Edition / New York * Cincinnati * Chicago / American Book Company

16mo. Cloth.
Contains one illustration by Howard Pyle not previously published, as follows:

p 32   "The Meeting of Cortes and Montezuma"   p 4.0 x 3.0
                                                     Karst, Sc.

Copyright, No. 5358, Jan. 12, 1894.

1894

The Autocrat / Of the Breakfast-Table / By Oliver Wendell Holmes / With Illustrations by / Howard Pyle / I / (publishers' seal) / Cambridge / Printed at the Riverside Press / MDCCCXCIV.

Two volumes. Bound in vellum.
8vo.
Edition of 250 copies. Large. Paper.
Contains fifteen full page photogravure illustrations and forty-four headings and tailpieces, or a total of fifty-nine illustrations by Howard Pyle not previously published, as follows:

Copyright, No. 46600, Oct. 17, 1893. Deposited Nov. 4, 1893.

1895

GREAT MEN'S SONS, by Elbridge S. Brooks. G. P. Putnam's Sons, New York, 1895.

12mo. Cloth.

Contains, p. 69, one illustration by Howard Pyle, first published in *Wide Awake*, May, 1886, and later in "Storied Holidays," Elbridge S. Brooks, D. Lothrop & Co., Boston, 1887.

1895

THE TRUE STORY OF GEORGE WASHINGTON, by Elbridge S. Brooks. Lothrop Publishing Company, Boston, 1895.

8vo. Square. Cloth.
Contains one illustration by Howard Pyle, first published in *Wide Awake*, July, 1887.

1895

(Decoration) Stops / of Various / Quills (Decoration) / By W. D. Howells / Illustrated by / Howard / Pyle / (publishers' seal) / New York / Harper and Brothers / MDCCCXCV.

8vo. Cloth.
A Limited Large Paper Edition of this work signed by author and artist was issued in 1896.

Contains three full page illustrations, twenty headpieces, thirteen tailpieces and eighteen initials, or a total of fifty-four illustrations by Howard Pyle, first published in *Harper's Monthly*, March, 1893 (18), Dec., 1894 (21), March (3) and Sept., 1895 (12).

Contains also twenty-five headpieces, fourteen tailpieces and decorations and five initials, in all a total of forty-four illustrations by Howard Pyle not previously published, as follows:

Title page decoration			p 1.7 x 0.4
Title page decoration			p 1.3 x 0.4
Table of Contents, Heading			p 3.5 x 1.5
p	II	Tailpiece	p 1.0 x 0.5
	v	Tailpiece	p 1.7 x 0.7
	VI	Headpiece	p 3.6 x 1.5
		Tailpiece	p 2.0 x 0.8
	VIII	Headpiece	p 3.5 x 1.0
	x	Tailpiece	p 1.3 x 0.7
	XIV	Tailpiece	p 1.6 x 0.8
	xv	Initial D	p 0.4 x 0.4

p	xx	Headpiece	p 3.5 x 1.9
		Initial J	p 0.4 x 0.4
		Tailpiece	p 2.2 x 0.8
	xxi	Tailpiece	p 1.3 x 1.8
	xxiv	Headpiece	p 3.5 x 1.5
		Tailpiece	p 2.0 x 2.3
	xxv	Headpiece	p 3.5 x 1.3
	xxvi	Tailpiece	p 1.5 x 0.8
	xxviii	Headpiece	p 2.9 x 1.8
	xxix	Headpiece	p 3.5 x 1.6
	xxx	Headpiece	p 3.5 x 2.2
		Tailpiece	p 3.5 x 2.2
	xxxi	Headpiece	p 2.7 x 1.4
		Initial T	p 0.4 x 0.4
	xxxii	Headpiece	p 3.5 x 1.6
		Tailpiece	p 1.7 x 1.8
	xxxiii	Headpiece	p 3.5 x 1.9
	xxxiv	Headpiece	p 3.5 x 2.0
	xxxv	Headpiece	p 3.5 x 1.7
	xxxvi	Headpiece	p 3.5 x 1.0
		Tailpiece	p 1.6 x 2.2
	xxxvii	Headpiece	p 3.5 x 1.8
		Initial L	p 0.4 x 0.4
	xxxviii	Headpiece	p 3.5 x 1.0
		Initial O	p 0.4 x 0.4
		Tailpiece	p 1.3 x 1.5
	xxxix	Headpiece	p 3.6 x 1.9
	xl	Headpiece	p 3.3 x 1.7
	xli	Headpiece	p 3.5 x 1.5
		Tailpiece	p 0.5 x 0.7
	xlii	Headpiece	p 3.5 x 1.1
	xliii	Headpiece	p 3.5 x 1.8
		Tailpiece	p 1.3 x 0.2

Copyright, No. 39945, Aug. 3, 1895. Deposited Oct. 25, 1895.

1895

The Parasite, A Story, by A. Conan Doyle. Harper & Brothers, Publishers, New York, 1895.

12mo. Cloth.

[183]

Contains four illustrations by Howard Pyle, first published in *Harper's Weekly*, Nov. 10, 17, 24, Dec. 1, 1894.

1895

HISTORY OF THE UNITED STATES, by E. Benjamin Andrews. New York / Charles Scribner's Sons, New York, 1895.

12mo. Cloth. Four volumes.
Vol. I contains two illustrations by Howard Pyle, first published in *Scribner's Magazine*, May, 1893.

1895

MODERN ILLUSTRATION, by Joseph Pennell. George Bell & Sons, London, 1895.

8vo. Three quarters morocco.
Japan Paper Edition, 125 copies.
Contains three illustrations by Howard Pyle, first published in *The Century*, Dec., 1893, and "The One Hoss Shay," Oliver Wendell Holmes, Houghton, Mifflin & Co., Boston, 1892.

1895

* The Novels and / Tales of Robert / Louis Stevenson / Kidnapped / * Published in / New York By / Charles Scribner's / Sons ** 1895 *

8vo. Cloth. Uncut.
Contains one illustration by Howard Pyle not previously published, as follows:
Frontispiece "I saw him pass his sword through the
                    mate's body"   p 3.0 x 4.3

1895

* The Novels and / Tales of Robert / Louis Stevenson / The Merry Men / and Other Tales / and Fables * Strange /

Case of Dr. Jekyll / and Mr. Hyde ** / * Published in / New York by / Charles Scribner's / Sons ** 1895 *

8vo. Cloth. Uncut.
Contains one illustration by Howard Pyle not previously published, as follows:

Frontispiece "He put the glass to his lips and drank at
one gulp"　　　　　　　　　　　　　　　p 2.9 x 4.1

1895

* The Novels and / Tales of Robert / Louis Stevenson / David Balfour / A Sequel to "Kidnapped" / * Published in / New York By / Charles Scribner's / Sons ** 1895 *

8vo. Cloth. Uncut.
Contains one illustration by Howard Pyle not previously published, as follows:
Frontispiece "Will you forgive my having followed you?" p 3.0 x 4.3

1896

In Ole / Virginia / By / Thomas Nelson Page / Illustrated / By / W. T. Smedley, B. W. Clinedinst, / C. S. Reinhart, A. B. Frost, / Howard Pyle and / A. Castaigne / New York / Charles Scribner's Sons / MDCCCXCVI (title surrounded by decorations)

12mo. Cloth.
Contains two illustrations by Howard Pyle not previously published, as follows:

p 206 "The gigantic monster dragged the hacked and
headless corpse of his victim up the staircase" p 4.0 x 5.5
222 "A man in it, standing upright, and something
lying in a lump at the bow" p 4.0 x 5.5
Copyright, No. 55950, Oct. 9, 1896. Deposited Oct. 10, 1896.

1896

THE HISTORY OF THE LAST QUARTER-CENTURY, by E. Benjamin Andrews. Charles Scribner's Sons, New York, 1896.

8vo. Cloth. Two volumes.

Contains, in Volume I, three illustrations by Howard Pyle, first published in *Scribner's Magazine*, May, July, Oct., 1895.

1896

Vol. IX. Writings of Harriet Beecher Stowe
Oldtown Folks / and / Sam Lawson's Oldtown / Fireside
Stories / By / Harriet Beecher Stowe / In Two Volumes /
Volume I / (cut) / Cambridge / Printed at the Riverside
Press / MDCCCXCVI.

8vo. Cloth binding. Paper label.
Autograph Edition, 250 copies.
Contains one illustration by Howard Pyle not previously published,
as follows:

Sub-title page vignette, Old Natick Church   p 2.5 x 2.5
    Copyright, No. 62468, Nov. 16, 1896. Deposited Jan. 2, 1897.

1896

Vol. X. Writings of Harriet Beecher Stowe
Oldtown Folks / and / Sam Lawson's Oldtown / Fireside
Stories / By / Harriet Beecher Stowe / In Two Volumes /
Volume II / (cut) / Cambridge / Printed at the Riverside
Press / MDCCCXCVI.

8vo. Cloth binding. Paper label.
Autograph Edition of 250 copies.
Contains two illustrations by Howard Pyle not previously published,
as follows:

Sub-title page vignette, Sam Lawson's House   p 2.5 x 2.5
Frontispiece, Sam Lawson telling stories   p 3.0 x 4.4
    Copyright, No. 62469, Nov. 16, 1896. Deposited Jan. 2, 1897.

1897

HUGH WYNNE, FREE QUAKER, by S. Weir Mitchell, M.D.,
LL.D. The Century Co., New York, 1897.

4to. Large. Paper.

Edition of 60 copies each signed by the author.

Two volumes.

Illustrated with the twelve illustrations by Howard Pyle used in the original publishing of the story in *The Century*, Nov., 1896, to Oct., 1897, and reproduced in full size as used in *The Century;* also the same twelve pictures in reduced size same as used in the trade editions of 1897 and 1899.

1897

Vol. V. Works of Francis Parkman
LaSalle and the Discov- / ery of the Great West * / France and England in / North America. Part Third / By Francis Parkman * * * * / In Two Volumes / Vol. I / (cut) / Boston * Little Brown / and Company * MDCCCXCVII.

8vo. Half levant morocco.
Limited Edition, 300 copies.
Vol. V.
Contains one illustration by Howard Pyle not previously published, as follows:

p 132   Father Hennepin Celebrating Mass   p 3.6 x 5.7
   Copyright, No. 46914, Aug. 21, 1897. Deposited Aug. 21, 1897.

1897

Vol. VI. Works of Francis Parkman
LaSalle and the Discov- / ery of the Great West * / France and England in / North America. Part Third / By Francis Parkman * * * * / In Two Volumes / Vol. II / (cut) / Boston * Little Brown / and Company * MDCCCXCVII.

8vo. Half levant morocco.
Limited Edition, 300 copies.
Vol. VI.
Contains one illustration by Howard Pyle not previously published, as follows:

p 173   Assassination of LaSalle [1]   p 3.6 x 5.7
   Copyright, No. 46914, Aug. 21, 1897. Deposited Aug. 21, 1897.
   [1] Reproduced in "The Struggle for a Continent." Pelham Edgar, Little Brown & Co., Boston. 1902.

1897

Vol. XI. Works of Francis Parkman
A Half-Century of / Conflict * * * * * / France and England in / North America. Part Sixth / By Francis Parkman
* * * / In Two Volumes / Vol. I / (cut) / Boston * Little
Brown / and Company * MDCCCXCVII.

8vo. Half levant morocco.
Limited Edition, 300 copies.
Contains one illustration by Howard Pyle not previously published, as follows:

p 73   The Return from Deerfield [1]   p 3.6 x 5.7
Copyright, 64257, Nov. 19, 1897.   Deposited Nov. 29, 1897.

1897

GEORGE WASHINGTON, by Woodrow Wilson. Harper & Brothers, New York, 1897.

8vo. Cloth.
Contains twenty full page illustrations, one headpiece and six endpieces by Howard Pyle, first published in *Harper's Monthly*, Jan. (4), Mar. (3), May (5), July (7), Sept. (4), and Nov. (4), 1896.

1897

The First / Christmas / Tree / By Henry / Van Dyke /
Illustrated by How- / ard Pyle / Charles Scribner's Sons /
New York MDCCCXCVII (title enclosed in decorated border)

8vo. Cloth.
Contains two illustrations by Howard Pyle, first published in *Scribner's Magazine*, Dec., 1891.

Also two illustrations by Howard Pyle not previously published, as follows:

p 24   "The fields around lay bare to the moon" [2]   p 4.2 x 6.4
60   "Then Winfried told the story of Bethlehem"   p 4.2 x 6.5
Copyright, No. 62651, Nov. 8, 1897. Deposited Nov. 8, 1897.

[1] Reproduced in "The Struggle for a Continent." Pelham Edgar, Little Brown & Co., Boston. 1902.
[2] Reproduced in "The Blue Flower." Henry Van Dyke, Scribner, New York. 1902.

1897

"Quo Vadis" / A Narrative of the Time / of Nero * By
Henryk Sienkie / wicz * * Translated from the Polish /
By Jeremiah Curtin * * * * / New Edition / With Maps
of Ancient Rome, and Photogravures from Pictures / by
Howard Pyle, Edmund H. Garrett, and Evert / Van
Muyden, and from Ancient Scriptures / Volume ——— /
(publishers' seal)/ Boston * Little Brown / and Company *
MDCCCXCVII.

8vo. Vellum binding. Two volumes.
Illustrated Edition, 250 copies.
Contains six illustrations by Howard Pyle not previously published,
as follows:
Vol. I.

1	p 34	"Lygia and Vinicius in the Garden of Aulus"	p 3.6 x 5.6
2	348	The Punishment of Chilo by Vinicius	p 3.6 x 5.6

Vol. II

3		Frontispiece, Nero Holding a Golden Lute, with Rome in Flames	p 3.5 x 5.5
4	204	"Peractum est!"	p 3.5 x 5.6
5	266	The Conversion of Chilo	p 3.7 x 5.7
6	317	"Quo Vadis, Domine!"	p 3.6 x 5.7

Copyright, No. 64263-4, Nov. 9, 1897. Deposited Nov. 11, 1897.

1898

Vol. XV. Works of Francis Parkman
Montcalm and Wolfe * / France and England in / North
America. Part Seventh / By Francis Parkman * * * /
In Three Volumes / Vol. III / (cut) / Boston * Little
Brown / and Company * MDCCCXCVIII.

8vo. Half levant morocco.
Limited Edition, 300 copies.
Contains one illustration by Howard Pyle not previously published,
as follows:

p 141   The Fall of Montcalm [1]   p 3.6 x 5.8

Copyright, No. 7145, Jan. 22, 1898. Deposited Jan. 24, 1898.

[1] Reproduced in "The Struggle for a Continent." Pelham Edgar, Little Brown & Co., Boston. 1902.

1898

THE BOOK OF THE OCEAN, by Ernest Ingersoll. The Century Co., New York, 1898.

8vo. Square. Cloth.
Contains two illustrations by Howard Pyle, first published in *The Century*, April and Sept., 1895.

1898

THE STORY OF THE REVOLUTION, by Henry Cabot Lodge. Charles Scribner's Sons, New York, 1898.

8vo. Cloth. Two volumes.
Contains twelve illustrations by Howard Pyle, first published in *Scribner's Magazine*, Jan. to Dec., 1898.

1898

ODYSSEUS, THE HERO OF ITHACA, by Mary E. Burt. Charles Scribner's Sons, New York, 1898.

12mo. Cloth.
Contains six illustrations by Howard Pyle, first published in "The Story of the Golden Age," James Baldwin, Charles Scribner's Sons, New York, 1887.

1898

SILENCE AND OTHER STORIES, by Mary E. Wilkins. Harper & Brothers, New York, 1898.

16mo. Cloth.
Contains one illustration by Howard Pyle, first published in *Harper's Monthly*, Feb., 1892.

1899

OLD CHESTER TALES, by Margaret Deland. Harper & Brothers, New York, 1899.

16mo. Cloth.
Contains sixteen illustrations by Howard Pyle, first published in *Harper's Monthly*, April to Dec., 1898.

1899

GOOD FOR THE SOUL, by Margaret Deland. Harper & Brothers, New York, 1899.

24mo. Cloth.
Contains frontispiece illustration by Howard Pyle from *Harper's Monthly*, May, 1898.
Story and illustration published in "Old Chester Tales," Margaret Deland, Harper & Brothers, New York, 1899.

1899

Janice / Meredith / A Story of the / American Revolution / ———— / By / Paul Leicester Ford / Author of / The Honorable Peter Stirling / ———— / With a Miniature by Lillie V. O'Ryan and / Illustrations by Howard Pyle and his Pupils. / ———— / Vol. ———— / ———— / New York / Dodd, Mead & Company / MDCCCXCIX (boxed rule and ornamental border around title)

8vo. Cloth. Two volumes.
One illustration by Howard Pyle not previously published, as follows:

Vol. II p 228   "They scrambled up the parapet and went over the crest, pell mell, upon the British."

P 3.5 x 5.2

Copyright, No. 2520, Jan. 5, 1899. Deposited Jan. 25, 1899.

1900

To Have and / to Hold / By / Mary Johnston / Author of "Prisoners of Hope" / with Illustrations by Howard Pyle, E. B. Thompson, / A. W. Betts, and Emlen McConnell / (publishers' seal) / Boston and New York / Houghton,

Mifflin and Company / The Riverside Press, Cambridge /
1900 (boxed double rule around title)

12mo. Cloth. Uncut.

Contains one illustration by Howard Pyle not previously published,
as follows:

Frontispiece, "Why don't you end it?"   p 3.5 x 5.3
    Copyright, No. 7246, Jan. 10, 1900.

1900

The Man with the Hoe / and Other Poems / By / Edwin
Markham / Decorated by Howard Pyle / New York /
Doubleday McClure Co. / 1900

8vo. Cloth. Uncut.

Contains one full page illustration and sixty-four headpieces, etc.,
or a total of sixty-five illustrations, etc., by Howard Pyle not previously published, as follows:

p I	Headpiece [1]	p 2.4 x 0.7
	Frontispiece	p 3.9 x 5.9
v	Headpiece—Dedication	p 3.8 x 0.7
VII	Headpiece—Prefatory Note	p 3.8 x 0.6
IX	Headpiece—The Contents	p 3.8 x 1.4
I	Headpiece—The Man with the Hoe	p 3.9 x 2.3
4	Headpiece—A Look into the Gulf	p 3.7 x 1.8
6	Headpiece—Brotherhood	p 3.8 x 0.5
7	Headpiece—Song of the followers of Pan	p 2.0 x 0.4
8	Headpiece—Little Brothers of the Ground	p 3.8 x 1.7
10	Headpiece—Wail of the Wandering Dead	p 3.8 x 1.7
13	Headpiece—A Prayer	p 3.5 x 1.5
15	Headpiece—The Poet	p 3.8 x 1.7
17	Headpiece—The Whirlwind Road	p 2.8 x 0.7
18	Headpiece—The Desire of Nations	p 3.7 x 0.7
23	Headband—(Reproduced five times)	p 3.8 x 0.4
24	Headpiece—The Goblin Laugh	p 2.7 x 0.9
25	Headpiece—Poetry	p 3.8 x 1.7
26	Headpiece—A Meeting	p 2.7 x 0.7
27	Headpiece—Infinite Depths	p 3.8 x 1.5
28	Headpiece—A Leaf from the Devil's Jest-Book	p 3.8 x 1.7
30	Headpiece—The Paymaster	p 2.7 x 1.2

[1] Reproduced in "Modern Pen Drawings." Charles Holme, The Studio, London. 1901.

[1] Reproduced in "Modern Pen Drawings." Charles Holme, The Studio, London. 1901.

Copyright, No. A2812, Jan. 31, 1900. Deposited Jan. 31, 1900.

1900

Vol. V. Works of John Lothrop Motley
Netherlands Edition / ———— / The Rise of / The Dutch
Republic / A History / By / John Lothrop Motley /
D.C.L., LL.D. / Corresponding member of the Institute
of France, Etc. / Vol. V / (seal) / New York and London /
Harper and Brothers Publishers / 1900

8vo. Buckram binding. Uncut.
Limited to 500 copies.
Contains one illustration by Howard Pyle not previously published,
as follows:

Frontispiece—Assassination of William of Orange   p 3.3 x 4.9
                (Signed by Howard Pyle)

Copyright, No. A9950, April 19, 1900. Deposited May 1, 1900.

1900

Vol. XIII. Complete Writings of Nathaniel Hawthorne
A Wonder Book for / Girls and Boys / and / Tanglewood
Tales / By / Nathaniel Hawthorne / (cut) / Boston and
New York / Houghton, Mifflin and Company / The River-
side Press, Cambridge / MDCCCC.

8vo. Buckram binding. Paper label. Uncut.
Autograph Edition, 22 volumes.
Limited to 500 copies.
Contains six illustrations by Howard Pyle not previously published,
as follows:

Frontispiece—A Thousand Miles a Day   p 3.2 x 4.8
                (Signed by Howard Pyle)

[1] Reproduced in "Modern Pen Drawings." Charles Holme, The Studio, London. 1901.

Title page vignette   p 2.6 x 3.4

    p 42   "Behold it then!" cried Perseus   p 2.8 x 5.4

    284   Theseus caught the monster off his guard   p 3.2 x 4.8

    304   "Who are you?" thundered the giant   p 3.2 x 4.8

    512   "Let me hasten onward"   p 3.2 x 4.9

Copyright, No. A29930, Dec. 10, 1900. Deposited Dec. 20, 1900.

1901

Sir Christopher / A Romance of a Maryland / Manor in
1644 / By / Maud Wilder Goodwin / Author of "The
Head of a Hundred," "White Aprons," / "The Colonial
Cavalier," etc. / Illustrated by / Howard Pyle, and Other
Artists / * / Boston / Little, Brown, and Company / 1901

12mo. Cloth.

Contains one illustration by Howard Pyle not previously published,
as follows:

Frontispiece—"'Let me go to him!' she shrieked, in her
                    anguish of soul"   p 3.5 x 5.3

Copyright No. 6648, April 6, 1901. Deposited April 6, 1901.

1901

The / Odes & Epodes / of / Horace / Latin text edited by
/ Clement Lawrence Smith, A.M., LL.D. / Dean of the
Faculty of Arts & Sciences / and Professor of Latin in /
Harvard University / With versions, paraphrases and /
explanatory notes by eminent / Scholars, Statesmen and
Poets / With an introduction by / Archbishop Ireland /
Issued by the Bibliophile Society / for Members only /
Boston 1901 (title surrounded by decorative design by
Howard Pyle)

8vo. Boards.

Edition 467 copies. Handmade paper. Nine volumes.

Contains one title page (used in eight volumes), one sub-title page
(used in two volumes) and three full page illustrations from paintings,
or a total of five illustrations by Howard Pyle not previously published, as follows:

Vol. I	Title page (used in eight volumes)	p 3.3 x 6.1
I	p 20 The Poet at Twilight	p 3.5 x 5.8
		W. H. W. Bicknell, Sc.
II	Part II Sub-title page (used in two volumes)	p 3.5 x 5.9
		· W. H. W. Bicknell, Sc.
IV	Part I Frontispiece—"Euterpe"	p 2.3 x 5.5
		W. H. W. Bicknell, Sc.
	(Autograph signature by Howard Pyle)	
VI	Horace Reading to Maecenas	p 3.4 x 5.7
		W. H. W. Bicknell, Sc.

Copyright: Vol. I, No. A28657,   March 3, 1902.   Deposited: June 25, 1902.
            Vol. II, No. A36160,   June 25, 1902.   Oct. 24, 1902.
            Vol. IV, No. A37684-5, July 11, 1902.   Oct. 24, 1902.
            Vol. VI, No. A41958,   Sept. 18, 1902.   Oct. 24, 1902.

1901

Captain / Ravenshaw / or, / The Maid of Cheapside / A Romance of Elizabethan London / (rule) / By / Robert Neilson Stephens / Author of "Philip Winwood," "A Gentleman / Player," "An Enemy of the King," etc., etc. / Illustrated by / Howard Pyle / and others / (rule) / (3 line quotation) / (rule) / (seal) / Boston: L. C. Page & / Company Publishers. MDCCCCI. (title boxed with dotted border)

12mo. Cloth.

Contains one illustration by Howard Pyle not previously published, as follows:

Frontispiece—"There was exchange of thrust and parry"[1]   p 3.3 x 5.0
Copyright, No. 15822, Aug. 28, 1901. Deposited Aug. 27, 1901.

1901

A HISTORY OF AMERICAN ART, by Sadakichi Hartmann. L. C. Page & Company, Boston, 1901.

12mo. Two volumes.

Vol. II, p. 103, contains illustration by Howard Pyle, first published in "Captain Ravenshaw," Robert N. Stephens, L. C. Page & Co., Boston, 1901.

[1] Reproduced in "A History of American Art." Sadakichi Hartmann, L. C. Page & Co., Boston. 1901.

1901

Modern Pen Drawings, European and American.
Edited by Charles Holme, The Studio, London, 1901.

4to. Leather.
Limited Edition of 300 copies.
Contains three illustrations by Howard Pyle, first published in
"The Man with the Hoe," Edwin Markham, Doubleday McClure
Co., New York, 1900.

1901

Character Sketches / of Romance, Fiction / and the
Drama * * * / A Revised American Edition / of the
Readers' Handbook / By / The Rev. E. Cobham Brewer,
LL.D. / Edited by / Marion Harland / ——— / Volume
H / (cut) / (double rule) / New York. Selmar Hess, Pub-
lisher / (rule) / MCMI. / (double rule) / (initial C at
beginning of title in red)

4to. Half leather.
Contains one illustration by Howard Pyle not previously published,
as follows:

Frontispiece—Lorna Doone   p 5.0 x 7.7

Parts as published, as well as edition of 1892, did not have this
illustration, but it appears in edition of 1901.
Parts as published forming Volume II.

Copyright, No. 44325, Oct. 31, 1892. Deposited May 26 to Aug. 23, 1892.

1902

A History of / The American / People * By / Woodrow
Wilson / (seal) / Alumni / Edition / New York & London
/ Harper & Brothers / Publishers MDCCCCII.

8vo. Board. Cloth back. Five volumes.
Edition of 350 copies.
Signed by Woodrow Wilson.
Contains thirty illustrations in Volumes I, II and III by
Howard Pyle, first published in *Harper's Monthly*, Jan., 1881; Jan.,

April, 1884; April, 1889; May, 1893 (2); Mar., Nov., 1896; April, 1897 (2); Jan., Feb. (2), Mar. (3), April (4), May, June, Aug. (3), Oct. (2), Nov. and Dec. (2), 1901.

Also one illustration by Howard Pyle not previously published, as follows:

Vol. III, p 99   Inauguration of Washington at New York [1] p 3.7 x 5.6
Copyright, No. A41677–81, Sept. 16, 1902. Deposited Oct. 25, 1902.

1902

THE STRUGGLE FOR A CONTINENT. Edited from the Writings of Francis Parkman, by Pelham Edgar, Ph.D. Little, Brown & Company, Boston, 1902.

12mo. Cloth.

Contains three illustrations by Howard Pyle previously published, as follows:

p 220   "Assassination of La Salle."

First published in "La Salle and the Discovery of the Great West," by Francis Parkman, Little, Brown & Co., Boston, 1897.

p 284   "The Return from Deerfield."

First published in "A Half Century of Conflict," by Francis Parkman, Little, Brown & Co., Boston, 1897.

p 446   "The Fall of Montcalm."

First published in "Montcalm and Wolfe," by Francis Parkman, Little, Brown & Co., Boston, 1897.

1902

HARPER'S ENCYCLOPAEDIA OF UNITED STATES HISTORY. Based upon the plan of Benson John Lossing, LL.D. With a Preface on the Study of American History by Woodrow Wilson, Ph.D., LL.D. Harper & Brothers, New York, 1902.

8vo. Half morocco. Ten volumes.

Contains sixty-three illustrations in the ten volumes by Howard Pyle first published as follows:

[1] Reproduced in Vol. V, Documentary Edition, "A History of the American People." Woodrow Wilson, Harper, New York. 1918.

Harper's Monthly, Nov. (2), Dec., 1879; April (4), June, 1880; Jan., 1881 (3); Nov., 1882 (5); Mar. (3), April (3), June (2), July (3), Aug., Oct. (3), Nov., 1883 (2); Jan., April, 1884; June, 1885 (2); July (4), Aug., 1886; Feb., 1888; April, 1889 (2); May (3), June, 1893; Jan., July, Nov., 1896; Jan., Mar. (2), Oct., Dec., 1901 (2).

Harper's Young People, July 13, Aug. 3, Aug. 17, 1880; May 10, 1881.

Harper's Weekly, Oct. 22, 1881.

Contains one illustration by Howard Pyle first published in "Building the Nation," by Charles C. Coffin, Harper, New York, 1883.

1902

The Blue Flower / By / Henry Van Dyke / (four line quotation) / Illustrated / New York / Charles Scribner's Sons / MDCCCCII.

12mo. Leather.
Edition 500 copies.
Contains two illustrations by Howard Pyle previously published as follows:

p 278   "The fields around lay bare to the moon."

First published in "The First Christmas Tree," by Henry Van Dyke, Charles Scribner's Sons, New York, 1897.

p 288   "It poised for an instant above the child's fair head," etc.

First published in "The Oak of Geismar," by Henry Van Dyke. *Scribner's Magazine*, Dec., 1891.

First reproduced in "The First Christmas Tree," by Henry Van Dyke, Scribner's, New York, 1897.

Contains one illustration by Howard Pyle not previously published, as follows:

p 196   Then the old man's lips began to move   c 3.4 x 5.3
Copyright, No. A44631, Oct. 21, 1902.

1902

A Report of the truth concerning / the last sea-fight of the Revenge / By Sir Walter Raleigh, Knight. / The / Riverside / Press (title surrounded by ornamental border with Pyle illustration in center of page).

4to. Board covers.

Edition of 300 copies.

Contains one illustration by Howard Pyle not previously published, as follows:

Illustration in center of title page   p 3.7 x 5.9

1903

The Bibliomania / or / Book-Madness / History * Symptomes / and * Cure * of / This * Fatal * Disease / By / Thomas Frognall Dibdin / (ornament in colors) / Boston / The * Bibliophile * Society / MCMIII. (title in gold and colors and surrounded by ornamental border)

8vo. Boards. Handmade paper.

483 copies. Four volumes.

Contains one illustration by Howard Pyle previously published, as follows:

Vol. I   Frontispiece—Caxton at his Press   3.7 x 6.4
                                        Etched by W. H. W. Bicknell, Sc.

which was copyrighted and copy deposited before this book and published in Portfolio of Etchings, by W. H. W. Bicknell, Bibliophile Society, Boston, 1903.

Contains three illustrations by Howard Pyle not previously published as follows:

Frontispiece

Vol. II   "Friar" Bacon in his Studio [1]   3.7 x 6.4
                                    Etched by W. H. W. Bicknell, Sc.

   III   Erasmus reading to Colet and More [1]   3.8 x 6.4
                                    Etched by W. H. W. Bicknell, Sc.

   IV   Izaak Walton [1]   3.8 x 6.4
                                    Etched by W. H. W. Bicknell, Sc.

Copyright, Vol. I, No. A63494, July 7, 1903. Deposited June 17, 1903.
Copyright, Vols. II–IV, No. A64266–8, July 26, 1903. Deposited June 17, 1903.

1903

Etchings / ———— / By W. H. W. Bicknell / After original
Paintings / By / Howard Pyle / ———— / The five paint-

[1] Reproduced in "Portfolio of Etchings," by W. H. W. Bicknell, Bibliophile Society, Boston, 1903.

ings after which these etchings / are executed were made
exclusively for / The Bibliophile Society / and no reproductions of them in any form are / distributed outside of the
membership. The / subjects are all protected by copyright.

Contained in portfolio. Limited to 302 sets.
Each picture signed by Howard Pyle and W. H. W. Bicknell.
Contains three etched illustrations by Howard Pyle, first published
in "Bibliomania or Book Madness," The Bibliophile Society, Boston,
1903, as follows:

1	Roger Bacon	10.5 x 17.8
2	Erasmus, Colet and More	10.5 x 17.9
3	Isaac Walton	10.5 x 17.8

Contains also two etched illustrations by Howard Pyle not previously published, as follows:

4	Caxton at his Press [1]	10.2 x 18
5	Richard de Bury Tutoring Young Edward III	10.4 x 18

Copyright No. 1, No. F15398, Aug. 20. Deposited Aug. 24, 1903.
Copyright No. 2, No. F16007, Oct. 2. Deposited Sept. 29, 1903.
Copyright No. 3, No. F15399, Aug. 20. Deposited Aug. 24, 1903.
Copyright No. 4, No. F14467, June 11. Deposited June 11, 1903.
Copyright No. 5, No. F16681, Nov. 18. Deposited Nov. 18, 1903.

1904

Breviary Treasures / ———— / The Eclogues of / Vergil
* * * / Translated by Baron Bowen / * / Privately printed
by / Nathan Haskell Dole / Boston (title surrounded by
decorated border in color)

8vo.
The Athenian Edition.
100 copies. Royal Japanese vellum.
Contains one illustration by Howard Pyle not previously published,
as follows:

Frontispiece—(No title)   p 3.0 x 5.0

Copyright, No. 104408, Dec. 21, 1904. Deposited Jan. 28, 1905.
───────
[1] Reproduced in "Bibliomania or Book Madness," Bibliophile Society, Boston, 1903.

1904

Vol. X. Lowell's Works

The Poetical Works / of / James Russell Lowell / In
Five Volumes / Volume II / The Biglow Papers / First
Series / (cut) / Cambridge / Printed at the Riverside
Press / MCMIV.

8vo. Half levant morocco. Uncut.
Limited Edition of 1,000 copies.
Contains one illustration by Howard Pyle not previously published,
as follows:

p 60   Hosea and the "cruetin Sarjunt"   p 3.2 x 4.8
   Copyright, No. A95490, Aug. 17, 1904. Deposited Aug. 30, 1904.

1904

Vol. XI. Lowell's Works

The Poetical Works / of / James Russell Lowell / In Five
Volumes / Volume III / The Biglow Papers / Second
Series / (cut) / Cambridge / Printed at the Riverside
Press / MCMIV.

8vo. Half levant morocco. Uncut.
Limited Edition of 1,000 copies.
Contains three illustrations by Howard Pyle not previously published, as follows:

p 6   Hosea and the Parson   p 5.0 x 3.4
  82   Zekle and Huldy   p 3.3 x 5.0
214   "Sunthin in the Pastoral Line" [1]   p 3.3 x 5.1
   Copyright, No. 95491, Aug. 17, 1904. Deposited Aug. 30, 1904.

1904

How to Draw. A Practical Book of Instruction in the
Art of Illustration, by Leon Barritt. Harper & Brothers,
Publishers, New York, 1904.

8vo. Oblong. Cloth.
Contains two headpieces by Howard Pyle first published in *Harper's Weekly*, Dec. 19, 1896.

[1] Reproduced in "Snow Bound." J. G. Whittier, Houghton, Mifflin & Co., Boston. 1906.

A HISTORY OF THE UNITED STATES, by Wilbur F. Gordy.
Charles Scribner's Sons / New York, 1904.

8vo. Cloth.
Contains seven illustrations by Howard Pyle first published in
Scribner's Magazine, May, 1893; Jan., Feb., June, July and Nov.,
1898; May, 1902.

1905

THE ISLAND OF ENCHANTMENT, by Justus Miles Forman.
Harper & Brothers, New York, 1905.

8vo. Cloth.
Contains four illustrations by Howard Pyle first published in
Harper's Magazine, Sept. and Oct., 1905; also marginal decorations
on title page from *Harper's Magazine*, Aug., 1905.

1905

THE LINE OF LOVE, by James Branch Cabell. Harper &
Brothers, New York, 1905.

8vo. Cloth.
Contains ten illustrations in color by Howard Pyle first published
in *Harper's Magazine*, Aug., 1903 (4); April (3) and Oct., 1904 (3).

1905

The / One Hoss Shay / With its Companion Poems / by /
Oliver Wendell Holmes / Illustrated in Color by / Howard
Pyle / (publishers' seal)/ Boston and New York / Houghton Mifflin and Company / The Riverside Press, Cambridge / MDCCCCV.

12mo. Cloth.
Contains sixty-six illustrations in color, same as used in edition of
1892 in black, also two decorations not previously published, as
follows:

Publishers' Note   c.p 2.7 x 1.4
Tailpiece   c.p 1.3 x 0.3

The painting of the pictures for this edition was done in water color by Howard Pyle.

1905

HISTORY OF THE UNITED STATES, by Thomas Wentworth Higginson. Harper & Brothers, New York, 1905.

12mo. Cloth.

Contains one illustration by Howard Pyle, first published in *Harper's Monthly*, Oct., 1883, and later in "A Larger History of the United States of America," Higginson, Harper & Brothers, New York, 1886.

1906

SNOW BOUND. A Winter Idyl, by John Greenleaf Whittier. Houghton, Mifflin & Company, Boston, 1906.

8vo. Cloth.

Contains one illustration by Howard Pyle, "Our Uncle, Innocent of Books," first published in Vol. XI, Lowell's Works, Houghton, Mifflin Co., 1904, with title, "Sunthin in the Pastoral Line."

1907

The First Book of / The Dofobs / (cut) / Printed for the / Society of the Dofobs / Chicago: MDCCCCVII.

8vo. Board.

Edition of 50 copies.

Contains one illustration by Howard Pyle not previously published, as follows:

Frontispiece—"Dofobius"   p 4.5 x 3.6

1907

GALLANTRY, AN EIGHTEENTH CENTURY DIZAIN, by James Branch Cabell. Harper & Brothers, New York, 1907.

8vo. Cloth.
Contains four illustrations in color by Howard Pyle, first published in *Harper's Magazine*, April (2) and May, 1907 (2); also top and side decorations on title page, first published in *Harper's Magazine*, Aug., 1905.

1907

DULCIBEL, A TALE OF OLD SALEM, by Henry Peterson. John G. Winston Co., Philadelphia, 1907.

12mo. Cloth.
Contains three illustrations in color by Howard Pyle, first published in *McClure's Magazine*, Nov., 1906, where they were used as illustrations for "The Hanging of Mary Dyer," by Basil King.

1909

CHIVALRY, by James Branch Cabell. Harper & Brothers, New York, 1909.

8vo. Cloth.
Contains nine illustrations in color by Howard Pyle, first published in *Harper's Magazine*, Aug., 1905; Jan., 1906 (2); Dec., 1907 (2); March and May, 1908; and April, 1909 (2); also top and side decorations on title page, first published in *Harper's Magazine*, Aug., 1905.

1909

LINCOLN AND THE SLEEPING SENTINEL, by L. E. Chittenden. Harper & Brothers, New York, 1909.

16mo. Cloth.
Contains frontispiece by Howard Pyle, first published in *Harper's Magazine*, Sept., 1907.

1910

HARPER'S BOOK OF LITTLE PLAYS, by Margaret Sutton Briscoe, John Kendrick Bangs, Caroline A. Creevey, Margaret E. Sangster and Others. Harper & Brothers, New York, 1910.

12mo. Cloth.
Contains nine illustrations by Howard Pyle, first published in *Harper's Young People*, Dec. 18, 1883.

1910

THE WORKS OF WILLIAM MAKEPEACE THACKERAY, by his daughter, Lady Ritchie. Harper & Brothers, Publishers, New York, 1910.

8vo. Board sides, cloth back, paper label.
Centenary Biographical Edition. Twenty-six volumes.
Limited to 491 copies.
Contains, in Volumes I, III, X, XII and XVI, five illustrations in color by Howard Pyle, first published in *Harper's Magazine*, Dec., 1906, March, 1907, Aug., 1906, June, 1908, and July, 1911.

1912

ON HAZARDOUS SERVICE. Scouts and Spies of the North and South, by William Gilmore Beymer. Harper & Brothers, New York, 1912.

8vo. Cloth.
Contains four illustrations in color by Howard Pyle, first published in *Harper's Magazine*, June, Sept. and Nov., 1909, and June, 1911.

1912

THE BUCCANEERS, by Don C. Seitz. Harper & Brothers, New York, 1912.

8vo. Cloth.
Contains one illustration and one headpiece by Howard Pyle, first published in *Harper's Magazine*, Jan., 1911, also tailpiece, first published in *Harper's Magazine*, Aug., 1905. Also insert in cover by Howard Pyle, taken from illustration in *Harper's Magazine*, Dec., 1902.

1912

THE WILMINGTON SOCIETY OF THE FINE ARTS. Catalog of Pictures by Howard Pyle. Wilmington, Delaware, 1912.

8vo. Paper cover.
Contains thirteen illustrations by Howard Pyle, first published in *Harper's Monthly*, Dec., 1895; *Harper's Magazine*, Dec., 1902; Dec., 1905 (2); April, 1907 (2); Dec., 1907; Jan., 1908; May, 1908; Aug., 1908; Aug., 1909; Dec., 1909; Jan., 1910.
Contains also portrait and sketch of Howard Pyle.

1912

FOUNDERS OF OUR COUNTRY, by Fanny E. Coe. American Book Company, New York, 1912.

12mo. Cloth.
Contains one illustration by Howard Pyle, first published in *Harper's Fourth Reader*, Harper & Brothers, New York, 1888.
Copyright, No. 330519, Dec. 31, 1912.

1913

THE SOUL OF MELICENT, by James Branch Cabell. Frederick A. Stokes Company, New York, 1913.

8vo. Cloth.
Contains four illustrations in color by Howard Pyle, first published in *Harper's Magazine*, Dec., 1903 (on cover), Aug., 1904 (2), and Dec., 1905.

1913

ETCHINGS, by W. H. W. Bicknell. The Bibliophile Society, Boston, 1913.

Portfolio of eight etchings.
Title sheet has insert picture by Howard Pyle, first published in *First Year Book*, Bibliophile Society, Boston, 1902.

1914

THEATRICAL BOOKPLATES, by A. Winthrop Pope. H. Alfred Fowler, Kansas City, 1914.

16mo. Paper covers. Edition 150 copies.
Contains reproduction full size of large bookplate, The Players, engraved by E. D. French, 1894.

1915

SOME AMERICAN COLLEGE BOOKPLATES, by Harry Parker Ward, A.M. Columbus, Ohio, 1915.

8vo. Cloth.
Edition 500 copies signed by author.
Contains, p. 370, Reproduction Bookplate designed by Howard Pyle for the Yale Club. Engraved by E. D. French, 1905; p. 478, Reproduction Bookplate designed by Howard Pyle for The Players. Engraved by E. D. French, 1894.

1915

AROUND OLD CHESTER, by Margaret Deland. Harper & Brothers, New York, 1915.

16mo. Cloth.
Contains on front cover in colors illustration by Howard Pyle, first published in *Harper's Monthly*, May, 1898; also illustration from *Harper's Monthly*, July, 1898.

1915

STORIES OF LATER AMERICAN HISTORY, by Wilbur F. Gordy. Charles Scribner's Sons, New York, 1915.

12mo. Cloth.
Contains three illustrations by Howard Pyle, first published in *Scribner's Magazine*, March, July, August, 1892.

1915

AMERICAN ART BY AMERICAN AUTHORS. P. F. Collier &
Son, New York, 1915.

Folio. Board.
Contains one illustration by Howard Pyle, first published in *Collier's Weekly*, June 2, 1906.

1918

A HISTORY OF THE AMERICAN PEOPLE, by Woodrow
Wilson, Ph.D., Litt.D., LL.D., President of the United
States. Harper & Brothers, New York, 1918.

8vo. Various bindings.
Edition of 400 copies autographed by Woodrow Wilson.

Documentary Edition

There are thirty-eight illustrations in Volumes I to VI, by Howard
Pyle. Thirty of them were previously published in the 1903 edition,
same work, and are from *Harper's Monthly*, Jan., 1881; Jan., April,
1884; April, 1889; May, 1893; Mar., Nov., 1896; April, 1897 (2);
Jan., Feb. (2), Mar. (3), April (4), May, June, Aug. (3), Oct. (3),
Nov., Dec., 1901; and one from the edition of 1902 not previously
published.

The illustrations not published in 1902 edition are from *Harper's
Monthly*, April, Oct., 1883 (2); June, 1892; May, 1896 (2); Feb., 1905;
and one from *Harper's Weekly*, Oct. 22, 1881.

1919

SAINT JOAN OF ARC, by Mark Twain. Harper & Brothers,
New York, 1919.

8vo. Cloth.
Contains four illustrations by Howard Pyle, first published in
Harper's Magazine, Dec., 1904. One of these illustrations inserted on
front cover of book.
Published May, 1919.

PROGRAMMES, BOOKPLATES, A PRINT,
A POSTER, MURAL DECORATIONS, AND
IMPORTANT EASEL PAINTINGS (NEVER
REPRODUCED) BY HOWARD PYLE

PROGRAMMES

1888

Season, 1887–88 / Grand Opera House—Wilmington, Del. / Tuesday Evening, May 29, 1888. / Mendelssohn's / Oratorio of "Elijah," / Rendered by the Tuesday Club, / Accompanied by the / Germania Orchestra, of Philadelphia, under the direction of / Mr. D. H. Morrison, of Philadelphia. / ——— / Soloists: / Soprano. ——— Miss Kate Currender, of Wilmington, Del. / Contralto, ——— Miss Gertrude Edmunds, of Boston, Mass. / Tenor. ——— Mr. Leonard E. Auty, of Phila., Pa. / Basso. ——— Mr. Clarence E. Hay, of Boston, Mass. / Organist. ——— / Mr. John Graig, of Wilmington, Del.

8vo. Paper cover.
Contains three illustrations or decorations by Howard Pyle not previously published, as follows:

Decoration on front cover with border	p 6.7 x 9.4
Headpiece, p. 3	p 4.3 x 2.3
Tailpiece	p 2.0 x 1.0

1889

Season, 1889–90. / Wednesday Evening, Dec. 18, 1889. / Handel's Oratorio / of / The Messiah / Rendered by the Tuesday Club, / Accompanied by a / Selected Orchestra / Under the direction of / Mr. W. W. Gilchrist, of Philadelphia. / ——— / Soloists: / Soprano, ——— Miss Kate Currender, of Wilmington, Del. / Contralto. ——— Mrs. S. F. Osborn, of Phila., Pa. / Tenor. ——— Mr. Leonard E. Auty, of Phila., Pa. / Basso. ——— Mr. W. E. Harper, of New York. / ——— / Accompanist. ——— Mr. Walter Hall, of Phila., Pa.

8vo. Paper cover.
Contains one illustration or decoration by Howard Pyle not previously published, as follows:

Decoration on front cover	p 6.0 x 8.8

B. J. Lang, Conductor / Twenty-third Season / First
Concert / Boston Music Hall / Wednesday Evening /
December Sixth / MDCCCXCIX / The Cecilia

8vo. (The date MDCCCXCIX on cover is an error.)
Programme, The Cecilia Society, Boston.
Decoration by Howard Pyle, not previously published.

Front cover   p 3.3 x 4.7

(Headpiece) / A. D. 1699 / Trinity Parish / Wilmington,
Del. / Bi Centennial / Commemoration. / Holy Trinity. /
Old Swedes, / Church. / Trinity Sunday, / May 28th,
A. D. 1899.

8vo. Folder.
Contains at top of front cover headband by Howard Pyle not
previously published, as follows:

Headpiece   p 4.7 x 5.0

Twelfth / Night / at / Eagleroost / Being a Revel with /
Maſque and Muſic / as enacted by the / Century Aſſocia-
tion / A°D · MCMVI.

8vo. Paper.
Contains three illustrations by Howard Pyle not previously published, as follows:

1 Front cover (with sub-title)   c 4.5 x 7.2
2 Title page   p 4.3 x 7.0
3 Headpiece   c 4.3 x 4.2

Centuria's Greetings / For January 6th 1906 / Ye Lord of
Miſrule / A Twelfth-Night Call / to One and All

8vo. Paper.
Contains two illustrations by Howard Pyle, not previously published, as follows:

1 Front cover (title)   p 4.4 x 6.4
2 Heading   p 4.3 x 2.2

1906

Two-Hundredth / Anniversary / of the Birth of / Benjamin Franklin / Franklin Inn Club / Philadelphia / Saturday, Jan. 6, 1906

12mo. Four pages.

Programme and menu.

On front cover is illustration by Howard Pyle not previously published, as follows:

1 Poor Richard   P 4.5 x 5.7

The title as given is printed above and at side of picture.

BOOKPLATES

1 1894 THE PLAYERS, New York. Engraved by E. D.
             French   2.8 x 5.4
             Reprinted in "Some American Bookplates," Henry P. Ward, Columbus, Ohio. 1915.
             Reprinted in "Theatrical Bookplates," A. Winthrop Pope, Kansas City. 1914.

2 THE PLAYERS, New York. Engraved by E. D. French 2.0 x 3.2

3 1899 FREDERICK HAINES CURTISS, Boston. Engraved
             by Sidney L. Smith   2.9 x 3.7

4 HOWARD PYLE, Wilmington, Del. Photogravure by
             Beck Engraving Co., Phila.   2.2 x 4.1

5 1905 EDITH KERMIT ROOSEVELT, Oyster Bay, N. Y.
             Engraved by Sidney L. Smith   3.2 x 2.7

6 1905 THE YALE CLUB, New York City. Engraved by
             E. D. French   3.2 x 5.1
             Reprinted in "Some American Bookplates," Henry P. Ward, Columbus, Ohio. 1915.

7 1908 KEATS-SHELLEY MEMORIAL, Rome. Engraved
             by Timothy Cole   2.6 x 5.2

8 1916 WILLARD S. MORSE, Seaford, Delaware. Engraved by W. H. W. Bicknell   3.0 x 4.7
             Originally drawn in 1901 for The Bibliophile Society, Boston, for frontispiece in *First Year Book*.

A PRINT AND A POSTER

THE DUPONT POWDER WAGON. The DuPont Powder
         Co., Wilmington, Del.

Print   27.0 x 21.0   Picture   18.3 x 14.0

1900   To Have and to Hold. By Mary Johnston. Hough-
         ton Mifflin & Co., Boston. Printed in black and
         red.

Poster   15.0 x 22.0   Picture   5.2 x 14.0

MURAL DECORATIONS

With location, size in inches and decimals, and date.

1905   *Mrs. Howard Pyle's House*, 907 Delaware Avenue,
         Wilmington, Delaware.

The Birth of Literature	110.5 x 65.0
Panel	11.5 x 65.0
The Genus of Art	115.0 x 65.0
Music	28.0 x 65.0
Panel	34.5 x 65.0
Panel	34.5 x 65.0
Drama	24.5 x 65.0

1906   *State Capitol*, Saint Paul, Minnesota

The Battle of Nashville	96.0 x 78.0

1907   *Essex County Court House*, Newark, New Jersey.

The Landing of Carteret	240.0 x 72.0

1910   *Hudson County Court House*, Jersey City, New
         Jersey.

Hendryk Hudson and the Half-Moon	396.0 x 84.0
Peter Stuyvesant and the English Fleet	296.0 x 84.0
Life in an Old Dutch Town	420.0 x 84.0
Dutch Soldier	72.0 x 84.0
English Soldier	72.0 x 84.0

IMPORTANT EASEL PAINTINGS (NEVER REPRODUCED)

With date, title, owner and measurement.

1901   Spring. Mrs. Daniel Moore Bates, Lewiston, Maine 12.0 x 30.0
1903   The Garden of Youth. Mr. Schwartz, Pittsburgh,
         Pa.   40.0 x 59.0
1906   The Landing of Carteret. Mrs. R. R. M. Car-
         penter, Wilmington, Delaware   55.0 x 21.0

1908 THE MIDSUMMER MOON. Mrs. Grant Campbell,
Short Hills, New Jersey   16.0 x 23.0
1909 THE ENCHANTED SEAS. Mr. George P. Bissell, Wilmington, Delaware   47.0 x 31.0
1909 MAROONED. The Wilmington Society of the Fine
Arts   60.0 x 40.0
1910 THE MERMAID. Mrs. Howard Pyle, Wilmington,
Delaware   41.0 x 59.0

Robin Shooteth His Last Shaft

The Merry Adventures of Robin Hood
Copyright, Scribner's, 1883

"Which Shall It Be First—Sausages or Pudding?"

Harper's Young People, January 25, 1887

Uncle Bear and the Great Red Fox

Harper's Young People, January 25, 188~
Copyright, Harper's, 188~

"There they sat, just as little children of the town might
sit upon their father's doorstep"

Otto of the Silver Hand
Copyright, Scribner's, 1888

"He gazed and gazed until his heart melted within him"

Harper's Young People, February 18, 1890

Peter Rugg Ye Bostonian

Scribner's Magazine, December, 1891

Ye Deacon

The One Hoss Shay

"Drew a circle on the ground with his finger-tips"

Harper's Young People, April 5, 1892

Vignette, The Cocklane Ghost

Harper's Magazine, August, 1893
Copyright, Harper's, 1893

Vignette, The Cocklane Ghost

Harper's Magazine, August, 1893
Copyright, Harper's, 1893

The Evolution of New York

Harper's Magazine, May, 1893
Copyright, Harper's, 1893

New York Colonial Privateers.
by Thomas A. Janvier

O F

New York Colonial Privateers

Harper's Magazine, February, 1895

By Land and Sea.

A Series of Three or Four Sketches by Howard Pyle.

By Land and Sea

Harper's Magazine, December, 1895

Copyright, Harper's, 1895

W

General Washington

Harper's Magazine, July, 1896
Copyright, Harper's, 1896

The Birds of Cirencester
by Bret Harte

The Birds of Cirencester

Scribner's Magazine, January, 1898

The·Yellow·of·the·Leaf

The Yellow of the Leaf

Harper's Magazine, November, 1900

Truth Leaves the Fairies' Wonderland

Harper's Magazine, December, 1900
Copyright, Harper's, 1900

Hope and Memory.
by Howard Pyle.

Hope and Memory

Century Magazine, November, 1901

Vivien

St. Nicholas, November, 1902
Copyright, Scribner's, 1903

wo Knights do battles
before Camilard ♜♜♜

Two Knights Do Battle before Camilard

St. Nicholas, March, 1903
Copyright, Scribner's, 1903

Sir Kay overthroweth his Enemies.

Sir Kay Overthroweth His Enemies

St. Nicholas, November, 1902

Copyright, Scribner's, 1903

ow one clad all in Black did a wonder before King Leode=grance of Camilard.

How One Clad All in Black Did a Wonder before
King Leodegrance of Camilard

St. Nicholas, November, 1902
Copyright, Scribner's, 1903

The Lady Guinevere

The Lady Guinevere

St. Nicholas, January, 1903

Subject Index of Illustrations

PIRATES

In Periodicals

Sea-Drift from a New England Port	Harper's, Dec. 1879
The Rose of Paradise	Harper's Weekly, June 11 to July 30, 1887
Buccaneers and Marooners of the Spanish Main	
	Harper's Magazine, Aug. and Sept., 1887
Morgan	Harper's, Dec. 1888
Jamaica, New and Old	Harper's Magazine, Jan. and Feb., 1890
Blueskin the Pirate	Northwestern Miller, Dec., 1890
Among the Sand Hills	Harper's Magazine, Sept., 1892
Evolution of New York	Harper's, June 1893
The Pirate's Christmas	Harper's Weekly, Dec. 16, 1893
The Sea Robbers of New York	Harper's, Nov. 1894
New York Colonial Privateers	Harper's, Feb. 1895
Jack Ballister's Fortunes	St. Nicholas, April 1894 to Sept. 1895
Tom Chist and the Treasure Box	Harper's Round Table, Mar. 24, 1896
The Ghost of Captain Brand	Harper's Weekly, Dec. 19, 1896
The Buccaneers	Harper's Round Table, June 29, 1897
How the Buccaneers Kept Christmas	Harper's Weekly, Dec. 16, 1899
Dead Men Tell No Tales	Collier's, Dec. 17, 1899
Captain Scarfield	Northwestern Miller, Dec. 1900
Colonies and Nation	Harper's, May 1901
The First Self-Made American	Everybody's, June 1902
Captain Goldsack	Harper's, July 1902
The True Captain Kidd	Harper's, Dec. 1902
The Fate of a Treasure Town	Harper's Magazine, Dec. 1905
The Ruby of Kishmoor	Harper's Magazine, Aug. 1907
The Cruise of the Caribbee	Harper's, Dec. 1907
The Mysterious Chest	Harper's, Dec. 1908
The Buccaneers	Harper's, Jan. 1911
Ye Pirate Bold	The Autograph, Jan., Feb. 1912

COLONIAL AND REVOLUTIONARY SUBJECTS

In Periodicals

One of Those City Fellows a Thousand Years Ago	Harper's Weekly, Sept. 8, 1877
The Battle of Monmouth Court-House	Harper's, June 1878
Last Revel in Printz Hall	Harper's, Sept. 1879
Old National Pike	Harper's, Nov. 1879
Sea-Drift from a New England Port	Harper's, Dec. 1879
Bartram and His Garden	Harper's, Feb. 1880
Some Pennsylvania Nooks	Harper's, April 1880
Old Catskill	Harper's, May 1880
Captain Nathan Hale	Harper's, June 1880
First Public Reading of the Declaration of Independence	
	Harper's Weekly, July 10, 1880
Women at the Polls in New Jersey in the Good Old Times	
	Harper's Weekly, Nov. 13, 1880

Christmas Morning in Old New York   Harper's Weekly, Dec. 25, 1880
Nancy Hansen's Project   Harper's Young People, April 13, 1880
Old Times in the Colonies
  Harper's Young People, Aug. 3, Aug. 17, Sept. 21, Oct. 5, Oct. 19, 1880
Story of the American Navy Harper's Young People, July 13, July 20, Aug. 3, 1880
Old Time Life in a Quaker Town   Harper's, Jan. 1881
A Glimpse of an Old Dutch Town   `Harper's, Mar. 1881
Tilghman's Ride from Yorktown to Philadelphia   Harper's, Nov. 1881
Surrender of Cornwallis   Harper's Weekly, Oct. 22, 1881
Hours with the Octogenarians Harper's Young People, May 10, 1881
Old New York Coffee-Houses   Harper's, Mar. 1882
Early Quakers in England and Pennsylvania   Harper's, Nov. 1882
The French Voyageurs   Harper's, Mar. 1883
An English Nation   Harper's, April 1883
The Hundred Years' War   Harper's, June 1883
Second Generation of Englishmen in America   Harper's, July 1883
The British Yoke   Harper's, Aug. 1883
The Dawning of Independence   Harper's, Oct. 1883
Last Days of Washington's Army at Newburgh   Harper's, Oct. 1883
Evacuation of New York by the British   Harper's, Nov. 1883
Christmas   Harper's, Dec. 1883
The Mysterious Guest   Harper's Weekly, Mar. 24, 1883
The First Visit of William Penn to America   Harper's Weekly, Mar. 31, 1883
Evacuation, 1783   Harper's Weekly, Nov. 24, 1883
Washington Taking Leave of His Officers   Harper's Weekly, Dec. 1, 1883
Birth of a Nation   Harper's, Jan. 1884
Our Country's Cradle   Harper's, Feb. 1884
Witchcraft   Harper's, Dec. 1884
Gunpowder for Bunker Hill   Harper's, July 1886
George Washington's Boyhood   Wide Awake, July 1887
Washington's Inauguration   Harper's, April 1889
In the Valley   Scribner's, Sept. 1889 to July 1890
Old New York Taverns   Harper's, May 1890
Quaker Lady   Harper's, Nov. 1890
Pastoral Without Words   Scribner's, Dec. 1890
The First Thanksgiving   Harper's Bazar, Dec. 5, 1891
A Maid's Choice   Harper's, Dec. 1891
Two Cornets of Monmouth   Harper's Weekly, Sept. 12, 1891
Peter Rugg Ye Bostonian   Scribner's, Dec. 1891
How the Declaration was Received in the Old Thirteen   Harper's, July 1892
Stopping the Christmas Stage Harper's Weekly, Dec. 10, 1892
Soldiering of Beniah Stidham   St. Nicholas, Dec. 1892
A Set of Sketches   Century, Dec. 1893
Evolution of New York   Harper's, May, June 1893
Unpublished Autograph Narrative by Washington   Scribner's, May 1893
Sea Robbers of New York   Harper's, Nov. 1894
Jack Ballister's Fortunes St. Nicholas, April 1894 to Sept. 1895
Paul Jones   Century, April 1895
A Business Transaction   Century, June 1895
The Constitution's Last Fight   Century, Sept. 1895
New York Slave Traders   Harper's, Jan. 1895
New York Colonial Privateers   Harper's, Feb. 1895

An Unwelcome Toast	Harper's Weekly, Dec. 14, 1895
Some Thanksgivingtime Fancies	Scribner's, Nov. 1895
Hugh Wynne, Free Quaker	Century, Nov. 1896 to Oct. 1897
In Washington's Day	Harper's, Jan. to Nov. 1896
Love at Valley Forge	Ladies' Home Journal, Dec. 1896
Assembly Ball	Harper's, Feb. 1897
Washington and the French Craze of '93	Harper's, April 1897
The Price of Blood	Collier's, Dec. 17, 1897
The Old Captain	Harper's, Dec. 1898
Small Game Better Than None	Harper's Weekly, Dec. 17, 1898
Story of the Revolution	Harper's, Jan. to Dec. 1898
Last Years of Washington's Life	Ladies' Home Journal, Oct. 1899
Man for the Hour	McClure's, Dec. 1899
Colonies and Nation	Harper's, Jan. to Dec. 1901
First Self-Made American	Everybody's, June 1902
Story of a Great-grandfather	Scribner's, Jan. 1903
The Great LaSalle	Harper's, Feb. 1905
The Minute Man	Collier's, Feb. 17, 1906
The Nation Makers	Collier's, June 2, 1906
Hanging of Mary Dyer	McClure's, Nov. 1906
Ruby of Kishmoor	Harper's, Aug. 1907
Pennsylvania's Defiance of the United States	Harper's, Oct. 1908
The Mysterious Chest	Harper's, Dec. 1908
When All the World Was Young	Harper's, Aug. 1909
The Salem Wolf	Harper's, Dec. 1909

MEDIAEVAL SUBJECTS

In Periodicals

The Merry Adventures of Robin Hood	Harper's Young People, Jan. 9 and 16, 1883
Dame Bridget's Prophecy	Harper's Young People, Jan. 4, 1887
Hugo Grotius and His Book Chest	Harper's Young People, Mar. 15, 1887
Men of Iron	Harper's Young People, Jan. 20, June 9, 1891
Maid Marian's Song	Century, Nov. 1895
The Birds of Cirencester	Scribner's, Jan. 1898
Margaret of Cortona	Harper's, Oct. 1901
Don Quixote	Century, Nov. 1901
King Arthur and His Knights	St. Nicholas, Nov. 1902 to Oct. 1903
The Castle of Content	Harper's, Aug. 1903
Peire Vidal, Troubadour	Harper's, Dec. 1903
The Stairway of Honor	Harper's, Jan. 1904
The Story of Adhelmar	Harper's, April 1904
The Charming of Estercel	Harper's, June 1904
The Sword of Ahab	Harper's, Aug. 1904
The Maid of Landevannec	Harper's, Sept. 1904
In Necessity's Mortar	Harper's, Oct. 1904
St. Joan of Arc	Harper's, Dec. 1904
The King's Jewel	Harper's Weekly, Dec. 10, 1904
Melicent	Harper's, Jan. 1905
The Fox Brush	Harper's, Aug. 1905
The Sestina	Harper's, Jan. 1906

The Second April	Harper's, April, May 1907
The Noble Family of Beaupertys	Harper's, July 1907
The Rat Trap	Harper's, Dec. 1907
The Choices	Harper's, Mar. 1908
A Princess of Kent	Harper's, April 1908
The Scabbard	Harper's, May 1908
Edric and Sylvaine	Harper's, Aug. 1908
The Satraps	Harper's, April 1909
The Castle on the Dunes	Harper's, Sept. 1909
The Second Chance	Harper's, Oct. 1909
Swanhild	Harper's, Jan. 1910
The Initial Letter	Harper's, April 1910
Ysobel de Corveaux	Harper's, Aug. 1910
Soul of Mervisaunt	Harper's, April 1910
The Dead Finger	Harper's, Sept. 1911
The Painted Pitcher	Harper's, Nov. 1911
The Evil Eye	Harper's, Feb. 1912
The Die of Fate	Harper's, May 1912

In Books

The Merry Adventures of Robin Hood
Otto of the Silver Hand
The Story of the Champions of the Round Table
The Story of Sir Launcelot and His Companions
The Story of the Grail and the Passing of Arthur

MYSTICAL OR ALLEGORICAL SUBJECTS

In Periodicals

The Star Bearer	Wide Awake, Dec. 1887
To the Soil of the Earth	Cosmopolitan, June 1892
Two Moods	Harper's, July 1892
Monochromes	Harper's, Mar. 1893
In Tenebras	Harper's, Feb. 1894
Stops of Various Quills	Harper's, Dec. 1894
Society	Harper's, Mar. 1895
Pebbles	Harper's, Sept. 1895
The Werewolf	Ladies' Home Journal, Mar. 1896
Love and Death	Harper's, Mar. 1897
Birds of Cirencester	Harper's, Jan. 1898
The Body to the Soul	Harper's, Aug. 1899
A Prelude	Harper's, April 1900
The Angel and the Child	Harper's, May 1900
The Yellow of the Leaf	Harper's, Nov. 1900
At the Turn of the Glass	McClure's, Dec. 1900
The Pilgrimage of Truth	Harper's, Dec. 1900
The Flying Dutchman	Collier's, Dec. 8, 1900
A Dream of Young Summer	Harper's, June 1900
Columbia Speaks	Collier's, Jan. 12, 1901
Hope and Memory	Century, Nov. 1901

FABLES AND FAIRY TALES

FRONTIER AND INDIAN SUBJECTS

In Periodicals

INDEX

INDEX—*Continued*

INDEX—*Continued*

INDEX—*Continued*

INDEX—*Continued*

INDEX—*Continued*

List of Those Who Contributed to the Publication of This Book

Mr. Stanley M. Arthurs
Mr. Clifford W. Ashley
Mrs. Henry Bancroft
Mr. John Bancroft
Mrs. John Bancroft
Mr. Joseph Bancroft
Mrs. Samuel Bancroft
Mr. William Bancroft
Miss Ethel Barksdale
Mrs. Hamilton M. Barksdale
Mr. Daniel M. Bates
Mrs. William S. Bergland
Miss Emily P. Bissell
Mr. George P. Bissell
Mrs. George P. Bissell
Mrs. John B. Bird
Mr. Henry B. Bradford
Mrs. Henry B. Bradford
Mr. Sidney G. Bradford
Mr. Harold M. Brett
Miss Gertrude Brincklé
Miss Elizabeth A. Bringhurst
Miss Ethel Pennewill Brown
Mr. Caleb E. Burchenal
Mr. Philip Burnet
Mrs. Philip Burnet
Mr. Henry M. Canby
Mr. George S. Capelle, Jr.
Mr. Walter S. Carpenter, Jr.
Mr. Sidney M. Chase
Mrs. Charles Copeland
Miss A. L. Crawford
Mr. B. Denver Coppage
Mrs. F. William Curtis
Mrs. John Wilcox Donaldson

Mr. Russell H. Dunham
Miss Marion G. Dunham
Mrs. Coleman duPont
Mr. Eugene duPont
Mrs. Eugene duPont
Colonel H. A. duPont
Mr. Henry F. duPont
Mrs. Irénée duPont
Mr. Pierre S. duPont
Mrs. William K. duPont
Mr. William H. Fenn
Mrs. William H. Fenn
Mrs. A. Lentilhon Foster
Miss Helen S. Garrett
Mrs. James N. Ginns
Mr. Philip R. Goodwin
Mr. John G. Haderer
Mr. Harry G. Haskell
Mr. William S. Hilles
Mrs. Charles B. Holladay
Mrs. William H. Laird
Mr. Charles A. MacLellan
Mr. Frank A. McHugh
Judge David T. Marvel
Miss Mary Askew Mather
Mrs. William G. Mendinhall
Mrs. Thomas Woodnutt Miller
Mr. Francis Newton
Mrs. Otho Nowland
Mr. Thornton Oakley
Mr. Samuel M. Palmer
Mr. Charles L. Patterson
Miss Elsie L. Patterson
Mrs. Howard Pyle
Mrs. William G. Ramsay

Dr. Charles L. Reese
Mrs. Charles L. Reese
Mrs. Richard Reese
Mrs. David J. Reinhardt
Miss Harriet R. Richards
Mrs. Charles G. Rumford
Mrs. Charles G. Rupert
Hon. Willard Saulsbury
Mrs. Willard Saulsbury
Mr. Frank E. Schoonover
Mrs. William Sellers
Mr. William F. Sellers
Mr. H. Rodney Sharp
Miss Jessie Willcox Smith

Miss Sarah K. Smith
Miss Alice P. Smyth
Mr. Henry J. Soulen
Mr. Harry E. Speakman
Mr. Herbert D. Stitt
Mrs. Frank Taylor
Mrs. Henry B. Thompson
Mr. Christopher L. Ward
Mrs. Alfred D. Warner
Mr. Alfred D. Warner, Jr.
Mrs. E. Tatnall Warner
Mrs. Irving Warner
General James H. Wilson
Mr. N. C. Wyeth